Argentina Cooks!

Treasured Recipes from the Nine Regions of Argentina

Expanded Edition

Shirley Lomax Brooks

HIPPOCRENE BOOKS, INC.
New York

Book design by Chikamura Design
Book cover photograph by Leo Gong
Food styling by Andrea Lucich

Argentine location photography on back cover courtesy of Asesor de
Gabinete, Secretaria de Turismo, Presidencia de la Nacion,
Republica Argentina.

Paperback Edition, 2014.

For information, address:
HIPPOCRENE BOOKS, INC.
171 Madison Avenue
New York, NY 10016
www.hippocrenebooks.com

ISBN-13: 978-0-7818-1333-4 (pb)
ISBN-10: 0-7818-1333-6 (pb)

ISBN-13: 978-0-7818-0997-9 (hc)
ISBN-10: 0-7818-0997-5 (hc)

Printed in the United States of America.

MIX
Paper from
responsible sources
FSC
www.fsc.org   FSC® C011935

Argentina Cooks!

Treasured Recipes from the Nine Regions of Argentina

Expanded Edition

For Peter, whose insights,
knowledge and Latin charm
made this book possible.

Acknowledgments

Argentina Cooks! is the culmination of twenty years research into the culinary and cultural heritage of Argentina. Smoothing the road was a cast of many. Among the people I want to thank are my wonderful relatives and friends in Buenos Aires. Josefa Rebaudo, my mother-in-law, got me started on this adventure when she gave me an old copy of a cookbook published in 1914, *La Cocinera Criolla*, for which I am exceedingly grateful; Josefa "Pichi" Rebaudo and Alicia Rebaudo provided recipes and insights into Argentine ingredients and techniques; Graciella Stasi and her husband Edwardo Stasi introduced me to the owner and manager of Parilla La Raya in Buenos Aires, Claudio Codina, who provided helpful advice and an entrée to leading vintners in Mendoza. Juan Carlos Rodriguez was also a great help in escorting us throughout the capital and its best restaurants.

In addition, I'm grateful to Shirlie Radcliff Corletti who put me in touch with Miguel Lorente, president of the San Jose, California Argentine Club, who introduced me to Andrea Celoria, Consul at the Argentine Embassy in Los Angeles, who made many phone calls and sent faxes on my behalf. Thanks to Señora Celoria I was able to interview key people in Argentina including Carlos Magnani, Secretaria de Turismo, Presidencia de la Nacion, Argentina in Buenos Aires. I am most appreciative for the assistance that all these people provided.

I am deeply indebted to the chefs and restaurant managers in Argentina who gave so generously of their time and talents, not to mention their signature recipes. In Buenos Aires I'm grateful to Mario Alonzo, chef at

Munich Recoleta; Bernardo Claus, formerly chef at Clark's; and Marcelino Acuña, chef at La Herradura. In Puerto Iguazú, my thanks go to Chef Xavier Sanchez and executive chef and manager, Pablo Lundhal, at the fabulous Garganta del Diablo in the Hotel Internacional. In Mar del Plata, I want to thank Raul Castro and the staff at Taberna Baska. In San Carlos de Bariloche, my thanks are due to the staff at Ahumadero Familia Weiss, and to Noemi Barchetta, chef, and Guillermo Kempin Pugni, manager at the Ristorante La Rondine in the Pan American Hotel. In Salta, I want to thank the owner of Mama Gaucha, Maria Ercilia Praguglia, and the manager and chef, Carmen Evelia Lopez. In Mendoza, I'm grateful to Estacion Miró owner, Sergio Sawa, and Daniel Bracamonte, manager at Parilla Sarmiento. A heartfelt thanks goes to my hosts at a number of bodegas in Mendoza including Susana Balbo, general manager of Winery Martins; Jose (Pepe) Galante, manager at Bodega Catena; and Rodolfo Reina Rutini, president of Bodega La Rural.

Special thanks are due to Maxine Schur for her artistic sensibility and wise counsel; Claire Lomax who was unflagging in spotting inconsistencies and for purifying my spelling and grammar; and Michael Chikamura, a graphic designer of rare intelligence and taste, who lent his talents to the design of this book. Susan Travis, my agent, and Carol Chitnis-Gress, managing editor at Hippocrene Books, each deserve a big thanks for their unfailing support, encouragement and counsel.

And surely no one has had more enthusiastic support than that provided by my family and friends in New

Mexico, California and Arizona: Jeffrey and Cheri Lenhert, Mimi Lomax, Carolyn Morris, Bojana Fazarinc, Joyce Lekas and Dean Elsie. Thanks also to the Beckers—Paul, Anne and Mutti—for their discerning palates and recipe contributions.

The contributions of my husband, Peter Rebaudo, to *Argentina Cooks!* can't be measured. He not only corrected my Spanish and charmed our hosts in Argentina, at the bottom of the funnel, he helped me test the recipes. His unerring good taste in food and wine, and his wide knowledge of Argentina and Argentine food, are integral to this book.

Shirley Lomax Brooks
Belmont, California

Argentina Cooks!
The Nine Regions of Argentina

When I first visited Argentina twenty years ago, it was as a bride meeting my Argentine husband's family for the first time. Argentina took me by surprise. I found it to be a highly sophisticated, industrialized nation, not the sleepy Latin American backwater that I, in my ignorance, expected. Another surprise: almost all Argentines were of European extraction and the country's ethnic composition was unlike any other in Latin America. And, instead of a laid-back *mañana* mentality, Argentines were a "here and now" kind of people who lived fully in the moment. Perhaps their live-for-today-and-tomorrow-be-damned attitude stemmed from the frequent political upheavals in the country. Or maybe it was a result of the runaway inflation that argued against saving for a rainy day. Whatever spirit drove Argentines to live in the present also impelled them to revel in the pleasures of superlative dining. Scrimping on food was simply not an option for an Argentine.

Because both my parents had been wonderful cooks— no doubt in rebellion against their British heritage—I learned very early to appreciate the difference between eating to live and living to eat. I enjoyed cooking and was accustomed to good food and lots of it. But I was completely unprepared for the sumptuousness of Argentine meals. In my husband Peter's home, breakfast may have been minimal, but lunch was gargantuan, tea was more than I could handle and dinner was beyond my comprehension. Menus were based on meat—mainly beef. Snacks were elaborate: deep-dish garlic or prosciutto and cheese pizza—the best I've ever had; meat, nut and fruit mixtures encased in pastry; thick slices of braised meat rolls filled with layers of onion rings, spinach, carrots plus slices of hard-boiled eggs and pimiento-stuffed olives; and for dessert, Viennese-style pastries with real whipped cream—none of that icky goo that comes from a can. These were the dishes I came to expect every day. For special occasions, chicken was featured. It was usually roasted on a spit and served with roasted potatoes and fresh garden vegetables that were grilled or steamed so they were still crunchy. Meals continued for three or four hours while family members engaged in heated polemics. Then it was time for a *siesta*.

Restaurant cuisine, while more varied and sophisti-cated, was just as satisfying as home-cooked meals. Peter's friends hosted dinner parties for us at their favorite restau-rants in Buenos Aires and the suburbs. Friendly arguments ensued at the table—not about yesterday's transportation strike or the latest on the "dirty war;" rather, Peter's old schoolmates debated passionately the merits of various restaurants. Meanwhile, the assorted sausages they ordered after the pasta turned out to be another appetizer, not the main course as I had thought. Then a huge tray loaded with unrecognizable "meats" arrived at our table. Feeling that I had stumbled Alice-like into a world where there was no tomorrow—a world where dieting was unknown—I watched my hosts in awe as they ordered and finished off course after course. In spite of the quan-tities of food consumed, everyone looked fit. I could only conclude that Argentines must exercise a great deal. Could it be the tango?

The Argentines I met at these dinners were warm and fun loving. They seemed happier and more relaxed than their North American counterparts—in spite of their tribulations. Yes, an indifferent bureaucracy guaranteed constant irritation. Yes, triple-digit inflation and a general lowering of the standard of living caught the middle class in an economic vise. And yes, petty graft was common as in any industrialized society. Yet, the average Argentine (Peter's friends fell into this category) threw up his hands in resignation, complained without angst, "what can you do?" then took another bite of sausage.

When I returned to Argentina eighteen years later, I was stunned by the changes that had taken place. Today, the peso is pegged to the dollar and prices are high. The middle class is squeezed as never before. Argentina has the highest proportion of psychiatrists in the world and it's a rare Buenos Aires resident who hasn't been analyzed. Maybe as a consequence, Argentina has evolved as the center of Latin American "magical realism" in literature. But there is also a sense of stability that was absent before. The only thing that hasn't changed is the intensity with which Argentines approach the table.

In the past, our travels within Argentina had been limited because of the size of the country and the great distances involved in getting from one place to another. This time, Aerolinas Argentina (the national airline of Argentina) offered a low-cost air pass that made it possible for me to travel to virtually every province and sample local cuisine that wasn't to be found elsewhere. To my great surprise, I discovered that Argentina was not *one* country, but *many*.

With its nearly three million square miles, Argentina presents tremendous regional diversity— gastronomically as well as geographically. And each region looks and feels different from the next—from pristine alpine lakes to wild Atlantic seacoasts, from painted deserts and steaming jungles to freezing, glacier-studded landscapes at the bottom of the world, and from grassy plains where millions of cattle and sheep graze to the tallest mountain in South America—Mount Aconcagua at 23,200 feet.

Tucked away in the snow-capped mountains, surrounded by cobalt lakes in the Patagonian Andes, is an Italian restaurant of great finesse and restraint. Though best known for its dishes prepared from local game, La Rondine and its superior Ossobuco would be quite at home in the Lombard region of Italy.

The Atlantic coastal area of Patagonia—with its rich marine mammal life that has seen little change since Darwin's visit—is the sheep-raising country of Argentina. Here, we dined on a succulent milk-fed lamb that was marinated simply in olive oil before grilling over hot coals and seasoned only with salt and pepper. The delicate flavor and texture of lamb grazed strictly on local salt marshes needs no further enhancement.

Near the crystal glaciers of the far south, bordering Tierra del Fuego and Antarctica, cozy Welsh teahouses dot the landscape. The hot English tea and traditional Welsh cakes are a welcome respite from the cold winds that sweep down the Patagonian steppes. Made from a mixture of flour, butter, sugar, milk, currants and allspice, the cakes are cooked on a hot, oiled griddle rather than baked.

In the wine country of Mendoza and San Juan, we were treated to private tastings of world-class Cabernets and Chardonnays. Unlike tastings in California wineries, these were the epitome of proper form—spitting the wine in discreet straw-filled baskets instead of swallowing it.

At an *estancia* in the rough and ready Pampas, we were feted with an *asado* of grilled fork-tender steaks, juicy sausages, crusty ribs, and delicious organ meats of every kind. I had always been a little squeamish about innards so I was astonished to find that I thoroughly enjoyed *chinchulines* (sheep and beef intestines grilled over an open fire) with their crisp, crunchy potato chip-like texture.

The tropical dreamscape of Puerto Iguazú with its voluminous, mist-shrouded waterfalls, was the backdrop for another unusual repast: giant fish, fresh from the Río Iguazú, and tropical fruits picked that morning in the rain forest surrounding our hotel. Among the treats were mangoes, papayas, bananas, coconuts, hearts of palm, avocados, starfruit, and all kinds of melons. Some of these fabulous fruits found their way into local meat dishes with delightful results.

The intact colonial city of Salta in the far northwest—a short hop from the majestic wonder of Mount Aconcagua—was the scene of a delectable Indian-inspired meal of *humitas* (a kind of tamale made with fresh corn) and *locro* (beef stew with wheat berries, fresh summer squashes, peppers and tripe).

Italian and Spanish influences are also present in the cuisines of the northern territories. The ruin of a Jesuit mission in a Misiones jungle was the romantic site of one

Spanish-style picnic. After a long, sweaty hike, we gobbled up gourmet sandwiches of *jamon crudo* (delicately cured ham) and *queso fresco* (soft white cheese) wrapped in a buttery, freshly baked *media luna* (a flaky, croissant-like bread that is slightly sweetened). Thirsty after the saltiness of the sandwiches, we washed them down with not quite cold Quilmes beer (the major Argentine brand).

Fresh dining adventures awaited us in the seaside playground and major port city of Mar del Plata. In a memorable Basque seafood restaurant, we enjoyed a dish that seemed to be the very essence of the sea. Set before us was a soupy dish of rice with tiny, baby squid in their own ink. These are a rarely available seasonal delicacy, but we were in Mar del Plata at precisely the right time. Although the color was dauntingly dark, the aroma that wafted upward was irresistible. As I took my first hesitant taste, I became aware that the waiters were watching me surreptitiously. Not knowing if they were amused at my hesitation or merely anticipating sighs of pleasure—and not one to be undone by a strange dish—I took another taste and discovered that this unusual concoction was, indeed, seductive. The waiters smiled at one another with satisfaction.

While touring the picturesque rivers and mountains outside Córdoba, we discovered a Viennese patisserie featuring ethereal pastries that were wonderfully light with a crème de cassis-flavored filling. With the pastries, we drank Viennese coffee—dark and rich topped with a dollop of slightly sweetened whipped cream.

Everywhere we traveled, we found marvelous things to eat that were prepared with pride and love. I was very glad to find that Argentina is still a star of the first magnitude when it comes to the art of dining. So it is with sincere pleasure that I share my Argentine adventures in cooking and eating with other lovers of fabulous food.

Table of Contents

Tête-à-tête with a small section of Iguazú Falls as a backdrop.

Introduction

Argentine cuisine is little known outside the country. Because Argentina does not have a long tradition of committing recipes to paper, most recipes have been handed down in families. And because cooking has long been the domain of servants in upper class Argentine homes, it is only in the past decade that the elite have come to consider the creation of things to eat an art form. Most in the middle class still look upon cooking as a job to be endured; it's the eating they're interested in.

Until recently, there's not been much opportunity for North Americans to meet an Argentine or become curious about their country, culture or cuisine. It surprises most North Americans that Argentina is the second largest country in area in Latin America— that only Brazil is bigger. Another surprise: Argentina is as long as the United States is wide. What's more, Argentina possesses incredible natural beauty that few outside the country have even heard of.

Buenos Aires, Argentina.

This low profile—especially in the culinary department—is probably because most Argentines are blatantly nationalistic and see no reason to leave their country. As a result, there aren't many expatriates here bringing recipes with them. In addition, travel between Argentina

Mar del Plata in peak season.

Dusk on the Pampas.

and North America is limited because of the distance—it's over eight thousand miles from Buenos Aires to San Francisco. All considered, it's no wonder that Argentina remained isolated and shrouded in mystery until several years ago when the country went to war with the British over the Falkland Islands—or the *Islas Malvinas* as the Argentines would have it. And when Madonna's role as Eva Perón in the movie *Evita* again landed Argentina on the front pages of newspapers around the world, *real* demystification began.

What's so special about Argentina? Peru has more quaint, ethnic charm. Brazil has better beaches. Colombia has emeralds. But Argentina has the earth as its wealth— a vast dry river-bottom with fertile, humus-laden soil that's 200 feet deep. With its special growing conditions, Argentina boasts an abundance of superior, inexpensive foodstuffs—especially meat.

Argentina is the world's largest producer of grass-fed beef, as well as corn and wheat. And it's fifth in wine production. The grasslands of the Pampas produce incomparable lamb and kid. Argentina's long Atlantic coastline is the source of superb seafood including scampi, baby eel, clams, crab, flounder, hake and other white-fleshed fish. Its profusion of freshwater fish from the rivers and lakes of the Andes (20-pound rainbow trout are not uncommon), and wild game from Patagonia—deer, boar, partridges, pheasants and pigeons—provide tantalizing tastes of nature's provender. As if such largess were not enough, Argentina's poultry are strictly free-range.

Also, while the population of Argentina and its culinary heritage are primarily of European origin, Argentina is a cultural crossroad. The variety of countries and national cuisines represented is astonishing: Basques and Galicians from Spain, Jews from Eastern Europe, immigrants from every corner of the British Isles and almost every country on the continent—France, Italy, Germany, Austria and Switzerland. Add to those the latecomers from Yugoslavia, Greece and the Levant. Each group brought to Argentina

The old swimming hole in the foothills outside Cordoba.

its own special dishes. Ethnic recipes were adopted and adapted by other groups. Exotic staples from local Indian tribes soon found their way into Creole cuisine—among them arrowroot, sago, plantains, bananas, sweet potatoes, oranges, prickly pears, mangoes, squashes, melons, maize, potatoes, turkeys and cassava—creating a melange of Creole and New World flavors and textures. About the same time, tropical Afro-Portuguese dishes migrated across the rivers in the north to add another exotic layer to a cuisine that was already complex. It is this cross-pollination of cultures, along with Argentina's super-abundance and quality of raw ingredients that make Argentine food so special.

Some oddities are worth noting. The combination of fruits and nuts in meat stews is quite common in Argentina. And Argentines are absolutely mad about frogs. Higher on the scale of exotica, and an unusual feature of Argentine cuisine, are indigenous animals such as rhea, nutria, guinea pig, cuy and armadillo.

Modern equipment in Mendoza's wine cellars.

Some unusual cooking techniques probably originated with the gauchos. One calls for coating large pieces of meat with sugar and searing them with a hot poker until the sugar forms a glass-like shell. Still, Argentina's mainstream cuisine is based on standard techniques and ingredients that are available in the United States. Most will not seem strange to North Americans.

Argentine celebrations call for a great *asado* (literally "roast"). Similar in style to a Texas barbecue, the typical *asado* includes high-quality beef, pork and lamb spitted whole and cooked over a large open fire or *parrilla* grill. In addition, one can expect huge beefsteaks, juicy ribs, perhaps a melting leg of veal plus crispy, juicy chicken and a variety of succulent sausages and organ meats. Salads and vegetable dishes are served as token accompaniments.

Chimichurri sauce—a piquant mixture of oil, vinegar, chopped parsley and seasonings—is obligatory at an *asado*.

The Argentine wine industry is exploding and will soon be a strong competitor to California and Chilean wines in the United States. The Cabernets and Merlots of Mendoza and the Chardonnays of Salta are outstanding. Argentines drink wine with every meal except breakfast. Even children are permitted some wine. It might be thought that this permissiveness would lead to overindulgence, but I have yet to see a tipsy Argentine. Next to wine, the national drink of Argentina is *yerba mate*—a so-called Paraguayan tea that Argentines and Uruguayans sip from decorated gourds through silver straws.

Salta; Argentines most intact colonial city.

Our culinary tour will take us to the major provinces and cities in Argentina: Buenos Aires, the Pampas, Mar del Plata, the Patagonian Andes and San Carlos de Bariloche, the Patagonian Atlantic, Córdoba, Misiones and Iguazú, Salta and the great northwest, and finally, Mendoza, the wine capital of Argentina. Recipes are organized according to regions. They come from all over the country and represent many traditions. There are certain dishes that are only available locally. *Fideos con Estofado* (Noodle and Beef Stew), for example, is a Sunday meal found only in the Río de la Plata area. Some *criollo* (creole) dishes are seldom seen in home kitchens today because of their special requirements. *Chanfaina*, for example, requires fresh pork blood, which is not readily available to the home cook. However, I have included the recipe for its historical significance.

Recipes for desserts, preserves and breads also are limited because most home cooks buy these fresh from the many excellent bakeries and *patisseries* located in every city, town and village in Argentina.

Recipes have been adapted where necessary so that home cooks should have no trouble reproducing them. Signature recipes from renowned Argentine chefs are highlighted and reproduced without change. However, preparation notes include suggested substitutions for hard-to-find ingredients as well as notes on origins, helpful hints, and purchasing, handling and storage information.

I believe Argentina offers one of the most sensual and satisfying dining traditions in the world. Even the most demanding gourmets will find the cuisine intriguing. But there is much more to Argentine food than the brief sampling contained on these pages. The book is merely intended to give a sense of the culinary range of that vast land and its extraordinary cuisine by focusing on the specialties of the different regions. I hope you will enjoy your tour of the gastronomic capitals of Argentina and trust that Argentina's seductive cuisine will soon become a regular feature of your culinary repertoire.

Buen Apetito!

Mate: The National Drink of Argentina

The romantic image of gauchos gathered around a camp-fire sipping *mate* from a gourd through a silver straw is part of every Argentine's cultural heritage. Because this image is so universally held, and the imbibing of *mate* is such a widespread custom throughout Argentina, *mate* has achieved mythic status.

Similar to tea, *mate* is made from the dried, cured leaves of the *Ilex paraguayensis* or Paraguayan holly tree and delivers a powerful caffeine kick. Unlike tea, *mate* is steeped in a hollowed out gourd the size of a large baby food jar. The leaves are usually crushed coarsely with some of the stems and placed in the gourd. The gourd is then filled with hot (not boiling) water and drunk imme-diately—no further steeping is required. The tea is sipped from the handheld gourd through a thin silver tube (*bom-billa*) that strains out the leaves. Some Argentines prefer their *mate* cold or with the addition of sugar. Occasionally, some spike it with brandy.

Frequently, the gourd and *bombilla* are decorated ornately in silver and gold. Then they become items for display, not mere utensils. My husband's uncle had one made of the hard shell of a rhea egg, which was displayed on a golden tripod when not in use.

Relished at any time of the day or night, *mate* is also a ceremonial drink passed in a single container around a circle of friends. Given the amount of caffeine that *mate* is purported to contain, it's no wonder that Argentines are famous for keeping late hours.

Mate can be purchased in Latin American grocery stores under the name *Yerba Mate*. Health food stores are another good source. Try to get it as fresh as possible; dusty packages are an indication of age. While *mate* can be made according to package directions, in Argentina the rules for making it can be quite complicated—much like a Japanese tea ceremony.

If you don't have the traditional paraphernalia, you can still make *mate* in a teapot as follows: Rinse the pot with boiling water, add one teaspoon of *mate* leaves per cup and pour in boiling water. Let the tea steep for five minutes, strain and serve. To drink cold, make the *mate* double strength and pour it over ice cubes. Add sugar if desired.

Lago Hesse in the Patagonian Andes.

How to Cook the Argentine Way

The recipes in this book have been collected over twenty years. They have come from friends, family and leading chefs throughout Argentina. They include my interpretations of recipes in a 1914 Argentine cookbook, *La Cocinera Criolla*, given me by my mother-in-law, Señora Josefa Rebaudo. The book stood alone among Argentine cookbooks—locally or abroad—up until the 1990s. But its instructions were exceedingly sketchy—*Take some beef and some onions and cook it until done*. This became my inspiration to explore and expand upon Argentine cuisine and to introduce it to North Americans.

Argentine food categories are arbitrary, overlapping and therefore confusing. For example, a *puchero* is a kind of stew that has large cuts of meats and vegetables and lots of thin broth. A *locro* is another kind of soupy stew that is thickened with grains or hominy grits. *Guisos*, *carbonadas* and *cazuelas* are additional stew categories. But I fail to find any significant differences among them. Even so, in this book I have used the popular names given to me when I learned to make the various dishes.

Cook's Tips

Traditional Argentine cooking depends on excellent raw materials, not spices nor condiments.

In Argentina, *verdura* refers to all vegetables. In Spain it refers to green-leafed produce only.

When a recipe calls for parsley, use the Italian broad leaf variety.

Butter is always unsalted. The best butter for Argentine cooking—indeed, any cuisine—is a European style such as Plugra. The higher fat content and lower water content of these butters impart a richer flavor.

Large eggs are the standard for Argentine dishes. Raw eggs should be refrigerated until used. Then they will be easier to separate and will thicken homemade mayonnaise faster. Wash the shells before breaking the eggs to protect against salmonella. (The presence of salmonella bacteria in raw eggs is very rare, however, the possibility must be considered when consuming raw eggs.)

All-purpose flour is the standard for pastries.

Herbs are fresh unless otherwise indicated.

Use coarse salt such as sea salt or kosher unless otherwise specified.

Use freshly ground black pepper unless otherwise specified.

Sugar is granulated unless otherwise specified.

For deep-frying, Argentines use a deep flameproof casserole or skillet.

For cooking, you can make use of lesser grades of olive
oil. Canola oil, light vegetable oils or grapeseed oil
also are recommended.

Some recipes call for lard. Use the best quality available.

Tear salad greens into bite-sized pieces with your hands
rather than cutting them with a knife which bruises
the delicate leaves and makes them bitter.

Make sure salad greens are perfectly dry before dressing
them. Using a salad spinner or hand drying and storing
in a cloth bag with lots of paper towels work well.

Peeling tomatoes is much easier if you puncture the skin
in several places and submerge the tomatoes in
boiling water for several minutes.

Removing the skin from peppers is best handled by
charring the skins over an open flame and then
steaming the peppers in a paper bag. An electric
broiler is an alternative but it tends to cook the flesh
of the pepper too much.

Garlic should be fresh and cut with a knife rather than
using a garlic press. Be careful that the garlic doesn't
burn when cooking.

Egg whites should be whipped by hand in an unlined
copper bowl with a balloon whisk for maximum
volume. If you don't have one, use any metal bowl
except aluminum.

When greasing pans or molds, use butter for hot dishes and oil for cold.

When unmolding hot foods, allow them to stand for five minutes before turning them out on another dish.

Rinse meat and poultry under cold running water before cooking to remove any bacteria. And be sure to thoroughly wash any cutting boards, knives and other implements—including your hands—that may have come in contact with meats or poultry. Some people swear by the effectiveness of using ½ teaspoon of vitamin C in the wash water.

Have meat at room temperature before cooking. The exception is previously frozen raw meat which should be cooked as soon as the juices begin to run.

Always heat the skillet before adding the oil for sautéing.

A mixture of butter and vegetable oil in a hot skillet or casserole will prevent the butter from burning.

Never pierce cooking meats or poultry. Use tongs for turning.

When browning meats, don't let the pieces touch or they will stew instead of sauté.

For turning a whole chicken while browning, insert a wooden spoon in the cavity.

To avoid losing juices, always let steaks, roasts and whole poultry rest before serving (from 5 minutes

for the smaller cuts up to 20 minutes for the larger
roasts and whole poultry).

Heat milk slowly and stir constantly to prevent its
separating and forming a skin on top.

To keep whipped cream from deflating, whip it in a
metal bowl (not aluminum) with a balloon whisk
over a second bowl of ice.

The secrets of a good sauce are gentle simmering over
low to medium heat—never high—and thorough
skimming and straining.

Deglazing is the process of making a sauce by boiling
down pot liquids and stirring the hardened materials
on the sides and bottom of the pot into the liquid.
The process may include adding other seasonings
and liquids such as wine or spirits.

For a smoother mixture when making a roux, add flour
to melted butter off the heat. Stir in any liquid
added to a sauce base off the heat as well.

To avoid curdling your sauce, add a little hot sauce to a
cold mixture two tablespoons at a time.

To correct a too-thick sauce, heat until simmering, and
then beat in a little cream or stock, a spoonful at
a time.

For a too-thin sauce, blend a teaspoon each of flour
and soft butter and beat it into the sauce off the
heat. When the sauce is smooth, simmer it for
several minutes.

When glazing fruit for desserts, use a mixture of boiled-down fruit jellies or preserves. Use red currant, strawberry or raspberry for red fruits, and apricot for other fruits.

To achieve a shiny finish, glaze the top of pastry with an egg wash.

For kitchen weights, use clean bricks wrapped in heavy-duty foil.

STORAGE

To keep raw meat fresh, rub it with oil before refrigerating it. Meat needs to breathe. If wrapped in butcher paper, loosen the paper for ventilation. The plastic wrap used at the supermarket is ventilated so it's safe to reuse, but don't wrap meat in unventilated plastic wrap.

To keep raw fish fillets fresh, rinse them with fresh lemon juice and water, dry thoroughly, wrap and refrigerate.

GENERAL

Cooking times given are approximate as exact timing depends on many hard-to-gauge factors: equipment, size and age of meats and vegetables, etc.

For Fresh Hearts of Palm
  Earthy Delights
  JT Hoagland
  4180 Keller Road
  Holt, MI 48842
  Phone: (517) 699-1530
  E-Mail: ed@earthy.com

  D'Artagnan
  E-Mail: tina@dartagnan.com

For Rhea or Ostrich Meat
  Ostrich Growers
  Worldwide Web: www.ostrichgrowers.com

  Experience Argentina
  Phone: (888) 336-6586
  Fax: (203) 740-1226
  E-Mail: Cust-Serv@experienceargentina.com

CHAPTER 1

Buenos Aires:

A Culinary Affair to Remember

Buenos Aires

 The sophistication and charm of Buenos Aires are unexpected by first-time visitors. Those expecting whitewashed walls and red-tiled roofs are in for a shock. Buenos Aires looks and feels as if a great European city had been dropped into the middle of a grassy South American plain alongside a river so wide that it seems like an ocean. Called by many the *Paris of the Southern Hemisphere*, Buenos Aires is the federal capital of Argentina and the most cosmopolitan city in the whole of Latin America.

In part, Buenos Aires is a grand old lady—elegant, chic but with the patina that only age can bring. At the same time, it's like a huge theme park—a man's town reeking of leather, polished wood and the costly perfumes of beautiful women who are more in control than it would seem. Bubbling underneath the highly polished veneer lies a wild Latin passion for life. The color, energy and unexpected sexiness of the city are intoxicating, making it one of the most exciting cities on the planet.

Porteños (natives of Buenos Aires) are prone to awaken every morning in anticipation of the day ahead—knowing they'll have a wonderful day and evening filled with scintillating experiences and fabulous food.

A sprawling metropolis of over five million citizens, Buenos Aires pulsates to the seductive rhythm of the tango. In springtime (October through early December), Buenos Aires weather is delightful—the sun's warmth is complemented by soft breezes that ripple through the plane trees lining the city's sidewalks. Fall is almost as pleasant with its colorful falling leaves. At other times, the weather is similar to North America's East Coast—muggy and hot in summer, cool and wet in winter but without the ice or snow. Whatever the season, though, visitors are entranced by Buenos Aires' tree-lined streets, its mixture of Belle Époque and Euro-moderne architecture, its stylishly dressed citizens, the charming *barrios* with their cobblestone streets and sidewalk cafés, the late nightlife usually ending at dawn, the aura of sexual tension, and the palate-stirring dining experiences.

La Boca, the shipyard district of Buenos Aires, brings out the local tango dancers.

Despite Buenos Aires' ubiquitous potholes in sidewalks and streets, it's small wonder that the haunting strains of the tango, "My Beloved Buenos Aires," can bring tears to the eyes of Argentine expatriates. With its virtues and defects, Buenos Aires is more than just a city. It is a romantic idea. Its culture, art and bustle are highly stimulating. Its nightlife is spectacular. Europeans and North Americans find it amazing to discover fifty or more restaurants open until sunrise—especially if they like good food and have no cholesterol problems. Indeed, Buenos Aires is one of the world's best cities for excellent dining as acknowledged by articles in the *New York Times* and many other U.S. published periodicals.

Between-meal snacks are equally special. Outside the city, about thirty miles south, is Quilmes. Home of the nation's Quilmes beer, Quilmes features shady riverside recreation areas and numerous restaurants on the edge of a small but modern town of neat houses, clipped hedges and mowed lawns. Ice cream is the specialty of the area. In my experience, Quilmes ice cream is the richest, creamiest, tastiest blend of fruits and flavors to be found on this or any other planet.

In the opposite direction from Buenos Aires is the Delta del Paraná—one of the four largest estuaries in the Americas—and the Port of Fruits. Here, you can buy just-picked fruits, homemade sweets and local crafts.

Much of the excitement of Buenos Aires stems from the seriousness with which *Porteños* savor the pleasures of the table. Pleasurable they are, when you consider the wealth of superior restaurants and appetizing edibles of every stripe including the foods of France, Spain, Italy, Germany, China, Japan, Africa, Thailand, the United States and the Middle East, to name a few. A profusion of pizza restaurants, with exotic names such as *Los Inmortales*, turn out some of the best pizzas anywhere—including Italy. A dozen or so of the city's most prestigious restaurants look out on the cemetery where Eva Perón and members of the upper classes are interred in grand theatrical style—a zoning situation that seems odd to visitors who don't appreciate the unique attitude of Argentines to life and death and dinner.

Porteños fill the restaurants at lunchtime from one to three in the afternoon. Beautiful women in expensive copies of the latest Paris fashions dine lightly on seafood salads. Macho, much-too-good-looking men in high-style Italian suits must have their *bife* before they are sufficiently energized to engage in *piropo*—flirtatious and frequently naughty comments made to attractive women as they pass. The dinner hour—usually around 10 P.M.—finds most restaurants at capacity, too. Predominant among the restaurants are those serving Italianate dishes with Spanish flair.

If not out on the town, *Porteños* prepare sumptuous meals at home. Home dining usually mirrors the Spanish-Italian bias and is also a late evening event. While the home menu is much more limited than restaurant fare, the home cook always does justice to the excellent quality of Argentine foodstuffs from local markets and draws much more on the traditional repertoire for inspiration. As is true of all Argentina, the emphasis in Buenos Aires—whether in a restaurant or at home—is on beef.

Argentines claim to have the best meat in the world, and *Porteños* insist that theirs is the best in Argentina. Buenos Aires has been called the "belly-button of Argentina" because it is the gastronomic center of the country as well its cultural and political hub. As such, BA—as it is called in the local vernacular—has access to a wide and exotic variety of both traditional and regional dishes. While fashion affects what *Porteños* eat, the selection usually comes down to three choices: meats, pizza and pastas, or haute cuisine.

Most of the people prefer the *asado*. Beef ribs grilled until they are medium rare or medium are the preferred cut. Then there is the offal—kidney, sweetbreads, heart and chinchulines—and a variety of sausages. Patagonian lamb is always available and offers tender, lean, cholesterol-free meat that can be eaten without guilt. The same is true of *cabrito*—baby goat. *Porteños*—all Argentines—prefer pork in the form of ribs or filets cooked well done.

Every region has its own version of empanadas, and those of Buenos Aires feature knife-cut or ground meat. They can be hot or cold, sweet or savory, fried or baked.

More Italian than Italy, the pizzas baked in the brick ovens of Buenos Aires' pizzerias are a must before or after a movie. Avenida Corrientes is where you will find the city's best pizzas in traditional pizzerias. In the old days, *Porteños* would lean on the bars in small pizza shops along Corrientes to savor a slice of mozzarella with *fainá*—a thin cake-like mixture of semolina flour—with a glass of wine. These shops were completely without amenities—floors covered in discarded napkins—but some of them endured and eventually became restaurants. Today, they continue to serve up world-class pizza.

Pasta is served everywhere in Buenos Aires—from the most humble hole-in-the-wall, where you can order a generous serving of *Spaghetti al Pommodoro* for just a few dollars to the elegant, expensive eatery where one of Argentina's best chefs offers *nuevo* concoctions such as sweetbread ravioli in vodka sauce.

Haute cuisine reaches its zenith in Buenos Aires. Fresh seafood such as rare black hake is flown in from areas bordering the cold southern Atlantic. Mountain trout are kept fresh and swimming in clear tanks until they are ordered. Huge Tierra del Fuego king crab—steamed in an herb and shellfish infusion and served with a fresh garlic alioli—is as good as it gets. And spring-time brings to Buenos Aires the best of early lamb and

Happy hour at a small cafe in Buenos Aires.

veal, along with specialty produce such as fiddlehead ferns, squash blossoms, fresh hearts of palm and baby zucchini.

Because obtaining exceptional raw materials is no problem in Buenos Aires, French chefs who work throughout Argentina are creating an exquisite new cuisine that is both modern and tantalizing; consider Wild Mushroom Sauté with Porcini Polenta, Venison with Wild Berry Conserve, a creamy Risotto with Scallops and Arugula, Rare Breast of Duckling with Mandarin Orange Sauce, or tiny Segovia-style Piglets so tender they can be cut with the rim of a plate.

Gourmets will appreciate the array of fine, homemade cow's milk and goat's milk cheeses, as well as Italian-style mozzarella and Argentine-made French-style cheeses such as Saint Paulin, Reblechon or Camembert.

Among the strictly Argentine inventions are *dulce de batatas* (sweet potato jelly) and *dulce de leche* or milk jam. Sweet potato jelly is usually served atop cheese as a dessert.

Milk jam is made by combining fresh milk, sugar and vanilla, and stirring constantly until the mixture boils down and achieves a peanut butter-like consistency and color. It is used as a filling and frosting for any number of desserts.

It is with total justification that Buenos Aires makes a claim as a gourmet capital. The recipes that start on page 30 feature some of the best of Buenos Aires' gustatory pleasures.

A DAY IN THE LIFE OF A PORTEÑO

Denizens of Buenos Aires, the federal capital of Argentina, start their day with a modest breakfast of *media lunas*—a toothsome but slightly sweeter, breadier version of crois-sants. They wash them down with *café con leche*—strong Brazilian coffee diluted with milk or cream.

The main meal of the day is a lunchtime *asado;* a variety of grilled meats that Argentines usually eat at a *parrilla*—a restaurant specializing in grilled fare. This *asado* usually features five or six courses starting with sausages, beef empanadas or a pasta dish. Next are *chinchulines*—a variety of delectable organ meats served in succession and accompanied by a salad of watercress mixed with fresh hearts of palm. A course of *chorizos* and *morcillas* (beef and pork sausages and blood sausages) arrive soon thereafter. This course is usually followed by a thick, butter-tender steak broiled "à-point" (medium rather than rare) and served with crisp oven-roasted or French-fried potatoes. As an alternative to beef, the main event might be milk-fed lamb or kid, whose succulence and tenderness defy description. Crusty French bread, *chimichurri* sauce, roasted marinated peppers and a premium Argentine Cabernet from Mendoza accompany the *asado*.

Dessert consists of a selection of tiny, jewel-like pastries or *alfajores*—buttery cookies rolled in sweetened shredded coconut. As a final touch, *café cortado*—espresso with milk or cream—is enjoyed with dessert.

Teatime is observed much as in the United Kingdom with pastries and savories. But, instead of English tea, *mate* is served. *Mate* is a kind of tea made of the dried, cured leaves of the *Ilex paraguayensis* tree—a type of holly—and sipped from a gourd through a silver straw. The basic ingredient, *yerba mate*, is available in the United States in Hispanic markets.

An Argentine innovation at teatime is a thick slice of *matambre* on an equally thick slice of bread. *Matambre*—Spanish for "hunger killer" and more than equal to the task—is a roulade of the outer layer of flank steak marinated and filled with parboiled carrots, fresh raw spinach, hard-boiled eggs, stuffed green olives, Parmesan cheese and spices. It is then simmered in a rich beef broth until tender. *Matambre* can be sliced crosswise and served hot. Most Argentines, however, prefer it cooled in the broth and then weighted after which it is sliced about a half inch thick and served cold or at room temperature.

Those who dine circumspectly at lunch or tea can look forward to dinner at about 10 P.M. Typically, this is a lighter affair than lunch, consisting of a meat, fowl or fish dish, salad, potatoes, a light dessert and, of course, bread and wine. While vegetables don't play a big part in *asados*, they are frequently an accompaniment at the dinner table. Favorites include tomatoes, green beans, sweet potatoes, carrots, artichokes, chard, asparagus, summer squash, cauliflower, beets, broccoli, zucchini, peas and mushrooms. Most vegetables are served boiled or steamed al dente in the Italian/California style and dressed simply with a combination of olive oil, grapeseed oil and wine vinegar plus salt and pepper. Vegetable fritters also are popular.

An Argentine favorite at dinner is *milanesa*. This is a thin, pounded beefsteak dipped in egg and minced garlic then rolled in a zesty mixture of breadcrumbs and spices. It is quickly sautéed in a skillet and served with fresh lemon wedges. Some Argentines like their *milanesa* topped with a fried or poached egg. Another variation is Milanesa à la Napolitana—a layer of fresh sliced tomatoes capped by melted cheese atop the sautéed steak. *Papas al Horno* (oven roasted potatoes) and a simple salad of greens with large chunks of boiled beets dressed with oil and vinegar complete the meal.

The day ends with a coffee or cognac at a favorite café such as Tortoni. Then, depending upon one's age or marital status, the night with all of its possibilities begins.

A NIGHT ON THE TOWN

Your evening starts with a wine spritzer or cocktail somewhere with *élan.* It may be the avant-garde Renault Museum where Buenos Aires' high society rendezvous. Or, you might prefer an espresso at one of many bars on the Avenida Corrientes with their vaguely dangerous ambiance suggesting the fomenting of revolutions. Follow with a quiet stroll and browse through the bookstores which are open until late in the evening. Some claim that Umberto Eco, author of *The Name of the Rose*, found the idea for his famous novel in one of these bookstores.

When dinnertime finally arrives around 10 P.M., consider a full-scale *asado* at one of the city's fine *parillas*. Or perhaps you'd enjoy California-Italian style cuisine in one of twenty chic restaurants housed in recycled warehouses at Puerto Madero on the south side of the Río de la Plata—purported to be the world's widest river. Or maybe you have a yen for Italian or classic *criollo* fare in one of the city's revered restaurants in the Recoleta District such as Lola, Caruso or Munich Recoleta. Further out at the Carritos de la Costanera on the north riverside, you might dine on the legendary sweetbreads with herbs they serve at Los Años Locos. If steak is on your mind, you'll never forget La Cabana's prime porterhouse marinated in olive oil and coarse salt and grilled precisely to your specifications. Better yet, let the chef decide; you won't be disappointed.

After dinner, head for the Hard Rock Café, La Luna or La Casona del Conde de Palermo for rock and roll, which *Porteños* adore. For discotheque dancing, there's Elo Cielo or Pachá. But the night is not yet over. Even though it's 3 A.M., there's still the Planetarium on the Arcos del Sol where you can join in with crowds of *Porteños* singing and dancing until dawn.

Finish the evening with a cognac in one of the cafés on Avenida Porco where musicians, journalists and actors hang out. Later, when the sun just approaches the eastern horizon and the morning papers hit the sidewalks, it's time for strong coffee and a *media luna*. It's also the perfect time to recall Robert Frost's *Acquainted with the Night*: "A bright clock against the sky/Proclaimed that time was neither good nor bad/I've been one of those/Who knows what the night is."

In Buenos Aires, there will always be another night.

IF YOU'RE VISITING BUENOS AIRES . . .

This is anything but a complete list of Buenos Aires' better restaurants. Locals recommended some of them. Others I stumbled upon strictly by chance. Some are humble and some are extremely haute with prices to match. But for those visitors to Buenos Aires who have no other point of reference, the following restaurants won't disappoint.

Bice—a chic, new riverfront restaurant that is a branch of the famed Bice Restaurant headquartered in Milan. Northern Italian cuisine is featured.

El Repecho de San Telmo—housed in an 1807 building. Specialties are seafood and filet mignon.

La Bourgogne in the Alvear Palace Hotel—haute cuisine restaurant featuring a master chef, Jean Paul Bondoux. Here you will find incredible classic French cuisine made with Argentine ingredients.

La Cabaña—claims the best beef in the world.

La Herradura—a former stable adjacent to Palermo Park's racetrack in the suburb of San Isidro. Roast suckling pig and baby lamb are on the menu.

La Raya—a typical *parrilla* in business since 1944—provides a complete *Asado al Horno.*

Lola—a trendy establishment in the fashionable Recoleta restaurant district facing out on Recoleta Cemetery where Eva Perón is buried.

L'Orangerie in the Alvear Palace Hotel—where high society stops for breakfast, tea, or Sunday brunch.

Los Años Locos—a traditional *parrilla* in the old riverfront district. Specialties are larded suckling pig and baby beef.

Los Inmortales—a pizza palace founded in 1950. It pays reverent homage to Carlos Gardel—the famed Argentine tango singer and movie star.

Munich Recoleta—another popular old-time restaurant in the Recoleta district.

Plaza Mayor—a well-known Spanish seafood restaurant in the Barrio Norte. The specialties are *Cazuela de Pulpo* (Octopus Stew) and Paella.

Rose Petal Cocktail

LA ROSITA

Although Argentines seldom indulge in hard liquor, the rosita is a favorite among the diplomatic corps. This recipe comes to me from my good friend, Paul Becker, formerly of Buenos Aires and now a gentleman farmer in Saratoga, California.

INGREDIENTS

3 ounces Holland gin

3 ounces brandy (Fundador or comparable Spanish brandy)

2 teaspoons grenadine

1 teaspoon lemon juice

1 jigger Crême de Rose (optional)

6 gardenia or rose petals

6 maraschino cherries

6 pieces lemon peel

Serves 6

Directions

Shake gin, brandy, grenadine, lemon juice and Crême de Rose (if used) in a cocktail shaker with 8 ice cubes for at least 1 minute. Put 1 flower petal into bottom of each chilled cocktail glass and add the drink mixture. Garnish with a cherry and a piece of lemon peel.

Beef, Currant and Almond Empanadas

EMPANADAS DE CHORIZO AL HORNO

Empanadas are to Argentines what sandwiches are to North Americans. Made from plain or puff pasty, these delightful turnovers are filled with varieties of chopped, cooked meat, poultry, seafood, cheese and vegetables. Empanadas provide a hearty snack any time of day or evening and are a wonderful way to use leftovers. Two ingredients are almost always present no matter what the main ingredient is: one or two pimiento-stuffed green olives and a sliver of hard-boiled egg.

There are many exotic recipes for empanada pastry and fillings. This particular empanada recipe originated in the Northwest Territories— one of the few places in Argentina where the Indian influence prevails. Hence, it is one of the spicier empanada choices. The recipe came to Buenos Aires from Salta when migration from the provinces to the big city was at its height in the 1930s.

Pastry Directions

Sift the flour, baking powder and salt into a large bowl. Cut the fat into small pieces and rub into the flour with your fingertips to form a coarse meal. Mix with cold water until the dough is stiff but not dry. Gather the dough into a ball, cover it with waxed paper and refrigerate it for 1 hour. Roll the dough out on a floured surface until it is about ⅛ inch thick. Cut it into 16 circles that are 4 to 5 inches in diameter, using a bowl as a guide. Cover and keep cool until ready to use.

PASTRY

4 cups flour

2 teaspoons baking powder

1 teaspoon salt

1½ cups lard or ¾ cup each lard and butter

FILLING

- 2 tablespoons currants
- ½ cup finely chopped onions
- 1 tablespoon olive oil
- ½ cup water
- 1-pound boneless sirloin steak cut into ¼-inch cubes
- 2 tablespoons blanched, coarsely chopped almonds
- 1 teaspoon crushed dried chili pepper
- 3 garlic cloves, finely minced
- ½ teaspoon paprika
- ¼ teaspoon ground cumin seeds
- ½ teaspoon salt
  Freshly ground black pepper

ASSEMBLY

- 2 hard-boiled eggs, each cut lengthwise into 8 wedges
- 32 pimiento-stuffed green olives
- 1 egg, beaten with ½ teaspoon water

Makes approximately 16 turnovers

Filling Directions

Soak the currants in 1 cup boiling water for 10 minutes and drain thoroughly. Combine the onions, olive oil and water. Boil over high heat until the water is completely evaporated. Add the meat cubes and sauté, stirring constantly until they are browned on all sides. Stir in the currants, almonds, chili, garlic, paprika, cumin, salt and pepper. Set aside and cool.

Assembly Directions

Spoon 2 tablespoons of the meat mixture across the center of each circle of pastry, leaving ¼ inch at the edges. Press an egg slice and whole olive into one end, and another olive into the other end. Moisten the edges of the pastry with the beaten egg and fold the pastry over to make a turnover, pressing the edges together firmly. Curve the turnover slightly to form a crescent shape, then turn about ¼ inch of the pastry back over itself, pinching it between your thumb and forefinger to form a rope-like pattern around the edges. Prick the tops of the turnovers several times with fork-tines and brush with the remaining egg mixture. The empanadas are now ready to bake, or may be frozen. If frozen, let them thaw for 3 hours at room temperature before baking.

Preheat the oven to 400°F. Place the empanadas on a Silpat-lined or greased cookie sheet at least 2 inches apart. Bake for 10 minutes. Reduce the heat to 350°F and bake for 30 more minutes, or until golden brown. Transfer the empanadas to a heated platter and serve immediately.

Caviar-Stuffed Timbale

TIMBALES RELLENO

Here is a delicate first course that is a good example of Argentine finesse in the kitchen—as served at the prestigious Alvear Palace Hotel in Buenos Aires.

Directions

Preheat the oven to 350°F. Cut fillets into pieces, season with salt and pepper and sprinkle with lemon juice. Marinate in the refrigerator for 15 minutes. Remove fillets from the refrigerator and process in a food processor with cheese, saffron, egg whites and Jerez. Butter the small molds and fill them ¾ full with the fish mixture. Make a hollow in the center of each timbale and place a teaspoonful of caviar in the cavity. Cover the molds with the remaining fish mixture. Top the molds with aluminum foil. Place the molds in a baking pan filled ¾-full with water. Bake for 20 to 25 minutes, or until set. Unmold each timbale on individual serving plates topped with warm lemon cream sauce (recipe follows) and garnish with a sprig of fresh dill. Alternatively, chill both the timbales and sauce and serve cold.

Directions for Lemon Cream Sauce

Melt the butter in a saucepan over medium heat. Add the shallots and sauté until lightly browned, being careful not to burn the butter. Add the wine and turn the heat to high. Boil until the mixture is reduced by half. Add the chicken stock and lemon juice. Continue boiling until the sauce is again reduced by ⅓. Add the cream and reduce the heat to low. Continue cooking, while stirring, until the sauce is slightly thickened. Remove from the heat and strain. Stir in the lemon zest and salt and pepper. Serve warm or cold.

INGREDIENTS

1   pound fillet of sole or hake
    Salt and pepper to taste
1   tablespoon lemon juice
6   tablespoons cream cheese
    Saffron powder
2   egg whites
1   tablespoon Jerez or other
    dry Spanish sherry
    Butter for greasing the
    molds
2   tablespoons fresh caviar
1   recipe lemon cream sauce
    Sprigs of fresh dill

SAUCE

1   tablespoon butter
¼   cup chopped shallots
1   cup dry white wine
3   cups chicken stock
½ to ¾ cup lemon juice
¾   cup heavy cream
1   tablespoon grated
    lemon zest
    Salt and white pepper
    to taste

Serves 6

Cold Vegetable Soup

GAZPACHO

This recipe for gazpacho is a delightful first course in hot weather. It also can be served in lieu of salad any time of the year.

Directions

Lay crackers in a bowl. Cover well with warm water and let stand until soft. Drain and break the crackers into pieces, discarding the water. Mix the soaked crackers with the onion, bell pepper, tomato and sardines. In another bowl, beat the vinegar, paprika, minced parsley, basil, salt and pepper into the olive oil with whisk until the mixture thickens slightly. Mix the dressing with the sardine mixture and the tomato juice and garnish with parsley.

INGREDIENTS

4   saltine crackers
    Warm water
1   medium red onion, minced
1   green bell pepper,
    chopped
1   large tomato, chopped
1   6-ounce tin sardines,
    drained, boned and
    shredded
¼   cup red wine vinegar
1   tablespoon sweet paprika
2   tablespoons minced
    parsley
2   tablespoons minced
    fresh basil
    Salt and pepper to taste
½   cup olive oil
1 ½ cups tomato juice or
    vegetable juice
    Sprig of parsley

Serves 4

Frog Soup

SOPA DE RANA

Argentines are crazy about frogs. Gigantic ones are the norm in Buenos Aires markets. If you enjoy frogs' legs and your fish or gourmet market has access to them, try the following recipe for an unusual taste treat.

Directions

Remove all meat from the frogs, reserving the legs. Chop the carcass meat and liver. Heat the olive oil in a heavy pot until it is smoking. Add the garlic, onion, carrot, parsley, basil and celery leaves. Stir on medium heat until the vegetables are lightly browned. Turn down the heat and add the tomato, mushrooms and chopped frog meat. Continue cooking for about 5 minutes. Add the water, chicken broth and wine. Bring slowly to a boil and simmer until the meat is very tender, about 30 minutes.

Remove the mixture from the heat and strain, discarding the meat and vegetables. Return the broth to the pot and season to taste with salt and pepper. Add the reserved frog legs and simmer until tender, 15 to 20 minutes. Remove the frog legs and set aside to cool. When cool enough to handle, remove the meat from the frogs' legs, shred it and return it to the pot. Reheat soup over medium heat. Stir in breadcrumbs and garnish with a dollop of crème fraiche. Serve hot with toast fingers.

INGREDIENTS

1   dozen frogs
3   tablespoons olive oil
3   garlic cloves, minced
1   medium red onion, minced
1   carrot, minced
1   sprig parsley
1   sprig basil
2   tablespoons chopped
    celery leaves
1   tomato, chopped
4   mushrooms, chopped
3   cups water
2   cups chicken broth
1   cup white wine
    Salt and pepper to taste
2   tablespoons dry
    breadcrumbs
3   tablespoons crème fraiche
4   slices French bread,
    toasted and cut into 1- by
    3-inch pieces

Serves 4 to 6

Sole in Vinaigrette Sauce

MERLUZA EN ESCABECHE

The waters off the long coastline of Argentina in the South Atlantic are brimming with excellent fish and shellfish. Among them are sole, flounder, hake, red snapper, seabass, crab, squid and prawns. Since the simplest preparations are best for fruits of the ocean, the recipes for preparing them are not as numerous or as varied as those for meat and poultry.

In Argentina, the *escabeches*—or lightly pickled white fish—are especially appreciated. Originating with the Spanish, *escabeche* has evolved in Argentina to include local herbs and vegetables. In some localities, *pescado en escabeche* is made by the keg and sold in delicatessens. Any meat, poultry or fish can be used in *escabeche*, and the sour sauce comes in several varieties. This recipe is typical of Buenos Aires and Mar del Plata.

Directions

Rinse the fish and pat it dry. Cut the fillets into 12 pieces and sprinkle them with salt. Let the fish rest at room temperature for 1 hour. Rinse and dry the fillets then dredge them in flour, shaking to remove the excess. Sauté the fillets in 3 tablespoons of olive oil until they become opaque, about 5 minutes per side. Arrange the cooked fillets in a shallow dish. Make the marinade by mixing 1 cup olive oil with the garlic, cornichons, hard-boiled eggs, capers, parsley, vinegar and salt and pepper to taste. Pour the marinade over the cooked fillets and marinate them at room temperature for at least 1 hour. When ready to serve, drain the fillets and place them on top of the lettuce leaves.

Striped Bass Buenos Aires Style

CORBINA À LA PORTEÑA

Here is a simple recipe for baked fish calling for striped bass. However, any firm-fleshed white fish can be substituted.

Directions

Preheat the oven to 350°F. Dredge the fish slices in flour. Pour ½ cup olive oil in a baking dish and arrange the fish slices on top. Sauté the onions in the remaining 1 cup olive oil until soft. Add tomatoes, green bell peppers, bay leaf, oregano, salt and pepper. Simmer the mixture until it is thick and well blended. Pour the sauce over the fish and bake for 20 minutes or until the fish flakes easily with a fork. Discard the bay leaf. Transfer the fish to a heated platter and sprinkle with parsley.

INGREDIENTS

3 to 3½-pound striped bass, cleaned, boned with head and tail removed, cut into 1½-inch slices

1 cup flour

1½ cups olive oil

2 medium onions, chopped

2 tomatoes, peeled and chopped

2 green bell peppers, sliced

1 bay leaf

1 teaspoon dried oregano

Salt and pepper to taste

1 tablespoon minced parsley

Serves 4

Chicken in Cognac Sauce

POLLO EN SALSA DE COGNAC

This dish probably originated in France and the recipe migrated down the Mediterranean coast to Cataluña before making its way to Argentina. If you can find it, use a Spanish brandy in this dish. A medium-priced Fundador is perfect but a little hard to find.

INGREDIENTS

4   cups chicken stock
1   stewing hen, split in half
    Salt and pepper to taste
1   whole onion, peeled with
    3 cloves inserted in the
    flesh
1   large carrot, coarsely
    chopped
1   tablespoon fresh thyme
    Parmesan cheese

Directions

Pour the chicken stock into a large stockpot. Place the hen in the pot along with salt, pepper, onion, carrot and thyme. Bring the hen barely to a boil and simmer until tender. When the hen is done, remove it from the heat and set it aside to rest in the pot until the sauce is ready.

Preheat the oven to 400°F. Remove the hen halves from the broth and place them skin-side up in the baking dish. Reserve the broth for use in the sauce.

Directions for Cognac Sauce

Melt the butter in a saucepan and stir in the flour. Add the chicken broth, cognac, salt and pepper. Cook while stirring over a medium heat for several minutes or until the mixture is thickened. Set aside and keep warm until ready to use, or store in the refrigerator for up to a day. Spoon cognac sauce over the hen and top with a sprinkling of Parmesan cheese. Brown uncovered in the oven for about 10 minutes.

SAUCE

1   tablespoon butter
1   tablespoon flour
6   tablespoons reserved
    chicken stock
3   tablespoons cognac or
    brandy
    Salt and pepper to taste

Serves 4

Simple Roast Squab

POLLITO AL HORNO

Rosemary and lemon lend a subtle perfume to
what is the simplest of roast squab recipes.
Cornish game hens or small poussin chickens
may be substituted.

Directions

Preheat the oven to 350°F. Season the cavities of the
squabs with 1½ teaspoons salt and 1 teaspoon pepper.
Place the lemon slices, rosemary and garlic inside the cavities. Mix together the oil and the remaining 1½ teaspoons salt and 1 teaspoon pepper. Rub the mixture on
the skin of the squabs. Place the squabs breast-side up in
a flameproof casserole (preferably earthenware). Cover
the casserole and place it in the oven, basting periodically
with wine. Roast the squabs until they are tender (the legs
will move easily in their sockets), golden brown outside
and pink inside, 50 to 80 minutes. Remove the squabs to
a warm platter and serve them plain or with a sauce of
your choice.

*Variation: After the squabs have rested for a few minutes, place them
on buttered croutons on a bed of roasted peppers (recipe page 55) and
garnish with watercress. Green grapes also make a nice garnish.*

INGREDIENTS

4   squabs, cleaned and
    trussed
1   tablespoon coarse kosher
    or sea salt
2   teaspoons freshly ground
    pepper
8   lemon slices
4   fresh rosemary sprigs
4   garlic cloves, peeled
    Olive oil
¼   cup white wine or dry
    sherry

Serves 4

Creole Roast Turkey

PAVITA RELLENA À LA CRIOLLA

In the old days, turkey was a specialty at the Contes Ristorante in Buenos Aires. This restaurant featured turkeys that, according to legend, grew bigger than anywhere else. Only the maitre d'hotel was considered competent to cut the first slice from a prime roast turkey and serve it to the host or an honored guest. A less exalted waiter carved the remainder of the bird and served it to the other diners at the table.

INGREDIENTS

4   cups coarse kosher or sea salt
2   gallons water
10- to 12-pound turkey (not self-basting), preferably a hen
½ cup olive oil
¾ cup to 1 cup butter, melted

Directions

Make a brine solution by dissolving the salt in the water. Submerge the turkey in the brine for 4 to 6 hours in a very cool spot.

Preheat the oven to 325°F. Remove the turkey from the brine and rinse it thoroughly, inside and out. Pat the turkey dry, inside and out. Stuff the turkey (stuffing recipe follows) and truss it. If you have more stuffing than can fit in the turkey, bake it separately in a foil-covered pan at 325°F for 45 minutes. Rub the turkey all over with olive oil. Place it breast side down on a wire rack in a roasting pan. Add ¾ cup water to the pan. Roast uncovered for 2 hours, basting the back and legs several times with melted butter.

Remove the turkey from the oven and carefully turn it over so it is breast side up. Return the turkey to the oven, baste with the pan drippings and continue roasting for 1 to 1½ hours. To test for doneness, insert an instant-read thermometer into the thickest part of the thigh. When it registers 175°F to 180°F, the turkey is done. If the breast is not sufficiently browned, raise the heat to 400°F and continue to roast for another 5 to 10 minutes. Remove the turkey to a cutting board and let it rest for 30 to 40 minutes.

While gravy is unusual in Argentina, it can be made from the giblets, neck and pan drippings if desired. Cook the neck and giblets in water to make 3 cups of stock. Stir 4 tablespoons of flour into 4 tablespoons of drippings from the roasting pan. Add the stock and cook, stirring continuously, until the gravy thickens.

Persimmon and Sausage Stuffing

I developed this recipe for stuffing based on Argentine techniques and ingredients. The recipe calls for persimmons which are available in North America in the fall and early winter. They may be replaced with another fruit. I have used fresh peaches with great results. What fruit you use depends upon what's in season.

Directions

Soak the croutons or bread in milk or broth and allow them to absorb the liquid. Squeeze out the excess and fluff up the bread with a fork. In a skillet, heat the butter and sauté the onion until it is golden. Add the sausage meat and cook it until it has lost all its color, mashing with a potato masher to break it up. Remove the skillet from the heat. Add the croutons or bread, bay leaf, oregano, parsley, hard-boiled eggs, olives and persimmons. Season to taste with salt and pepper. Stir in the beaten eggs, mixing well. Stuff the turkey as directed in the previous recipe.

INGREDIENTS

2   8-ounce packages cheese
    and garlic croutons, or 8
    slices firm white bread
1½ cups milk, or chicken broth
2   tablespoons butter
1   medium onion, minced
1   pound pork sausage meat
2   bay leaves, crumbled
1   teaspoon dried crushed
    oregano
1   tablespoon minced parsley
2   hard-boiled eggs, finely
    chopped
½   cup pitted, chopped green
    olives
2   cups peeled, pitted, and
    chopped (into bite-sized
    pieces) fresh persimmons
    Salt and pepper to taste
2   eggs, lightly beaten

Serves 8 to 10

Tagliarini with Beef, Pork and Mushroom Sauce

TALLARINES CON TUCO À LA MUTTI BECKER

As the Spanish recipe title might indicate, this is a German twist on an Argentine favorite, courtesy of Señora Mutti Becker, who is the mother of my good friend, Paul Becker. Mother Becker moved to Argentina from the Black Forest area of southern Germany. She brought with her a husband, her five-year old son and a cooking talent beyond compare. She is now in her nineties and as lively as ever. Unfortunately, she never learned to speak Spanish in the 40 years she lived in Argentina, nor English during her ten-year stay in California. Because I don't speak German, I am at Paul's mercy when it comes to obtaining recipes from Mother Becker's famous kitchen. This recipe for *Tallarines con Tuco* is one he was willing to share. For this I am grateful, but I'm still working on him for some of Mother Becker's extremely wicked recipes for cakes and pastries.

The sauce for this noodle dish turns upside down the notion of sauced pastas. Instead of a watery, tomato sauce with a little meat—just enough for flavor—this dish is mostly flavorful chunks of beef and pork loin, with just enough sauce to keep the meat and mushrooms moist.

INGREDIENTS

- 1 pound lean beef (flatiron or chuck steak) cut into 1- by 1- by ½-inch cubes
- 1 pound pork loin, cut into 1- by 1- by ½-inch cubes
- 1 tablespoon olive oil
- 1 tablespoon butter
- Salt and pepper to taste
- 1 large onion, chopped
- 2 garlic cloves, minced
- ¼ pound porcini (dried Italian mushrooms), rehydrated in hot water for 30 minutes and drained (or ½ pound sliced fresh mushrooms)
- ¼ cup minced parsley
- 3 ounces tomato paste, dissolved in 1 cup water
- 2 chopped fresh oregano
- 1 bay leaf, crushed
- 1 teaspoon prepared mustard
- ½ cup dry vermouth
- 1 teaspoon ground thyme
- 1 pound tagliarini (small noodles)
- 2 tablespoons freshly grated Parmesan cheese

Serves 6

Directions

Brown the beef and pork cubes in oil and butter in a flameproof casserole. Season with salt and pepper while browning. Remove the meat when browned on all sides and keep it warm. Brown the onion, garlic and mushrooms in the remaining oil, adding some extra oil if necessary to keep the mixture from sticking. Add parsley and return the meat to the casserole. Stir in tomato paste, oregano, bay leaf, mustard, vermouth and thyme. Cover and simmer over low heat for 2 to 2½ hours. When the sauce is almost done, boil the tagliarini in 6 quarts of salted water for about 8 minutes or until it is al dente. Drain the tagliarini and keep it warm. Spoon the meat sauce generously over the tagliarini, sprinkle with Parmesan cheese and serve.

Veal Ravioli in Mushroom Sauce

RAVIOLI DE VITELLO CON FUNGHI

Pasta for ravioli must be soft and sticky. That means you must take your dough through the thinning process, cut it and stuff it individually before going on to the next piece. While you're working on one piece, make sure the rest of the dough is tightly covered in plastic wrap.

Directions
In a large skillet, put in 2 tablespoons of the oil and add the garlic. Cook on a medium heat, stirring, until the garlic is golden. Add the rosemary and stir. Add the veal and brown it thoroughly on both sides. Add salt and pepper and turn the meat several times. Add the wine and let it boil down to almost nothing while scraping the bottom of the pan with a wooden spoon. Transfer the meat mixture to a bowl and remove and discard the garlic.

INGREDIENTS

4   tablespoons olive oil
4   garlic cloves, peeled
1   teaspoon chopped dried
     rosemary leaves
1   pound veal, cut into strips
     Salt to taste
     Freshly ground black
     pepper to taste
¼   cup dry white wine
1½ cups shredded savoy cab-
     bage
2   egg yolks
1   recipe hand- or machine-
     rolled pasta dough
     (page 189)
     Mushroom cream sauce
     (page 194)

Serves 4 to 6

Pour 1 tablespoon oil in the skillet and add the cabbage. Turn up the heat to high and turn over the cabbage with a wooden spoon until it is thoroughly coated with the oil. Lower the heat, cover the skillet and simmer the cabbage for approximately 15 minutes or until it is limp. Turn the cabbage over occasionally so that it cooks evenly. Transfer the cabbage to a food processor and add the meat mixture. Process carefully to avoid reducing the mixture to pulp. Return the mixture to a mixing bowl and add the egg yolks, mixing well with a wooden spoon.

Cover half a sheet of freshly rolled pasta with mounds of ½ teaspoon each of the filling spaced 1 inch apart. Cover with the second half of the rolled pasta. Dip your finger in water and run it around the pasta so that no air is trapped. Press firmly to seal. Use a zigzag cutter to cut the sheet into squares, making sure that each piece is well sealed.

Bring 8 quarts of lightly salted water to a rolling boil. Add the pasta and 1 tablespoon of olive oil. (Avoid over-crowding the pot; cook in batches if necessary.) Reduce the heat and simmer, uncovered, until the ravioli rise to the top of the water, 5 to 6 minutes. Test by tasting to see if the ravioli are soft but still al dente. Drain the ravioli carefully and transfer them to a warm serving dish. Toss gently with a little olive oil and then with the mushroom sauce.

Beef Rolls à la Mutti Becker

NIÑOS ENVUELTOS À LA MUTTI BECKER

Here is another recipe from the kitchen of
Señora Mutti Becker—purveyor of German-
Italian-Argentine food extraordinaire.

Directions

Season both sides of the meat with salt and pepper, smear
a thin layer of mustard on the top side. Top each piece of
meat with a bacon slice, pickle slice and 1 tablespoon of
chopped onion. Roll the meat strips into a compact
package approximately 1½ inches in diameter and 4
inches long. Tie the rolls with sewing thread and fasten
the thread ends with a toothpick inserted into the end of
each roll. Sauté the rolls in oil and butter until brown on
all sides. Add ¼ inch hot water to the sauté pan. Cover
the pan and reduce the heat to low. Simmer for 1½ hours.
When done, remove the rolls to a heated serving platter
and remove the threads. Mix the cornstarch with the cold
water and add it to the pan juices. Stir over medium heat
until the sauce thickens. Remove the sauce from heat and
stir in the sour cream. Spoon the sauce over the meat rolls
and gnocchi.

INGREDIENTS

2 pounds sirloin or top round
   steak, pounded to ¼ inch
   thick and cut into 6 equal
   strips
   Salt and pepper to taste
2 tablespoons Dijon mustard
6 slices lean smoked bacon,
   thick cut
4 sour pickles, sliced lengthwise
1 medium onion, minced
1½ tablespoons olive oil
1½ tablespoons butter
   Hot water
1 tablespoon cornstarch
3 tablespoons cold water
2 heaping tablespoons sour
   cream
1 recipe gnocchi (recipe
   follows)

Serves 6

Potato Gnocchi
ÑOQUIS DE PAPAS

Many cooks in Argentina add eggs to their gnocchi. This recipe omits the egg because I believe that eggless gnocchi are lighter and tenderer. Gnocchi are usually served with *niños revueltos* but they are also very good with a roasted chicken, lamb or beef.

Directions

Boil potatoes in salted water until done, 20 to 30 minutes. When cool enough to handle but still warm, mash the potatoes until they become a smooth purée. Add flour, oregano and oil. Blend well until the dough is soft without kneading. If necessary, add a little more flour. Roll the dough into long, rope-like lengths, the thickness of a finger. Cut into pieces about 1½ inches in length and dust with flour. Press the tines of a fork across one end of each gnocchi to create ridges; indent the other end with your thumb. Let the gnocchi rest for at least an hour on a well-floured towel.

INGREDIENTS

2 pounds medium mealy potatoes such as russets, peeled
   Boiling salted water to cover
3 teaspoons crushed dried oregano
1½ cups flour
1 tablespoon vegetable oil
   Salt to taste
2 tablespoons grated Parmesan cheese

Serves 6

Bring a large pot of salted water to a boil and drop the gnocchi pieces in by the handful. When they rise to the top of water and stay afloat—2 to 3 minutes—remove immediately with a slotted spoon. Place the cooked gnocchi in a colander, drain them and keep them warm. Arrange the gnocchi on a serving platter around the beef rolls (page 47). Moisten the meat and gnocchi with the sauce and top with grated Parmesan cheese. Gnocchi may be prepared in advance and reheated in a microwave or moderate oven.

Filet Mignon in Egg Batter

Argentina is famous for its flavorful fork-tender beef. With beef production for export the largest industry in Argentina, Buenos Aires boasts the biggest refrigerating plant in the world. Buenos Aires is also famous for setting the most sophisticated meat table of any in the world. As far as beef is concerned, there is none finer anywhere—tender, melting cuts that need no knife with a rich, succulent flavor that is not found elsewhere in Latin America, save Uruguay with its similar grazing conditions. Fortunately for North American gourmets, our beef is exceptionally good and lends itself to cooking in the Argentine manner.

Churrasco Rebosado is an extremely rich dish that calls for light accompaniments such as a simple salad and rice.

Directions

Add flour to the beaten egg yolks all at once and continue to beat until smooth. Add milk to the mixture and stir in garlic, salt, pepper, marjoram and chilies. Carefully fold in the beaten egg whites. Dip the steaks in the batter, coating well. Heat the oil in a skillet until it smokes. Fry the coated steaks in the hot oil for 3 to 5 minutes per side, depending upon how well done you like your meat. Remove to a heated platter, dust with a little paprika and garnish with watercress.

INGREDIENTS

1 ½ cups sifted flour

4 egg yolks, beaten with a fork

½ cup milk

2 garlic cloves, minced

1 ½ teaspoons salt

½ teaspoon pepper

½ teaspoon crushed dried marjoram

¼ teaspoon crushed dried chili pepper

4 egg whites, beaten until stiff but not dry

8 beef filets or boneless sirloin steaks about ½ inch thick, trimmed of all fat

1 cup olive oil
Sweet paprika
Bunches of watercress or parsley for garnish

Serves 8

Roulade of Flank Steak and Vegetables

MATAMBRE

INGREDIENTS ▭▭

2-pound flank steak (thin outer
layer if possible), trimmed
of fat and gristle

½ cup red wine vinegar

3 garlic cloves, minced

1 tablespoon fresh thyme
leaves (or 1 teaspoon
crushed dried thyme)

2 tablespoons crushed dried
oregano

½ pound fresh spinach
leaves, washed, drained
and stems removed

4 to 5 carrots, scraped and
cut in half lengthwise
(if more than 1 inch in
diameter, parboil for 3 to
4 minutes)

4 hard-boiled eggs, cut
lengthwise into quarters

1 pound veal, cut in narrow
strips

½ pound salt pork, cut in
narrow strips

1 large onion, sliced ⅛ inch
thick and divided into rings

½ cup chopped parsley

1 tablespoon crushed dried
chili pepper

1 tablespoon coarse kosher
or sea salt

2 tablespoons grated
Parmesan cheese

8 cups beef stock

1 bay leaf

4 black peppercorns,
crushed

Serves 8 to 10

Literally translated, *matambre* means "hunger killer" and it's more than equal to the task. *Matambre* is usually cut in thick slices and served cold on an equally thick slice of crusty bread at teatime. And it is usually washed down with *yerba mate*. It is lovely to look at, with its many layers and colors made of thin flank steak, spinach, carrots, onions, hard-boiled egg slices and green olives. It is even better to eat, with its hearty beef essence, its fresh vegetable flavors and its spicy overtones.

Directions

Preheat the oven to 325°F. Butterfly the steak lengthwise and sprinkle both sides with vinegar, garlic, thyme and oregano. Cover and marinate for 12 hours in the refrigerator. Drain the steaks and lay them side by side, overlapping by about 2 inches. Pound the overlapping edges together to make a seal. Cover the meat with a thick layer of spinach leaves. Arrange the carrots with the grain of the meat in rows about 2 inches apart. Place eggs, veal strips and salt pork strips between the carrot rows. Scatter the onion rings over the filling and sprinkle with parsley, chili pepper and salt. Sprinkle the onion rings with Parmesan cheese and roll up the meat carefully with the grain (like a jellyroll). Secure the roll with skewers and string.

Place the *matambre* in a 12-quart, flameproof casserole or roasting pan. Add stock, bay leaf and crushed peppercorns. Cover and bring just to the boiling point. Turn off the heat and place the casserole in the middle of the oven. Simmer for about 2 hours or until the meat is tender but not falling apart.

To serve warm, let the *matambre* rest on a cutting board for 10 minutes. Remove the string and cut the *matambre* crosswise into 1-inch slices. Arrange the slices on a heated platter and moisten them with some of the pan liquid. To serve cold the following day, remove the matambre from the casserole after it has cooled. Press the *matambre* under weights until the juices drain off. Wrap it in foil or plastic wrap and refrigerate. When thoroughly chilled, cut the *matambre* crosswise into ½ inch thick slices and serve atop a thick slice of good French bread.

Breaded Beef Buenos Aires Style

MILANESA À LA PORTEÑA

Milanesa is every Argentine's favorite dish. While similar in concept to our chicken fried steak, it's quite different in taste and texture. And, in Argentina, there are as many ways to treat *milanesa* as there are cooks. Some top the finished dish with tomatoes. Some melt cheese on top. Others like theirs covered with sliced cooked eggplant and a spicy sauce. But most like it plain with a squirt of lemon—if you can call "plain" a dish with eleven ingredients.

The following is your basic Argentine *milanesa* made of beef. You can be creative and add any number of toppings. *Milanesa* is usually served with a salad and gnocchi or French-fried potatoes Argentine style.

INGREDIENTS

1½ pounds boneless sirloin,
  fat removed
1 egg, beaten lightly
2 garlic cloves, finely minced
½ teaspoon crushed dried
  oregano
¼ teaspoon crushed dried
  red chili peppers
¼ teaspoon salt
  Freshly ground pepper to
  taste
  Pinch of dried parsley or
  cilantro
½ cup dry breadcrumbs
¼ cup olive, grapeseed or
  peanut oil
1 tablespoon chopped
  parsley
  Lemon wedges

Serves 4

Directions

Slice the meat into ¼ inch thick pieces and pound them until they are about ⅛ inch thick (yields about 8 slices). Beat the egg lightly with a fork. Add garlic, oregano, red pepper, salt, pepper and dried parsley. Pour the egg mixture over the steaks and marinate them for 10 minutes, turning several times. Dip the steaks in breadcrumbs, turning several times to cover the steaks thoroughly, pressing the crumbs into the steaks with the heel of your hand. Heat the oil in a skillet and sauté the steaks on a medium setting until they are golden brown on both sides. Remove the steaks from the skillet, sprinkle them with fresh parsley and serve with lemon wedges.

Oven-Roasted Potatoes

PAPAS AL HORNO

In Buenos Aires, *Papas al Horno* are the first choice for meat accompaniments with French fries running a close second. I prefer the former—perhaps because you don't need a big pot of boiling oil to make it. Also, I think *papas al horno* taste even better with their salty, crispy brown outer crust and tender insides. And they couldn't be easier to prepare.

Directions

Preheat the oven to 500°F. Place the quartered potatoes in an oiled roasting pan in a single layer. Sprinkle the oil over the potatoes and keep turning them and basting them until they are thoroughly coated with the oil. Sprinkle the potatoes with 1 tablespoon salt and 1 table-spoon paprika and turn them again. Place the potatoes in the oven in an uncovered roasting pan. Roast for 20 min-utes. Turn the potatoes over with a spatula, scraping the bottom of the pan so that the potatoes don't stick. Sprinkle with the remaining 1 tablespoon salt and 1 table-spoon paprika. Continue roasting until potatoes are cooked through and nicely browned. If the potatoes are soft but not browned enough, place them under a broiler for several minutes.

INGREDIENTS

6 medium white potatoes,
   peeled and quartered
   lengthwise
½ to 1 cup olive oil or
   vegetable oil
2 tablespoons coarse kosher
   or sea salt
2 tablespoons sweet paprika

   Serves 6

Chard in Cream Sauce

ACELGAS EN CREMA

Even people who claim to hate vegetables enjoy this dish. Its combination of chard with onions, carrots and potatoes may seem like gilding the lily to North American cooks, but the result justifies the effort. The addition of cream raises homely vegetables to epicurean heights.

Directions

Melt the butter in a saucepan or skillet and sauté the onion, carrot and potato cubes until they are tender. Cut the chard (both stems and leaves) crosswise into thin strips. Stir the chard into the vegetable mixture and season to taste with salt and pepper. Cover and simmer over very low heat until the chard is tender, about 10 minutes. Stir in the cream and simmer, uncovered, for about 3 minutes. Remove the chard from the heat and place it in a serving dish. Sprinkle it with nutmeg and serve.

INGREDIENTS

3   tablespoons sweet butter
1   medium onion, finely
    chopped
1   medium carrot, julienned
1   medium potato, cut in ½-
    inch cubes
1 ½ pounds green Swiss
    chard, washed and
    drained
    Salt and freshly ground
    pepper
⅓ cup heavy cream
    Dash of freshly ground
    nutmeg

Serves 6

Roasted Marinated Peppers

Not to be missed, roasted, skinned, marinated peppers—both mild and hot—are a traditional accompaniment to grilled meats, especially *asado al horno*. Using different colored peppers— green, red, orange, yellow and purple—makes an attractive arrangement at the table. For an informal but delectable appetizer, pile several of the marinated pepper strips on top of a piece of bread or biscuits. If fresh herbs are not available, substitute dried ones. While not traditional, the addition of light soya sauce to the marinade adds just the right note.

Directions

Char peppers over a gas flame, on a barbecue or in a broiler. When evenly charred, put peppers in a paper bag and close it. This step steams the peppers and makes it easier to remove the skins. When cool enough to handle, peel off the skins and remove the seeds. Tear the peppers into strips about 1½ inches across at the widest point. Lay the strips in a single layer on a platter radiating them like spokes on a wheel, and sprinkle them with olive oil, vinegar, soya sauce, salt and pepper. Top with a sprinkling of basil, oregano, marjoram and chili pepper. If using dried herbs crush them between your fingers before adding. *Aji* may be served warm or can be made ahead and served chilled.

INGREDIENTS

6   large sweet peppers (or 4 bell peppers and 2 California green or pasilla chilies)

⅓   cup olive oil

¼   cup balsamic vinegar

2   teaspoons light soya sauce
    Salt and pepper to taste

1   teaspoon chopped fresh basil leaves (or ¼ teaspoon dried basil)

1   teaspoon chopped fresh oregano leaves (or ¼ teaspoon dried oregano)

1   teaspoon chopped fresh marjoram (or ¼ teaspoon dried marjoram)
    Pinch crushed dried chili pepper (omit if using green chilies)

Serves 6

Cauliflower Croquettes

CROQUETAS DE COLIFOR

Vegetables that are sauced or fried in a batter must be very young and fresh. This recipe comes from the kitchen of Señora Josefa Rebaudo. The batter may be used with other vegetables such as broccoli, green beans, summer squashes or parboiled carrots.

Directions

Cook the florets over medium heat in ½ cup milk and water to cover for 4 minutes. Drain and marinate the florets in olive oil, season with salt and pepper and let them cool. Make a batter of flour, egg yolks and remaining ½ cup milk, mixing well. Fold in the egg white. Dip the florets in batter and deep-fry briefly in oil until lightly browned. Drain on paper towels and serve.

English Sauce

An Argentine interpretation of an English sauce, *Salsa Inglesa* is a favorite topping for fish and vegetables. To avoid salmonella contamination, make sure the raw egg yolk used in this recipe is very fresh and the shell is clean before cracking.

Directions

Add the mustard, sugar and egg yolk to the water and beat the mixture well with a whisk. Add the oil and continue to beat until thickened. Beat in the milk and add vinegar a little at a time. Continue to beat for about 15 seconds more.

INGREDIENTS

1   teaspoon Dijon mustard
1   teaspoon sugar
1   raw egg yolk
2   teaspoons cold water
¼   cup olive oil
2   tablespoons milk
2   tablespoons white wine
     vinegar

Makes about ½ cup
of sauce

Orange Cake

TORTA DE NARANJA

Torta de naranja came to Argentina from Andalusia in southern Spain with the first wave of Spanish immigrants after the Conquest.

Directions

Preheat the oven to 300°F. Cream the butter and gradually add the sugar. Beat the mixture until it is light and fluffy. Add whole eggs and extra yolks one at a time, beating well after each addition. Stir in the flour and almonds and pour the mixture into 9-inch tube pan lined on the bottom with waxed paper. Bake for 1 hour, or until a clean broom straw or wooden toothpick inserted in the center of the cake comes out clean. Turn the cake out on plate and allow it to cool.

To make the frosting, mix confectioners' sugar with orange rind and orange juice until smooth. While still warm, spread the cake with the frosting.

INGREDIENTS

1   cup butter, softened
2   cups sugar
4   whole eggs plus 2 egg
    yolks
1¾ cups flour
1½ cups blanched and finely
    ground almonds
2   cups confectioners' sugar
    Grated rind of 1 orange
¼   cup orange juice

Serves 6 to 8

CHAPTER 2

The Pampas:
Land of the Gauchos

The Pampas

When the Spaniards abandoned their first primitive settlement at Buenos Aires for the easy life in Paraguay, they left behind cattle and horses that multiplied prodigiously in their absence. For centuries prior to the arrival of the Spanish, aboriginal people had transformed the natural environment of the Pampas by burning off scrub growth to make it easier to hunt wild game. The succulent native grasses that flourished as a result supported even more game—and eventually—the abandoned Spanish horses and cattle as well. One eighteenth-century visitor estimated the number of cattle in the area at 48 million.

Bordering the Atlantic Ocean and the Río de la Plata, and stretching north to Córdoba and the central Andean foothills, the pampas are the heartland of modern Argentina. Comprising the provinces of Buenos Aires, La Pampa and major portions of Santa Fe and Córdoba, the area is divided into a dry zone west, northwest and south of Buenos Aires, and a humid zone from Buenos Aires extending north to Paraguay, Brazil and Uruguay and south along the Atlantic coast to Mar del Plata and beyond. The dry zone is a sea of grass that extends for hundreds of miles in an arc around Buenos Aires. Scattered throughout these green plains are splendid *estancias* (cattle ranches) that are the domain of the landed oligarchy. As might be expected, the provinces of the Pampas are the center for cattle raising.

The Pampas is also the land of the gauchos—those tougher-than-nails cowboys whose independent self-reliant lifestyle instilled these homely virtues in generations of young, impressionable Argentine men.

Glorious tales of the gauchos are told to this day: that they perished only if their horses died underneath them, leaving them without food or shade; that they drank *caña* (raw spirits made of sugarcane) in quantities that would astonish the rest of humanity; that they were the descendants of Indians and early Spanish settlers; that they fought to the death with knives the size of small swords.

Today they seem less dangerous, less picturesque. But the gaucho who tended the fire at one *asado* had hot black eyes, skin like burnished leather and a large and frightening knife in his belt. In addition to his fiery occupation, he sang haunting songs that came to Argentina with the earliest settlers from Spain.

A gaucho sips *mate* while starting the grill for an *asado*.

The influence of the gauchos on the region and its food is still felt. Local cuisine is simple and hearty, with beef being the center of the culinary universe. A plate of *puchero*—"stew" in English but indicating much more than that—would be considered a peasant dish in other, less democratic countries. In the Pampas, it is eaten in the best restaurants as well as in cattlemen's huts.

The dish is remarkable for the gargantuan size of its ingredients: blocks of beef three to four inches square, whole onions, yams and potatoes, oversized carrots each the size of a turkey baster, thick ears of sweet corn, a large, meat-fringed bone replete with creamy marrow, and for extra flavoring, a sizable chunk of *chorizo*—a garlic-and herb-flavored sausage of a deep oxblood hue. In some kitchens, cooks added greens—cabbage and collards—at the last minute.

Then there's *Bife a Caballo*—Beefsteak on Horseback. Again, it is the quantity that counts, for the dish consists of nothing more than a thick rump steak large enough to cover a dinner plate, surrounded with very crisp fried onions and covered by two, three or four fried eggs, according to the diner's appetite.

Macho-sized steaks are the norm—enough to feed two trenchermen anywhere else. The tenderloin is called *lomo*; sirloin—which carries little fat—is known as beef *chorizo*, even though it's not a sausage. A T-bone steak—so common in the U.S—is not typical. It is available, however, in restaurants and hotels that cater to tourists from the States. A *bife*, which is the most common beef plate, is a large piece of meat with one rib attached. Argentines prefer their beef medium rather than rare, but it is so tender and juicy that one soon begins to cook it or order it the way the locals do.

Interestingly, prime beef is so common and, until recently, so reasonably priced it is rarely served on special occasions. Gala events usually feature chicken or duck. That isn't to say that beef is treated as ho-hum fare. In fact, because of beef's super-abundance, beef cookery has been elevated to a state of near perfection. Fortunately for the Argentines, they have never had to think about increasing yields with hormones or additives.

But there's nothing to compare with the Argentine *asado* prepared by a genuine gaucho. In Spanish, *asado* means merely a roast. But in the Pampas, it means a whole ox or sheep split down the center and roasted on huge iron stakes driven into the ground at an incline over a wood fire. The stakes, which run through the ribs of the animal, are turned from time to time, and the meat is frequently sprinkled with brine or a potent flavoring liquid made from garlic and herbs. Be warned, there is no gender equality here; the preparation of the meat for *asado* is strictly a male activity.

In the Pampas—indeed, throughout Argentina— most cuts of meat are simply marinated in a seasoned olive or grapeseed oil and then grilled over charcoal. Contrary to everything I thought I knew about cooking meat, Argentines salt their oil-coated beef prior to throwing it on the grill. I have to concede that the flavor is better and there's no appreciable loss of juices. At home in California, I now prepare all grilled meat in the Argentine manner to rave reviews from guests and family.

Empanadas Santa Fe Style

EMPANADAS SANTAFESINAS

PASTRY

4   cups flour
½   teaspoon baking powder
6   tablespoons cold lard or
    shortening
3   tablespoons sugar
6   egg yolks and 1 egg
    white, lightly beaten
2   cups lightly salted water

FILLING

2½ tablespoons lard
6   medium tomatoes, peeled,
    seeded, drained and
    coarsely chopped
1   large onion, chopped
4   tablespoons chopped
    pimiento
½   cup minced parsley
4   tablespoons sweet paprika
1   teaspoon sugar
1   pound beef tenderloin,
    roughly chopped
1   cup shredded cooked
    chicken
¾   cup chopped cooked
    bacon
1½ cups peeled, chopped
    cooked pork sausages
½   cup chopped plums or
    prunes
    Salt and pepper to taste
¼   cup red wine vinegar
3   garlic cloves, minced
1   bay leaf, crumbled
½   teaspoon ground cumin
1   teaspoon ground nutmeg
    Few drops Salsa Inglesa
    (page 57)

Here's an unusual empanada recipe gleaned from the files of a talented home cook from Santa Fe.

Pastry Directions

Sift the flour and baking powder together. Cut the lard into the flour with a pastry cutter or two knives until the mixture forms a coarse meal. Mound the mixture on a cookie sheet and make a well. Mix the sugar and eggs thoroughly and pour this mixture into the flour well, pulling the flour into the egg mixture with a fork. Add salted water a little at a time just until the dough holds together, discarding unused water. Remove the dough from the cookie sheet. Stretch or roll the dough to a thickness of ⅛ inch. Cut into 6-inch rounds. Cover with a damp towel and chill in the refrigerator until ready to fill.

Filling Directions

Melt 1½ tablespoons of lard in a large pot. Add tomatoes, onion, pimiento and parsley and sauté for about 5 minutes. Stir in the paprika and continue to cook over low heat for 2 minutes. Remove the mixture from the heat and stir in the sugar. In a skillet, add the remaining 1 tablespoon of lard and sauté the beef until it is lightly browned on all sides. Remove the beef from the skillet and add it to the pot along with the chicken, bacon, sausages and plum or prune pieces. Season with salt and pepper. Mix in the vinegar, garlic, bay leaf, cumin, nutmeg and *Salsa Inglesa*. Continue to stir over low heat until the mixture is cooked through but not dry.

Assembly Directions

Preheat the oven to 375°F. Place a heaping tablespoon of the filling in the center of each pastry circle. Add an egg quarter and an olive. Seal each empanada by folding half the pastry circle over the filling and pinching the edges together as described on page 33. Prick the top of each empanada with a fork. Place the empanadas 2 inches apart on greased or Silpat-lined cookie sheets and bake in the middle of the oven for 20 to 24 minutes, or until golden brown.

ASSEMBLY

4   hard-boiled eggs, cut
     lengthwise into quarters
10 pimiento-stuffed green
     olives

Makes 8 to 10 large
empanadas

Fried Bread

MIGAS DE PAN

Migas—originating in Spain—is the fate of yesterday's bread in Argentina. Whether eaten with drinks or before or with meals, *migas* are considered gourmet fast food in the Pampas. They are especially good with fried eggs.

Directions

Pour the olive oil into a jar, add crushed garlic, cover and set aside. Cut the crusts off the bread and discard. Cut the loaf into crouton-sized pieces and place them in a bowl. Add minced onions, bacon, salt, pepper and paprika and mix well. Sprinkle water over the bread gradually, tossing until the mixture is evenly dampened. Cover and set aside for at least 30 minutes. Heat the garlic oil together with the bacon fat in a skillet. When the oil is hot, cook *migas* in batches. Scoop up about 2 cups of the bread mixture and flatten it into a large ¼ inch thick round. Place it in the skillet and sauté over high heat for about 3 minutes on one side, turn the *migas* in sections and cook on the second side, again drizzling them with oil as needed until they are very crisp and well browned. Set aside to drain on paper towels. When cool enough to handle, break the *migas* into 2-inch pieces. Cook the remaining *migas* mixture in the same fashion. Serve immediately.

INGREDIENTS

1 cup olive oil
4 garlic cloves, crushed
1 large day-old loaf
   sourdough bread, unsliced
2 medium onions, minced
8 slices bacon, fried crisp
   and crumbled
   Bacon fat
1 teaspoon salt
1 teaspoon pepper
1 tablespoon sweet paprika

Serves 8

Cucumber Salad

Ensalada de pepinos is a refreshing first-course salad that can be served at lunch or dinner. Argentine cucumbers resemble English cucumbers; they have fewer seeds than those in the United States do. Either type can be used in this recipe but the English type is preferred.

INGREDIENTS

2   cucumbers, peeled (if
    waxed) and thinly sliced
1   teaspoon salt
2   medium tomatoes, peeled
    and chopped
2   tablespoons olive oil
    Juice from ½ lime
    Salt and pepper to taste

Serves 4

Directions

Mix cucumbers with salt and let stand for 30 minutes. Rinse and drain cucumbers thoroughly. Add tomatoes and toss with oil. Remove seeds from lime and squeeze lime juice over the salad. Season with salt and pepper.

Beef and Potato Soup

Traditional but extremely easy to prepare, *chupi* is a wonderfully comforting soup in winter.

INGREDIENTS

¼   cup vegetable oil
1   large onion, minced
1   red bell pepper, seeded
    and chopped
1   pound lean beef round or
    sirloin steak, coarsely
    chopped
3   medium white potatoes,
    peeled and cubed
1   tablespoon minced parsley
⅛   teaspoon cayenne
6   cups beef stock
2   teaspoon dried crushed
    oregano
    Salt and pepper to taste

Serves 6

Directions

Heat the oil in a large saucepan or flameproof casserole. Sauté onion and bell pepper until tender. Add the beef and sauté while stirring to break it up. When the meat is lightly browned, add potatoes, parsley, cayenne and stock. Season with oregano, salt and pepper and simmer covered for 30 minutes, stirring occasionally. Serve hot.

Roasted Quail
CORDONICES AL HORNO

Cordonices al Horno are wrapped and cooked in grape leaves, which are then unwrapped on the dish forming a decorative nest for the quail. You can find grape leaves in jars at specialty groceries or Middle Eastern markets, if not at your local supermarket.

Directions

Preheat the oven to 325°F. Salt the body cavity of each quail and place a quail liver inside. Sprinkle the outside of each quail with salt and pepper. Wrap each quail first with bacon and then with grape leaves. Top the quail bundles with rosemary sprigs. Roast uncovered for 30 to 45 minutes or until the meat is tender. Discard the rosemary and place the quail on serving dishes. Unwrap the quail and arrange the grape leaves in a nest around each bird before serving.

Variation: Place the cooked, unwrapped quail on roasted, marinated bell peppers; recipe on page 55.

INGREDIENTS

12 quail, cleaned
Salt
12 quail livers
Freshly ground pepper to taste
12 bacon slices
Grape leaves
Fresh rosemary sprigs

Serves 6

Pickled Squabs

Escabeche is one of the most popular treatments for fish and fowl in Argentina. It is usually served as a light luncheon dish or a first course at lunch or dinner.

Directions

Rinse and dry the hens then rub them inside and out with 1½ teaspoons salt and ¼ teaspoon pepper. Heat 2 tablespoons of the olive oil in a large skillet. Add the hens and brown them on all sides. Spread half the onions on the bottom of a flameproof casserole or Dutch oven. Arrange the hens on top of the onions in the casserole and cover them with the remaining onions. Mix together the remaining 1½ teaspoons salt, ½ teaspoon pepper plus the garlic, pimientos, bay leaves, vinegar, white wine, tarragon, chili peppers and the remaining oil. Add this mixture to the casserole. Add the bacon, bouillon cube and water and mix well. Finally, add the carrots, turnips, tomatoes, celery, paprika, cumin, oregano, thyme, rosemary, basil, parsley, cinnamon and cloves. Cover and simmer over low heat for about 1 hour, or until the hens are tender.

Remove the cooked hens and vegetables from the casserole with slotted spoon and place them in a deep bowl, hens on top. Boil the liquid in the casserole over high heat until it is reduced by half. Pour the reduced liquid over the hens, cover the bowl and refrigerate for 48 hours. When ready to serve, drain the hens and cut them into quarters. Serve each quarter on a lettuce leaf with a few stewed vegetables garnished with a chili flower, cherry tomato and radish slices.

INGREDIENTS

2   squabs or Cornish game hens, quartered
3   teaspoons salt
¾   teaspoon freshly ground pepper
1   cup olive oil
4   large onions, sliced or chopped
4   garlic cloves, minced
2   fresh or canned pimientos, julienned with seeds removed
4   bay leaves
½   cup wine vinegar
½   cup dry white wine
½   teaspoon fresh tarragon
3   small dried chili peppers, crushed
6   slices of bacon, chopped
1   chicken bouillon cube
1   cup water
4   carrots, chopped
2   turnips, chopped
4   tomatoes, chopped
½   cup chopped celery
1   teaspoon sweet paprika
½   teaspoon cumin
½   teaspoon dried oregano
1   teaspoon chopped fresh thyme leaves
1   teaspoon chopped fresh rosemary leaves
1   teaspoon chopped fresh basil leaves
3   tablespoons minced parsley
½   cinnamon stick
3   whole cloves
    Lettuce for garnish
8   fresh chili peppers, seeded and cut in flower shapes for garnish
8   cherry tomatoes for garnish
3   radishes, sliced for garnish

Serves 4 as a luncheon dish or first course

Roast Suckling Pig

LECHON ASADO

INGREDIENTS

1 suckling pig (15 to 20 pounds), cleaned, with hair, organs and eyeballs removed

STUFFING

Pig heart

Pig liver

Pig lights (lungs), optional

2 tablespoons salt

5 cups stale bread

2 eggs, beaten

¼ cup tomato sauce

¾ cup raisins soaked in sherry

¼ pound roasted chopped almonds

¼ pound toasted pine nuts

1 cup dried apricots

10 sprigs parsley

3 tablespoons rinsed and drained capers

1 tablespoon crushed dried chili pepper

2 teaspoons dried sage

2 teaspoons dried marjoram

Freshly ground pepper to taste

Sprinkling of lemon juice

In Spain, the ideal age for roast suckling pig is one month old, with a weight of four to seven pounds. But a piglet of this size will be difficult to find in North America—unless you're a pig farmer. Even in Argentina, the average size of a suckling pig is 15 to 20 pounds. I've adapted the recipe for the piglet to a slightly older and larger animal, as it is more likely to be available in the United States.

Stuffing Directions

Boil the heart, liver and lights in water with 1⅓ tablespoons salt until tender. Drain and finely chop. Soak the bread in water until soft. Squeeze the bread dry in a towel and add to the meat mixture. Stir in the eggs, tomato sauce, raisins, almonds, pine nuts, apricots, parsley, capers, chili pepper, sage, marjoram, 2 teaspoons salt, pepper and lemon juice. Mix thoroughly and stuff the pig with this forcemeat. Sew up the opening and truss the pig.

Marinade Directions

Make a marinade by mixing together lemon juice, garlic, wine vinegar, and olive oil, along with paprika, parsley and white wine. Pour the marinade over the pig and marinate for at least 1 hour. When ready to roast the pig, remove it from the marinade, reserving the marinade.

Roasting Directions

Preheat the oven to 425°F. Tie the pig legs in place so as to form a roasting rack as follows: Tie the hind legs together and pull them forward over the belly. Make sure the legs are parallel, not crossed. Pull the front legs back and position them next to the hind legs. Tie the 4 legs together under the pig—again, keeping the legs parallel to the body. Cover the ears and tail with foil.

Make several long diagonal slashes in the skin on one side of the backbone, being careful not to penetrate the meat. Place the roast on its haunches in a sturdy roasting pan (not a disposable aluminum pan) that is just large enough to hold it. A 20-inch pan works best. If necessary, prop up the head on a loaf pan.

Roast for 2 hours, basting every 20 minutes with the hot water, marinade and melted butter during the first hour. After that, baste with the pan drippings at 30-minute intervals and reseason with salt and pepper. After 2 hours of roasting, turn the heat up to 475°F and roast for 30 minutes more. The roast is done when a meat thermometer inserted in the thickest part of the rump reaches a temperature of 165°F to 170°F. Note that the temperature will continue to rise 5° to 10° after the roast is removed from the oven. Let it stand for 30 minutes then remove the foil from the tail and ears and the trussing string from the legs and body cavity. Replace the ball or block in the mouth

MARINADE

1 cup lemon juice
4 garlic cloves, minced
½ cup wine vinegar
1 cup olive oil
1 tablespoon sweet paprika
2 tablespoons chopped parsley
½ cup white wine

ROASTING

Hot water
Reserved marinade
¼ pound butter, melted
Kosher salt, to taste
Freshly ground pepper to taste

with an apple, orange or lemon. Garnish the ears with sprigs of watercress and place prunes or cranberries in the eye sockets.

When ready to serve, transfer the roast to a nest of lettuce or watercress on a serving tray. Accompany the roast with Gingered Orange Sauce, passed at the table (recipe follows). Serve with a crisp salad, crusty bread and a dry white wine such as a Sauvignon Blanc.

Sauce Directions

Melt the butter in a saucepan over medium heat. Add the shallots and sauté until lightly browned, being careful not to burn the butter. Add the wine and ginger. Turn the heat to high and boil until the mixture is reduced by half. Add the chicken stock, orange juice and lime juice. Continue boiling until the sauce is again reduced by ⅓. Remove from the heat and strain. Stir in orange zest and salt and pepper. Serve warm.

GINGERED ORANGE
SAUCE

1   tablespoon butter
¼   cup chopped shallots
¾   cup dry chopped fresh
     ginger
3   cups chicken stock
¾   cup orange juice
¼   cup lime juice
1   tablespoon grated orange
     zest
     Salt and pepper to taste

Serves 8 to 12

Rice with Pork
ARROZ CON PUERCO

Arroz con puerco is Argentine comfort food. What mashed potatoes and macaroni and cheese are to Americans, *arroz con puerco* is to Argentines. Originating in Spain, the dish has evolved with New World touches such as peanuts and pimiento. There are many different versions, some elaborate, some plain; this is one of the simplest.

Directions

Preheat the oven to 350°F. Sauté the bacon in a skillet until it's almost crisp. While still warm, roll each bacon slice around the tines of a fork to make curls. Drain them on paper towels and set aside. Pour off all drippings from the skillet, then measure a tablespoon of drippings and return it to the skillet. Add the pork cubes and brown them slowly on all sides. Remove the pork from the skillet and set it aside. Sauté the onion and garlic until soft then push it to one side of the skillet. Add the rice and sauté until golden, stirring constantly. Stir in the saffron, chicken broth and water. Bring the mixture to a boil then pour it into a 12-cup baking dish or flameproof casserole. Top with the browned pork, cover the casserole tightly and place in the oven. Simmer for an hour, or until all the liquid is absorbed and the rice is tender. Fluff the rice with a fork and transfer the mixture to a serving dish. Stand the bacon curls in a ring on top of the rice and spoon the cooked peas around the outside edge. Sprinkle the peanuts and pimiento on top. Serve with a green salad, bread and a dry white wine.

INGREDIENTS

8   slices bacon
2   pounds boneless lean pork
    shoulder, cut in 1-inch cubes
1   large onion, chopped
3   garlic cloves, minced
2   cups raw long-grain rice
¼   teaspoon crushed saffron
5   cups chicken broth
1   cup water
1   package (10 ounces)
    frozen peas, cooked,
    drained and buttered
¼   cup chopped peanuts
1   pimiento, diced

Serves 8

Pork Loin in Milk

LOMO DE CERDO CON LECHE

Pork cooked in milk came to Argentina through Italy when Italian immigrants brought with them the secret of making a delicious sauce out of slightly curdled milk.

Directions

Remove all visible fat from the pork and tie it into a compact bundle with a length of string. Place the pork into a flameproof casserole that is just large enough to hold it. Mix the milk with the lemon juice and pour it over the pork. The lemon juice will clabber the milk slightly while tenderizing the meat. Cover the casserole and leave it overnight in the refrigerator. Remove the casserole from the refrigerator about 30 minutes before cooking.

INGREDIENTS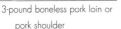

3-pound boneless pork loin or
   pork shoulder
4 cups whole milk, not
   skimmed
¼ cup lemon juice
   Salt and pepper to taste
2 tablespoons butter
1 tablespoon olive oil
2 garlic cloves, chopped
1 onion, chopped
½ cup diced pancetta
1 bay leaf, crumbled
½ teaspoon dried thyme
1 tablespoon prepared
   mustard
½ cup beef broth

Serves 6

Preheat the oven to 350°F. Remove the pork from the milk mixture and reserve the milk. Pat the pork with paper towels until it is dry and season it with salt and pepper. Heat the butter and oil in a skillet and brown the pork on all sides. Return the pork, along with the pan drippings, to the milk mixture in the casserole. Stir in the garlic, onion, pancetta, bay leaf, thyme, mustard and beef broth. Cover and bake for about 3 hours, or until the pork is tender. Check the casserole every 15 minutes to make sure the milk doesn't burn. Add more milk if necessary. When done, the pork should be tender and the sauce reduced to curds. Lift the pork onto a warm serving platter and remove the string. Slice the pork across the grain and keep it warm. Skim the fat from the casserole and spoon a small amount of the sauce over the sliced pork. Ladle the remaining sauce into a sauceboat and serve it at the table.

Pan-Grilled Steak

This recipe uses only two ingredients for the marinade, yet the results belie the simplicity. Of course, steak is at its best when it is well marbled. Cuts such as beef filet, New York steak, porterhouse or T-bone are recommended.

Directions

Marinate the steaks in olive oil for at least 30 minutes. Drain off the oil—leaving a light film of oil on the steaks—and salt the steaks on both sides. Heat a well-seasoned cast-iron skillet over a high setting. When hot add the steaks and char on one side. Turn the heat down to medium and continue cooking for about 3 minutes for medium rare. Turn the steaks with tongs and turn up the heat to high. Be careful not to cut into the steaks while turning so that you don't lose any of the juices. Sear the second side of the steaks, then turn the heat to medium and cook for another 3 minutes for medium rare. Add 2 to 3 minutes per side for well-done steaks. Serve with a green salad, *Aji Asado* (roasted marinated peppers, page 55), and *Papas al Horno* (roasted potatoes, page 53).

INGREDIENTS

4   beef steaks, 1 inch thick
½ cup olive oil
2   tablespoons coarse kosher
    or sea salt

Serves 4

Variations: If using an electric oven broiler, char one side of the steaks on a high broil on a preheated broiler pan with the rack as close as possible to the broiler element. When browned, turn steaks with tongs and brown the other side. Total cooking time with this method is about 5 minutes per side for medium rare.

Less time is required for gas broilers and outdoor charcoal barbecues. If using the latter, char meat directly on a rack over very hot coals on the hottest part of the barbecue, then move the meat to a cooler area of the rack over the drip pan leaving the barbecue lid open about one inch. Return the meat to the hotter area to char the second side and then move it back over the drip pan.

The Argentine spit-roasted barbecue originated with the gauchos—those fabled cowboys who tended the cattle that grazed the wide rolling plains of the Pampas, stretching like a sea of grass for thousands of miles. Rough and tough, these gauchos were accustomed to a hard life with primitive conditions. But they were proud of their heritage and fierce—even dangerous—when crossed.

Gauchos still ply their trade in the hinterlands, and you can find some remnants of their way of life in some of the estancia-like restaurants outside of Buenos Aires. Here, they build and tend the fires, then barbecue whole carcasses of various kinds for the busloads of tourists who come to experience the old ways and great food in a rustic setting.

The home-cooked *Asado Criollo* is an Argentine's favorite method of entertaining. And while it doesn't have quite the nostalgic ambiance of an *estancia*, it can be a memorable climax to a visit to Argentina. It's not too difficult to get invited to a home-based *asado* because Argentines are very friendly and welcome visitors from afar—even if communications must be conducted in sign language.

The home-based *asado* is an all-day affair that starts mid-morning and features a variety of grilled meats with traditional accompaniments. Building an open wood fire with a metal grating or spit is the first step. As guests start to arrive around noon they are served each course as it comes hot off the grill or spit. First come juicy beef or pork sausages. Then it's a course of *chinchulines*—those crunchy, salty grilled small intestines that taste wonderful if you don't know what they are. Other organ meats follow and will probably include kidney, sweetbreads, heart and sometimes mountain oysters. If entertaining a large group, the host will roast an entire quarter of beef or a whole lamb or pig on the spit. For smaller groups, steaks or whole baby lamb or kid are served. Served on the side will be a variety of salads, bread, *chimichurri* sauce and roasted, marinated peppers. Desserts are simple and usually consist of a fruit bowl, *alfajores* (filled cookies) or dainty pastries from the local *patisserie*.

The day and the *asado* end with the setting sun as if ringing down the curtain on the final act of a splendid *opera buffa*.

These sumptuous outdoor feasts are easy to duplicate on a charcoal or gas grill. The important thing at an *asado* is that everyone goes home completely sated.

Creole Barbecue
ASADO À LA PARRILLA CRIOLLA

This recipe is a classic of Argentine cookery. It is based on suggestions from Claudio Codina, owner of Parilla La Raya in Buenos Aires, and visits to several *estancia asados*.

The *estancia* version features a variety of meats marinated in olive oil, salted and roasted outdoors over a *parrilla* (brazier) and served with salads, sauces, bread and wine. *Asados* last for hours and always begin with grilled sausages—

either pepperoni, biroldo or longanizas. The former is available at most delis or supermarkets. The latter can be found in markets catering to Latin Americans. Don't hesitate to substitute whatever sausages you most enjoy. The sausages are served without accompaniment except for a glass of dry red wine. This course is merely to stave off starvation early on while guests wait for the other meats to cook. The next course is traditionally the *chinchulines* cooked to crisp, crunchy perfection and quashed with more red wine.

For a large *asado* with numerous guests, half or whole baby lambs, piglets or kid are grilled on spits or in the traditional manner where the animals are split in half and impaled on iron rods that have a crosspiece to keep them flat. The rods are thrust firmly into the ground at a 20-degree angle toward a wood fire about a foot away. They are basted with brine and their own fat while they are turned so both sides are nicely browned and evenly cooked—about 3½ hours. A split chicken is frequently added to provide a variety of flavors. Tripe cut into strips about one inch wide also is served along with grilled sweetbreads, kidneys, udders, mountain oysters and calves liver. After a simple dessert, coffee may be served. Most likely, guests will opt for *mate*—the green herb tea that is a must at any self-respecting Argentine *asado*.

If you have the room in your backyard, a great party can be built around an Argentine *parrilla*. To make one, dig a pit about 1 foot deep and about 3 feet long by 2 feet wide. Make sure this fire bed is level and cover it with a layer of sand. Surround it with bricks at ground level and cover it with an iron grate. You will also need a long three-pronged fork, and tongs for turning the meats and lifting them from the grill. Make sure you have heatproof mitts to protect your hands from the fire. You'll also need a small work table near the grill for cutting up cooked meats, a bowl of brine and a basting brush to baste the meats, plus a water-filled spray bottle to put out any flames.

When the wood or charcoal has turned to embers—in about an hour—the designated barbecue cook puts the meats on the grill in sequence so that they are served hot and crispy brown on the outside, red and juicy inside. To get it right requires considerable expertise, common sense and a watchful eye.

Meats are basted with brine made of water and salt or *chimichurri* sauce instead of a North American-type barbecue sauce. When the meat is seared on one side, it is basted and turned. The other side is then seared and basted. After that, the meat is turned and basted frequently until done. Argentine hosts usually allow about one pound of meat per person. English-cut short ribs are the closest to the Argentine cut of ribs. But instead of the long braising that is customary in North America, the ribs are marinated then grilled over hot coals. The result is delicious and is a totally different taste from braised short ribs.

For a complete and authentic Argentine *asado*, serve the meats with *chimichurri* sauce, *Aji Asado* (roasted marinated peppers, page 55), sour dough or French bread and several different salads. Obviously, all cooking times are approximate and depend upon the size and thickness of the meats selected.

INGREDIENTS

6 pounds beef ribs, cut in 2-
   to 3-inch lengths
   Chimichurri sauce
   (page 82)
2 cups olive oil
3 biroldo sausages
6 beef or pork sausages
   Beef or lamb chinchulines,
   cleaned
   Brine (6 tablespoons salt
   dissolved in 4 cups water)
   Coarse kosher or sea salt
   to taste
   Freshly ground pepper to
   taste
3 pounds lamb riblets
1 ½-pound flank steak
2 pounds rump, sirloin or
   chuck, cut into steaks

   Serves 10 to 12

Directions

The order of battle starts with marinating the meats. Marinate the ribs in *chimichurri* sauce for 2 hours in the refrigerator then marinate them in olive oil for at least 30 minutes. Set aside until ready to grill.

When ready to start serving grill the sausages over live coals for approximately 10 minutes per side. When done, cut in slices and serve immediately. Then grill the *chinchulines*, basting with brine until they are brown and crisp. Cut them into 3-inch lengths and serve hot off the grill. Next, remove the ribs from the marinade and drain, reserving the marinade. Season the ribs with coarse salt and pepper then place them on the grill. When they are brown and crisp on one side, turn them over and continue grilling until the other side is brown and crisp. Allow 6 minutes per side for medium rare, 8 minutes per side for medium and 10 minutes per side for well done. Serve immediately with *chimichurri* sauce.

Finally, marinate the lamb riblets, flank steak and rump, sirloin or chuck steak in the reserved olive oil for about 10 minutes. Drain and salt the lamb riblets then grill them until they are well done on both sides, about 8 minutes total. Serve immediately.

Remove the flank steak from the marinade and drain. Grill the steak—fat side first—for 4 to 5 minutes per side, basting several times with the brine. Slice the flank steak thinly across the grain and serve.

Remove the remaining rump, sirloin or chuck steaks from the marinade. Salt and grill them 4 to 6 minutes per side. When done, slice them thinly across the grain and serve.

In addition to *chimichurri* sauce, offer bread, a variety of salads, plus bowls of hard-boiled eggs, celery stalks, radishes and *Aji Asado* (roasted marinated peppers).

Chimichurri Sauce

CHIMICHURRI

Chimichurri is an absolute requirement for the famous Argentine *asado* or barbecue. The recipe for *chimichurri* that follows is only one of many, but it is typical of those you will find in the Pampas. Some locals use it as a salad dressing as well. And don't limit your *chimichurri* to *asado;* serve it with any broiled or roasted meat or poultry.

Directions
In a large jar, combine the oil, vinegar, paprika, garlic, parsley, peppercorns, oregano, bay leaves and salt. Cover the bottle and shake well to mix the ingredients. Refrigerate the *chimichurri* until ready to use. Moisten the cooked meats in each course with a little of the sauce and serve the remaining sauce in a sauceboat at the table.

INGREDIENTS

½ cup olive oil

1 ½ cups red wine vinegar

2 tablespoons hot paprika or 1 teaspoon cayenne pepper

4 garlic cloves, minced

1 bunch fresh parsley leaves, minced

1 teaspoon crushed black peppercorns

2 teaspoons dried oregano

2 bay leaves, crumbled

1 teaspoon salt

Makes about 2½ cups sauce

Kidneys in Wine Sauce

RIÑONES EN VINO BLANCO

Delicate lamb or veal kidneys are served frequently in the Pampas and other Argentine enclaves where these animals are plentiful. This recipe calls for a wine sauce but kidneys are equally delicious with a garlic sauce or cognac sauce.

Directions

Trim all membranes and excess fat from the kidneys. Marinate them for 15 minutes in vinegar. Remove the kidneys from the marinade and chop them coarsely. Season with salt and pepper. Heat the oil in a skillet and sauté the kidneys for about 2½ minutes per side. When lightly browned yet still tender and juicy, lift the kidneys out of the skillet, set them aside in a covered dish and keep them warm. Sauté the onion until it is soft in the oil remaining in the skillet. Add the parsley and sauté for about 1 minute. Add the potatoes, sage, and wine, mixing well. Return the kidneys to the skillet. Simmer just long enough to heat through. Serve immediately.

INGREDIENTS

2   veal kidneys
2   cups white wine vinegar
    Salt and pepper to taste
4   tablespoons olive oil
1   large onion, minced
4   tablespoons minced
    parsley
6   medium potatoes, freshly
    boiled and cubed
1   tablespoon chopped fresh
    sage leaves
1½ cups dry white wine

Serves 6

Veal and Vegetable Stew

CARBONADA CRIOLLA

INGREDIENTS

4 tablespoons olive oil

3-pound leg of veal, boned
   and cut into 2-inch cubes

¾ cup flour

1 large onion, minced

3 large tomatoes, peeled
   and chopped

1 bay leaf

½ teaspoon dried oregano

3 garlic cloves, minced

1 tablespoon tomato paste

1 teaspoon sugar

8 cups chicken stock

3 medium sweet potatoes,
   peeled and cut into 1-inch
   slices

1 medium winter squash,
   peeled and cubed

3 medium white potatoes,
   peeled and cut in half
   lengthwise

1 cup shelled peas

2 fresh jalapeño peppers,
   seeded and chopped
   (optional)

6 medium peaches, peeled
   and quartered (or 12
   canned Freestone peach
   halves)

½ pound zucchini, cut into
   1-inch slices

4 ears corn, cut in thirds

Salt and pepper to taste

Serves 6 to 8

Carbonada criolla has many versions, depending upon what is available and the cook's ethnic background. This version—based on veal—is typical of the Pampas. Other versions may feature beef, kid, lamb, chicken or pork. Sometimes beans, garbanzos or rice are incorporated to increase the number of servings.

When the *carbonada* is served in a hollowed out pumpkin or large winter squash, it makes a spectacular party dish.

Directions

Heat the oil in a large flameproof casserole. Dredge the meat with flour and brown it in oil. When browned on all sides, remove the meat from the casserole and keep it warm. Sauté the onion in the casserole until it's golden brown. Add the tomatoes, bay leaf, oregano, garlic, tomato paste, sugar, and mix well. Add the reserved veal and stock; cover and simmer gently for 45 minutes. Add the sweet potatoes, squash and potatoes; cover and simmer for an additional 30 minutes. Add the peaches, zucchini, corn, peas and jalapeños; simmer for 5 minutes more. If you are using canned peaches, cook them for 1 minute only. Season to taste with salt and pepper. Serve the *carbonada* in large rimmed soup plates with some of the juices from the casserole.

Variation: Add ½ cup rice or vermicelli during the last 25 minutes of cooking.

Variation: To serve the carbonada in a vegetable shell requires a 10 to 12-pound calabaza squash, a large Hubbard squash or a pumpkin. If you use this presentation method, eliminate the cubed winter squash in the recipe.

Preheat the oven to 375°F. Scrub the outside of the squash and cut a thick slice off the top for a lid. Scrape out seeds and stringy fibers. Brush the inside of the shell with melted butter and sprinkle with salt and pepper. Bake the shell on a baking sheet for 45 minutes or until it is tender but firm when pierced with a fork. Ladle the stew carefully into the shell and cover it with the lid. Bake for another 15 minutes to reheat all the ingredients. To serve, place the filled squash carefully on a large serving platter. Ladle the stew—along with a scoop of cooked squash from the shell—directly from the squash into individual serving dishes. Be careful not to break the shell when scooping out the cooked squash.

Pampas Stew with Beef and Chicken

PUCHERO CRIOLLO DE LAS PAMPAS

Pucheros are quite similar in concept to a New England boiled dinner. A standby of the rich and poor of Argentina, *puchero* is as simple or as complicated as the occasion requires. In the old days, *puchero* was a specialty in Argentine nightclubs for really big eaters after a hard night of tango dancing. One portion could consist of an entire calf's head—teeth, ears and all— surrounded by chicken parts, sausages, slices of boiled beef and assorted vegetables such as ears of corn, potatoes and sweet potatoes. Today, the ingredients are simpler and less unsettling to the uninitiated. This recipe features a thickened sauce—quite a departure from traditional *puchero* recipes.

Directions

Trim visible fat from the brisket. In a heavy kettle or Dutch oven, melt the fat from the brisket until you have approximately 2 tablespoons. Brown the brisket on all sides then remove it from the kettle. Add pepperoni along with salt, pepper, garlic, onion and celery. Sauté the mixture until the vegetables are almost tender. Return the brisket to the kettle and add the parsley and boiling water. Bring the contents of the kettle to a boil, lower the heat and cover. Simmer 2½ hours or until the meat is tender.

Add rutabaga, carrots, sweet potatoes, yams and white potatoes. Simmer, covered, for about 20 more minutes or until the vegetables are tender. Add corn and simmer 10 more minutes. Remove meats and vegetables to a large heated serving platter.

Skim the fat from the liquid in the pot if necessary. Blend the flour and water in a cup and stir in 1 or 2 tablespoons of the pot liquid. When thoroughly blended, beat the mixture into the liquid remaining in the pot with a wire whisk. Continue stirring over medium heat until the sauce thickens. Spoon 3 tablespoons of the sauce over the meats and vegetables and pour the remainder into a gravy boat to serve at the table. Serve very hot and offer olive oil, vinegar, salt, pepper and prepared mustard as condiments.

INGREDIENTS

3-pound beef brisket

2   tablespoons rendered fat
    from the brisket

½   pound pepperoni, sliced
    into ¼-inch rounds

1   teaspoon salt

¼   teaspoon freshly ground
    black pepper

4   garlic cloves, chopped

1   medium onion, chopped

½   cup chopped celery

2   sprigs parsley

4   cups boiling water

4   peeled rutabaga or yellow
    turnip, cut into 1-inch
    cubes

8   scraped carrots, cut into
    2-inch lengths

4   peeled sweet potatoes,
    quartered lengthwise

2   peeled yams, quartered
    lengthwise

4   peeled medium white pota-
    toes, quartered lengthwise

4   medium ears corn, cut into
    2-inch lengths

3   tablespoons flour

¼   cup water

Serves 8

Creole Sauce

This is a traditional sauce served with roasted or grilled meats.

Directions

Combine onions, tomatoes, jalapeño, garlic and parsley in a bowl. Season with salt and pepper. In a small bowl, make a paste with the mustard and a small amount of vinegar. Add remaining vinegar and beat in the oils with a whisk. Pour the mixture over the vegetables. Serve immediately or chill until ready to use.

INGREDIENTS

2   medium onions, minced
3   medium tomatoes, finely
    chopped
1   jalapeño pepper, seeded
    and finely chopped
4   garlic cloves, minced
2   tablespoons minced parsley
    Salt and pepper to taste
½   tablespoon dry mustard
3   tablespoons red wine
    vinegar
¼   cup olive oil
¼   cup grapeseed oil

Makes about 3 cups
of sauce

Creamed Chayote Squash

Creamed chayote squash served in its shell turns a simple vegetable into a spectacular poof at important dinners.

Directions

Preheat the oven to 475°F. Halve chayotes lengthwise. Remove pulp and mash it, taking care to preserve the shell. To the mashed pulp add the butter, whole egg, egg yolks, sugar, salt, mace and lime zest. If the mixture is too dry, mix in a little milk. Fold the egg whites into the mixture and spoon it into the chayote shells. Place the filled shells on a lightly greased cookie sheet and bake for about 5 minutes or until the filling is browned.

INGREDIENTS

3   chayote squash, washed
    and steamed until tender
3   tablespoons butter
1   whole egg, lightly beaten
2   egg yolks, lightly beaten
3   teaspoons sugar
1   teaspoon salt
1   teaspoon mace
1   tablespoon lime zest
    (grated rind)
½   cup milk if needed
2   egg whites, stiffly beaten
    to hold a peak

Serves 6

Quince Crescents

EMPANADAS DE MEMBRILLO

Quince paste can be homemade but it is available in most places—including Argentina—in cans. The canned product is quite acceptable for this recipe.

Directions

Preheat the oven to 350°F. In a large bowl combine the flour, baking powder and salt. Add the butter and quickly rub the flour and butter together with your fingertips until it forms a coarse meal. Add the water a few teaspoonfuls at a time and press and knead the dough gently until it can be gathered into a compact ball. If the dough seems too crumbly, moisten it with a little more water to make the particles stick together.

On a floured surface, roll out the dough into a large circle about ⅛ inch thick. Cut the dough into 4-inch circles. Use scraps and continue rolling and cutting rounds until all the dough has been used.

Place 1 tablespoon of quince paste in the center of each round. Moisten the edges of the round with water, fold the dough in half and press the edges with the tines of a fork to seal. Place the crescents on lightly greased cookie sheets and bake in the center of the oven for 15 to 20 minutes, or until they are golden brown. Cool the empanadas on a cake rack and dust them lightly with the confectioners' sugar before serving.

INGREDIENTS

1 ½ cups flour

½ teaspoon double-acting baking powder

½ teaspoon salt

4 ounces cold butter, cut into pieces

3 tablespoons cold water

1 cup plus 2 tablespoons canned quince paste

Confectioners' sugar

Makes 6 to 8 empanadas

CHAPTER 3

Córdoba:

Centuries of Sumptuous Living

Córdoba

Since the sixteenth century, Córdoba has offered scholars an oasis of learning and culture second to none. Today, it also provides an extravaganza of sights, sounds and sumptuous dining for the rest of us.

Lying between the Andes and the Pampas, Córdoba is a favorite destination for vacationing Argentines that is mostly overlooked by foreigners. This is a pity because both the city and the province are extraordinarily attractive. Throughout the province gentle rivers burble their way through the mountains and hill towns from the Sierras de Córdoba in the Andes foothills to the sea. The riversides are dotted with idyllic villages. Prosaically named—Primero (First), Segundo (Second), Tercero (Third) and Cuarto (Fourth)—the sparkling rivers are a major draw for visitors. On spring or summer weekends, the grassy knolls above the rivers are alive with local residents and vacationers picnicking on the exceptional local cheeses, crusty breads and Quilmes beer or table wines from Mendoza or San Juan.

The hundreds of small towns and villages of the Sierras de Córdoba offer a range of touristic and gastronomic attractions. La Calera, 11 miles west of the city of Córdoba, is an especially picturesque stop. After an obligatory visit to La Calera's simple seventeenth-century chapel, visitors pick up homemade salami and bread from roadside stands for impromptu picnics.

Further out in the Sierras de Córdoba, the grand resort of Villa Carlos Paz livens its holiday atmosphere with beach parties and rowing contests along the river and on the lakes, forays to the casino in the evening, and sophisticated dining at any time of day or night.

Candonga is 25 miles north of Córdoba. Its claim to fame is an eighteenth-century Jesuit chapel that is a minor masterpiece. Situated in a scenic, isolated canyon, the chapel was once part of the Estancia Santa Gertrudis— now an overgrown ruin. Candonga is known for its regional specialties including *Asado con Cuero* (beef, lamb or kid roasted in the hide), *locros*, empanadas and home-made desserts.

A little over 50 miles southwest of the city lies Villa General Belgrano, settled by the unrepatriated survivors of the German battleship *Graf Spee* that sank near Montevideo, Uruguay during World War II. With a stubborn refusal to assimilate, the community celebrates Octoberfest with the Teutonic fare one expects to find in Germany. A specialty is *Pescado à la Crema* (fish fillets under lightly salted whipped cream mixed with a mild white cheese). Another favorite is *Conejo en Vino Rojo* (rabbit braised in Merlot). Also available are other typical German dishes such as hot beer soup, tongue, sweetbreads and wild mushrooms in Chablis. As for poultry and game, the locals favor roast goose, duck and venison. Potato pancakes with applesauce and cream is a standby as are *Ternera à la Pepinilla* (veal in dill pickle sauce), and a vast array of sausages and smoked meats.

Therapeutic mineral waters attract world-weary *Porteños* to Mina Clavero. This important resort boasts verdant mountain landscapes with crystal streams and rocky waterfalls. Its hotels and restaurants offer exquisite haute cuisine as well as homely country-style dishes such as *locros, asados* and *pucheros*. Because many *Porteños* own vacation homes on the banks above Mina Clavero's Río de los Sauces, a number of specialty shops are located in the center of town to provide residents with fresh meats, produce, dry goods and canned and frozen foods. Home cooking here tends to the simple and traditional.

Well worth the one-hour drive from Córdoba is Río Ceballos-Sierra de Córdoba—a picturesque hamlet along the river of the same name that is the site of a remarkable Viennese pastry shop catering primarily to locals. For those who don't have access to homemade pastries, Confitería Vienesa's incredible edibles are everything a weary trekker could ask for in a teatime treat. Rich yet ethereal, these lightly sweetened pastries seem to float as you lift one to your mouth.

I still dream about a hazelnut cake made without flour and filled with stiffly whipped cream. And Spanish Wind Cake transports me to heaven. Its meringue shell filled with a mixture of heavy whipped cream, cognac and in-season berries is the height of decadence. Other favorites are *Dobos* cake or *Rigó Jansci*—a glazed, chocolate-filled confection. Linzer cake, filled with thick raspberry jam, also has many fans. Rounding out the possible selections are *media lunas*, palm leaves, fruit-filled coffee rings, strudels, apricot leaf cookies, tartlets and more. Washed down with dark Brazilian espresso *mit schlag*, these delicacies provide a fitting climax to the day's activities.

At the southeast corner of the province is the city of Córdoba. Founded in 1573, Córdoba is a university town and Argentina's second largest city after Buenos Aires. Since the early seventeenth century, Córdoba's churches and universities have been among the biggest, most beautiful and most respected in Latin America.

Córdoba is located on the south bank of the Río Primero 1,300 feet above sea level at the foot of the Sierra Chica. An important center for education, fine arts and architecture, Córdoba reeks of high culture and an appreciation for aesthetic values. Highlights of a walking tour include the city's many colonial buildings and

Colonial Córdoba.

riverside parks. Its sidewalk cafés are a pleasant place to while away the hours over espresso while discussing the politics of the day.

Córdoba boasts restaurants that have been in operation for more than a century. One local establishment, La Yaya Comidas del Campo (country food) has been at the same downtown address for over one hundred years. Here, the family's eighty-year-old grandmother still rules the kitchen and visits diners' tables to ask if they enjoyed their meals.

In the past, cuisine in the city ran from standard *criollo* fare—*carbonadas, locros,* and local versions of empanadas, *pucheros* and *asados*—to friuli sausages and the mild and creamy cheeses shipped in from the farming community of Caroya. And while Córdoba is more conservative than Buenos Aires, in the last ten years it has welcomed a spate of new restaurants featuring the experimental dishes of young chefs with original ideas.

The *Trucha en Chablis* (trout filled with a mousse of smoked trout in a fumet and Chablis reduction topped with a melange of sautéed wild mushrooms) from Guccio Restaurant represents this new breed at the high end. In the middle are dozens of chrome-plated operations where the kitchen is in full view, California-style, so that diners can watch the preparations of unusual dishes. In one such diner, we watched the chef prepare glazed oysters topped with sevruga caviar and roast squab with arugula on croutons. Another time—just so we could view the preparations—we ordered rare roasted breast of Muscovy duck with duck sausage rounds on wilted savoy cabbage, and a ravishing Scotch whiskey *crème brulée*.

As it is elsewhere in Argentina, the outdoor *asado* is the at-home favorite fare in Córdoba. But home cooks are also adept at turning out excellent *milanesas*, oven roasted leg of veal, tasty *locros*, outstanding ravioli and an unbelievable collection of empanadas.

To sum up, the living is very good in Córdoba. In my mind's eye, I always envision myself there, sitting by the river with a book in one hand and a glass of a pretentious wine in the other.

Estancia Jesuitica de Santa Catalina outside Córdoba.

Deep-Fried Bread

SOPAPILLAS

Sopapillas are served at breakfast or with *mate* at teatime.

Directions

Sift the flour and baking powder together twice. Place the lard and salt into a 2-quart measuring cup and add boiling water. Allow it to cool slightly until it is lukewarm, then stir in the beaten egg, mixing well. Work the sifted flour mixture into the egg mixture and knead until you have a smooth, elastic dough. Add flour a little at a time if necessary. Roll out the dough to about a ⅛-inch thickness and cut with cookie cutters to any shape desired.

INGREDIENTS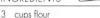

3   cups flour

2   teaspoons baking powder

3   tablespoons lard

¼   teaspoon salt

1   cup boiling water

1   egg, well beaten
    Lard or vegetable oil for
    deep frying

1   cup confectioners' sugar

Makes 8 to 10 sopapillas, depending upon the size of each

Heat the fat in a deep skillet or deep fryer until it's almost smoking. Add the *sopapillas* to the hot fat, one at a time. Fry until both sides are golden and drain them on paper towels. Transfer the *sopapillas* to a serving dish and sprinkle them with confectioners' sugar. Serve them with morning coffee or afternoon tea or *mate*.

Cheese Empanadas

EMPANADITAS DE QUESO

This is one of my favorite recipes for entertaining. Simple and easy to make, I usually make large batches and freeze them for cocktail parties. When unexpected guests arrive and I'm really in a hurry, I defrost frozen puff pastry from the supermarket instead of making it from scratch. It's every bit as good as homemade pastry, and I can join the guests while the *empanaditas* are baking.

Directions

Defrost and unfold the pastry. Slightly overlap each rectangle of pastry on a floured board and roll them out to a ⅛-inch thickness. Cut out rounds of dough that are approximately 2½ inches in diameter. An empty tuna can makes a perfect form. Refrigerate the pastry rounds until the filling has been prepared.

Preheat the oven to 400°F. Mix together the cheese, cayenne, onions and currants. Place a slightly rounded teaspoon of filling on each pastry round. Add an olive and piece of egg. Fold the pastry in half, moisten edges with water, press edges together and crimp the edges with your thumb and index finger, making sure that each *empanadita* is completely sealed. Place the *empanaditas* slightly apart on an ungreased baking sheet. Bake for 12 to 15 minutes, or until the cheese melts and the pastry is golden brown.

INGREDIENTS

3   1-pound packages frozen puff pastry

1½ cups chopped teleme cheese (or grated semi-soft Monterey Jack cheese)

½ teaspoon cayenne pepper

¼ cup thinly sliced green onions

¼ cup currants

24 small pimiento-stuffed green olives

4   hard-boiled eggs, cut into 6 wedges each

Makes about 24 empanaditas

Onion Salad

ENSALADA DE CEBOLLA

If you're out of salad fixings and short of time, you can always make a tasty salad out of a large onion, adding whatever vegetables or greens you have on hand. This simple salad is surprisingly mild tasting after the onions have been steeped in water. It can be served at room temperature, but I think it is best chilled.

INGREDIENTS

2 large onions (Maui or other mild flavored types), sliced crosswise about ¼ inch thick

Boiling water

1 teaspoon minced garlic

1 bunch parsley, stems discarded and finely minced

¼ cup olive oil

2 tablespoons red wine vinegar

1 dried chili pepper, crushed

Salt to taste

Freshly ground pepper to taste

4 radishes

4 large lettuce leaves, washed and dried

4 sprigs fresh mint

Serves 4

Directions

Separate the onion slices into rings and place them in a heatproof bowl. Pour boiling water over the onions to cover and let them steep for 30 minutes. Drain and squeeze out the excess water. Add garlic, parsley, olive oil, vinegar, hot pepper, salt and ground pepper. Marinate the mixture in the refrigerator for at least 1 hour.

Cut radishes into flowers by cutting 6 to 8 petal shapes starting at the tip and cutting back toward the stem end without detaching the petal from the radish. Place the radish flowers in a covered jar filled with ice water and chill until petals curl back toward the stem. Place a lettuce leaf on each serving dish. Divide the onion mixture into 4 portions and spoon them onto the lettuce leaves. Garnish with mint leaves and radish flowers.

Crudités with Romesco Dip

VERDURA À LA ROMESCO

Raw vegetables served as finger food with a dip
are as popular with Córdobans as they are with
North Americans. But instead of sour cream and
onion soup mix, this dip is an exotic mixture of
pulverized almonds, tomatoes, vinegar and
spices that originated in Spain.

Vegetable Directions
Arrange zucchini sticks in a small glass in the center of a
serving platter. Arrange cauliflower florets, cherry tomatoes and mushrooms around the zucchini sticks. Prepare
the dip as follows:

Dip Directions
Pulverize the almonds in a blender. Blend in the garlic,
cayenne pepper, salt, tomato and vinegar. When the mixture forms a fine paste, add half the oil 1 teaspoonful at a
time. Blend between each addition. Set the blender to its
lowest speed and blend in the remaining oil in a slow,
thin, continuous stream until the mixture has the consistency of mayonnaise. Chill. Serve in a separate bowl with
raw vegetables.

VEGETABLES

2 zucchini, washed, trimmed
   and quartered lengthwise
1 small cauliflower, washed,
   trimmed and separated
   into bite-sized florets
8 small cherry tomatoes,
   washed and speared on
   toothpicks
8 small fresh mushrooms,
   wiped and trimmed

ROMESCO DIP

¼ cup blanched, slivered and
   toasted almonds
1 teaspoon minced garlic
½ teaspoon cayenne pepper
1 teaspoon salt
1 small tomato, peeled,
   seeded and finely chopped
¼ cup red wine vinegar
1 cup olive oil

Serves 4

Orange Salad

ENSALADA DE NARANJA

This salad is especially good with roasted
poultry.

INGREDIENTS

4   medium oranges,
    separated into sections
    and each cut in 2 or
    3 pieces
1   small head romaine
    lettuce, torn into large
    pieces
1   small red onion, chopped
    Boiling water
¼   cup olive oil
1   tablespoon red wine
    vinegar
    Salt and pepper to taste
1   teaspoon dry mustard

Serves 4

Directions

Place orange and lettuce pieces in salad bowl. Blanch the
onions in boiling water for about 30 minutes. Drain and
squeeze the onions and discard the water. Add the onions
to the salad bowl. Chill in the refrigerator for at least 1
hour. Just before serving, beat oil, vinegar, salt, pepper
and mustard together with a wire whisk until slightly
thickened. Sprinkle over salad and toss.

Bread Soup

SOPA DE PAN

Sopa de pan is the Argentine way with a Spanish standard. Lighter soups such as this one are usually served as a first course in a multicourse dinner.

Directions

In a deep flameproof casserole, combine the short ribs, beef bones, water, onion, celery, carrot, parsley, garlic, salt and pepper. Bring the mixture to a boil and skim the top as scum rises to the surface. Simmer the mixture over medium heat for 2 hours. Remove it from the heat and strain. Pour 2 cups of strained broth into a skillet and carefully poach the eggs in it while basting them with the hot broth. Place a poached egg in each soup dish. Combine the poaching broth with the rest of the strained broth and strain again. Pour the broth over the eggs. Sprinkle the toast with cheese and place a slice in each soup dish. Reserve the beef for another use.

INGREDIENTS

2 pounds beef short ribs
   Several beef bones
   containing marrow
8 cups water
1 whole onion
1 whole stalk celery
1 whole carrot
2 sprigs parsley
3 garlic cloves, minced
3 teaspoons salt
1 teaspoon freshly ground
   pepper
6 eggs
6 slices French bread,
   toasted and buttered
¼ cup grated Parmesan
   cheese

Serves 6

Hake Fillets in Mustard Sauce

MERLUZA EN SALSA DE MOSTAZA

A piquant mustard sauce turns a simple dish of sautéed fish fillets into party fare. Some Argentine cooks add sliced pimiento and stuffed green olives as a garnish.

INGREDIENTS

3   pounds hake fillets (cod or
    sole may be substituted)
    Salt and pepper to taste
    Flour
1 ½ tablespoons butter
1 ½ tablespoons olive oil
6   boiled potatoes
    Mustard sauce (recipe
    follows)
2   tablespoons chopped
    parsley

Serves 6

Directions
Season the fillets on both sides with salt and pepper. Dredge them in flour, shaking off the excess. Sauté the fillets over medium heat in butter and oil until lightly browned. Remove the fillets to a serving platter and keep them warm while making the mustard sauce. Surround the fish fillets with boiled potatoes on a serving platter. Spoon the sauce over the fish and potatoes. Sprinkle parsley on top. Serve hot.

Mustard Sauce

SALSA DE MOSTAZA

INGREDIENTS

2   tablespoons butter
3   teaspoons prepared
    mustard
1   cup milk
1   cup beef stock
    Salt to taste
2   tablespoons cornstarch

Makes 2 cups of sauce

Directions
Melt the butter in a saucepan and stir in the mustard. Add milk and beef stock a little at a time. Stir in the salt and cornstarch. Cook the mixture over medium heat, stirring constantly until the sauce thickens and is smooth. Lower the heat and simmer for 5 minutes while continuing to stir.

Chicken in Sherry Wine

GALLINA EN PEPITORÍA

Pepitoría refers to poultry dishes that include raw or hard-boiled eggs. Originating in Spain, this dish with its savory sauce should be partnered with a watercress salad and a light red wine such as an Argentine Malbec or a French Beaujolais.

Directions

In a flameproof casserole, brown the chicken in butter and oil. Remove the chicken from the casserole and add the onions and garlic. Sauté the onions and garlic until they are soft. Sprinkle a bit of flour over the onion and stir until the mixture is smooth. Return the chicken to the casserole and add the parsley sprigs, bouillon cube, carrots, bay leaf, mint leaves and sherry. Cover and simmer over low heat until the chicken is tender, about 40 minutes. Remove the chicken from the casserole and place it on a warmed serving platter.

To make the sauce, strain the casserole juices through a sieve back into the casserole, discarding the vegetables. Add the egg yolk and stir it into the sauce until smooth. Return the chicken to the sauce and simmer it gently for several minutes to heat through. Be careful not to boil the sauce or it will curdle.

INGREDIENTS

1   fryer chicken, cut into
    serving pieces
2   tablespoons butter
1   tablespoon olive oil
1   large onion, chopped
2   garlic cloves, minced
2   tablespoons flour
4   sprigs parsley
1   chicken bouillon cube
1   carrot, peeled and
    chopped
1   bay leaf
6   mint leaves, whole
½   cup dry sherry wine (a
    Spanish fino such as La Ina
    or Tío Pepe)
1   egg yolk

Serves 4

Tongue Roman Style

LENGUA À LA ROMANA

Brought to Argentina by Italian immigrants, *Lengua à la Romana* is a favorite among Córdobans.

Directions

Boil the tongue in 2 quarts of water (or to cover) to which you have added bay leaf, marjoram, peppercorns, garlic and salt. Simmer gently until tender, 2½ to 3 hours. Remove the tongue from the liquid, reserving the liquid. Cool the tongue and remove the skin. Cut the tongue into thin slices on the diagonal and set aside. Brown the almonds in 1 tablespoon of butter and mash the mixture into a paste. Melt the remaining butter and stir in the flour. Gradually add 3 cups of the strained tongue broth. Simmer 5 minutes and add the almond paste, jelly, Madeira, raisins and sliced tongue. Simmer covered over low heat for 1 hour. Serve with steamed rice.

INGREDIENTS

1   medium-sized fresh beef or veal tongue
1   bay leaf
1   sprig fresh marjoram
4   whole black peppercorns
2   garlic cloves, minced
    Salt to taste
⅔   cup blanched, finely chopped almonds
3   tablespoons butter
2   tablespoons flour
2   tablespoons plum jelly
1   cup Madeira wine
¾   cup raisins

Serves 4

Beef Steaks with Tomatoes and Cheese

MILANESA À LA NAPOLITANA

Serve *Milanesa à la Napolitana* with fried or roasted potatoes and a green salad for a satisfying meal. Some cooks vary the recipe by omitting the tomatoes and cheese and topping the *milanesa* with fresh mushrooms sautéed with garlic and oregano. Another version calls for placing a slice of sautéed eggplant on top of the *milanesa*—with or without cheese.

Directions

Preheat the oven to 350°F. Prepare the steaks. When the steaks are cooked, place in a single layer on a heatproof platter or pizza pan. Place a slice of tomato on each steak and sprinkle with salt. Cut the teleme cheese into 8 chunks. Top each tomato slice with a chunk of cheese. Bake uncovered until cheese melts (about 10 minutes). Serve at once.

INGREDIENTS

1   recipe Milanesa à la
    Porteña (page 51)
1   ripe tomato, sliced
    Salt to taste
16 ounces teleme cheese (or
    any grated semi-soft white
    cheese)

Serves 4

Mixed Fry from La Yaya

FIESTA DEL CAMPO À LA YAYA

Argentines consume large quantities of the animal parts that most other nationalities throw in the garbage. This includes lungs, tripe, intestines, brains, tongues, cockscombs, feet, hearts, and mountain oysters. What's more, anything that walks, crawls or hops is fair game: snails, frogs, armadillos and guinea pigs. If Anglo Saxons could overcome their prejudices, they would be rewarded with some delicious protein bits that could become a habit. La Yaya restaurant has been dishing them up for over one hundred years.

Fiesta del Campo is a specialty at La Yaya restaurant, where the family's eighty-year-old grandmother runs a tight ship in her kitchen and dining room. Here, for the more adventurous cook, is Mama Yaya's favorite way of preparing some of the less intimidating morsels.

INGREDIENTS

2 cups flour
1 teaspoon salt
1 teaspoon cayenne
1 cup milk
2 eggs, beaten
6 slices calf's sweetbreads, skin and excess fat removed
6 slices calf's brains, skinned
½ cup vinegar (or lemon juice)
6 slices calf's liver
6 lamb kidneys, skinned
6 slices lamb's heart
Salt and pepper to taste
4 cups lard for deep-frying
6 artichoke bottoms, cooked
6 slices mild yellow cheese
6 slices eggplant, blanched
6 cauliflower florets, blanched
6 zucchini, sliced lengthwise into ¼-inch slices

Serves 6

Directions

In a large bowl combine the flour, salt, cayenne, milk and eggs. Beat until smooth and set aside. Soak the sweetbreads and brains in cold water for at least 1 hour. Blanch them over low heat in salted water to which vinegar or lemon juice has been added. After 20 or 30 minutes, remove the pan from the heat and allow the brains and sweetbreads to cool in the liquid. When cool enough to handle, drain them and remove the membrane and large veins.

Cut the liver, sweetbreads, brain, kidneys and heart into ½-inch pieces or slices. Season each with salt and pepper and dip them in the batter, turning them so they are well coated. Heat the lard in a deep skillet or deep-fryer until it is smoking. Fry the meats in the oil in batches until browned. Remove them from the oil and drain them on paper towels. Repeat the process with the artichoke bottoms, cheese, eggplant, cauliflower and zucchini. When all the ingredients are cooked, place them on a large heated platter, season with salt and pepper and pass at the table.

Roasted Kid, Creole Style

CABRITO CRIOLLO AL HORNO

Kid and lamb, if both are very young, are practically interchangeable in Argentina. But in most cases, kid is preferred because it was more available in Spain where the dish originated.

INGREDIENTS

4-pound leg or shoulder roast
   of kid (or lamb)
3 tablespoons butter
12 garlic cloves, crushed
4 tablespoons minced mint
   leaves
1 tablespoon crushed dried
   rosemary
   Salt and pepper to taste
½ cup olive oil
3 large white potatoes,
   peeled and halved
   lengthwise
1 cup dry white wine
   Lettuce leaves
1 pimiento, julienned

Serves 6

Directions

Preheat the oven to 325°F. Trim the roast of all but a thin layer of fat. Cream the butter with crushed garlic until well mixed. Add mint leaves, rosemary, salt and pepper and mix well. Spread the mixture on all sides of the roast. Place the roast in a roasting pan brushed with oil and surround the roast with potatoes. Baste the roast with wine and roast for 1 hour for rare (15 minutes to the pound). For medium rare, roast 1¼ hours. For well done, roast 1¾ to 2 hours. Baste every 20 minutes with wine and pan juices. Turn the potatoes over halfway through the cooking time.

Remove the roast to a carving board and let it stand for 15 minutes. Arrange the potatoes around the edge of a serving platter and keep them warm in a turned-off oven. Slice the roast and arrange the slices on the platter. Garnish the edges of the platter with lettuce leaves and strips of pimiento. Degrease the pan juices and spoon over the sliced roast.

Braised Beef, Genoa Style

MANZO À LA GENOVESA

INGREDIENTS

1 ½ ounces dried porcini mush-
    rooms
½   cup olive oil
3 ½-pound prime ribs of beef,
    boned, rolled and tied
1 ¼ cups red wine
½   cup beef stock
4   garlic cloves, minced
1   small onion, minced
2   carrots, finely chopped
2   stalks celery, finely
    chopped
3   sprigs parsley, finely
    chopped
3   cloves
7-ounce can Italian tomatoes,
    peeled, seeded, and
    drained, reserving juice
Salt and pepper to taste
3   tablespoons flour
1   cup water
3   cups cooked noodles

Serves 6 to 8

Sailors from Genoa jumped ship regularly in Buenos Aires in the late nineteenth and early twentieth century. They eventually migrated to less crowded locales and brought with them their favorite recipes from home.

Directions

Preheat the oven to 325°F. Soak the mushrooms in warm water for 30 minutes. Drain the mushrooms, straining and reserving the soaking liquid. Wipe the mushrooms dry, chop them and set aside. Heat the oil in a large, heavy flameproof casserole. Add the beef and brown it well on all sides. Add the wine and increase the heat slightly. Add the beef stock and continue cooking until the liquid has been reduced to about 1 cup. Add garlic, onion, carrots, celery, parsley, cloves, tomatoes, salt and pepper. Cover the casserole and place it in the oven for about 2½ hours. Add the juice from the tomatoes and the reserved mushroom soaking liquid after 1 hour of cooking. Check the dish at 20-minute intervals. If the liquid in the casserole starts to dry up, add more beef stock a little at a time.

Add the mushrooms and check the seasoning. Continue roasting, covered, until the meat is very tender. Remove the roast to a cutting board. Cut it into medium thick slices and arrange them on a hot serving platter. Keep the roast warm until you are ready to serve. Degrease the casserole juices and thicken them with flour mixed with water. Season to taste and moisten the meat slices with the sauce. Toss the remaining sauce with boiled noodles and serve with the meat.

Sausages with Lentils

CHORIZOS CON LENTEJAS

Lentils have been a food staple ever since biblical times when Esau sold his inheritance to his brother Jacob for a bowl of lentil soup. You might say that the Old and New Testaments meet in Argentina when lentils are served with pork sausages.

Directions

Heat the oil in a skillet. Fry the sausages in the oil until partially cooked. Remove the sausages from the skillet and cut them into small pieces. Pour off all but 2 tablespoons of the cooking fat and fry the lentils, onions, garlic and green pepper. Continue cooking over medium heat for 5 minutes, stirring occasionally. Return the sausages to the skillet and add tomatoes, salt and pepper. Cover and simmer until the sausage pieces are tender, 8 to 10 minutes.

INGREDIENTS

¼ cup olive oil

1 pound pork sausages (Spanish Butifarra if available; or sweet Italian sausages)

1 cup cooked lentils

1 onion, sliced

2 garlic cloves, minced

1 green pepper, roasted, skinned, seeded and chopped

2 tomatoes, peeled and quartered

Salt and pepper to taste

Serves 4

Brains à la King

SESO EN SALSA BLANCA

Brains are a delicacy much appreciated in France, Italy and, of course, Argentina. A basic component of Argentine ravioli, brains can also be sautéed or braised. In the United States, calf's brains are more common than lamb's, but both are equally good and can be used interchangeably. Like sweetbreads, brains are highly perishable and should be cooked within 24 hours of purchase. Otherwise, they can be kept an additional day when trimmed of all filament, soaked in salt water, blanched in salted water acidulated with vinegar or lemon juice, and refrigerated.

INGREDIENTS

2   calves brains
1   tablespoon salt per quart
     of water
1   tablespoon vinegar per
     quart of water
1   green bell pepper, minced
¼   cup minced celery
2   tablespoons minced onion
2   tablespoons butter
2   tablespoons flour
1   cup milk
1   fresh pimiento, chopped
     Salt and freshly ground
     pepper to taste
     Hot toast points or patty
     shells

Serves 6

Directions

Wash the brains in cold running water then place them in a bowl and soak them in several changes of cold salted water for an hour or longer. Drain and carefully remove the membrane with the tip of a sharp knife. Place the brains in a saucepan and cover with water. Add salt and vinegar to the water and bring the brains to a boil. Reduce the heat to low and simmer the brains, covered, for 20 to 30 minutes. Allow the brains to cool in the liquid then drain them, cut them into small cubes and set aside. Sauté the bell pepper, celery and onion in butter until they are golden. Stir in the flour and add milk. Cook the mixture over medium heat while stirring until thickened. Add the brains and pimiento and heat through. Add salt and pepper to taste then ladle the brains over toast points or fill patty shells. Serve immediately.

Creole Rice

ARROZ À LA CRIOLLA

Rice pilaf came to Spain from North Africa with the Moors who stayed for almost eight hundred years. When it migrated to Argentina, rice was considered merely a backdrop to meats, seafood and vegetables. That perception hasn't changed much and rice rarely has the status of a main dish as it does in the Orient.

Small quantities of long-grain rice are grown in northeast Argentina. Short-grain rice is imported from Italy and Spain. Both varieties are used in Argentina but a pilaf should be made with long-grain rice.

Directions

In a heavy saucepan, lightly brown the onion and rice in oil. Add the salt and the boiling water. Stir the rice with a fork, cover tightly, and simmer over a low heat for 20 to 25 minutes, or until the rice is tender and the water is completely evaporated. Fluff the rice gently with a fork.

INGREDIENTS

1   tablespoon minced onion
1   cup raw long-grain rice
1   teaspoon vegetable or
    olive oil
1   teaspoon salt
2   cups boiling water

Makes about 4 cups

Potato Balls

YAPINGACHOS

Yapingachos are a Lenten dish of cheese-filled mashed potato balls. They are usually served with just a salad and bread.

Directions

Boil potatoes in salted water until tender, about 30 minutes, then drain and mash. Add the salt, egg yolk and cornstarch and mix well. Sauté the onions in butter until they are golden. Add the Parmesan and cottage cheese, mixing well. Roll the mashed potatoes into 10 balls, putting some of the cheese and onion mixture in the center of each ball. Make sure that the ball is completely covered with the potato mixture. Flatten the balls slightly and sauté in hot shortening until well browned on both sides. Serve immediately.

INGREDIENTS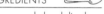

4   cups peeled and diced
    potatoes
½   teaspoon salt
1   egg yolk
2   tablespoons cornstarch
2   medium onions, chopped
2   tablespoons butter
½   cup grated Parmesan
    cheese
½   cup small-curd cottage
    cheese
¼   cup vegetable shortening

Serves 4

Asparagus in Mustard Cream

ESPÁRRAGOS CON MOSTAZA

This sauce is the perfect complement to most steamed or boiled vegetables that are served cold or at room temperature. Try it with cooked cauliflower, carrots, broccoli, leeks and green beans. In addition to asparagus, it's also good with raw cucumbers, tomatoes, celery and fennel.

Directions

Steam asparagus for 3 minutes. Drain and allow the asparagus to cool. In a bowl, beat the cream until it barely begins to thicken. Carefully fold the mustard and lemon juice into the cream making sure not to beat the cream. Place asparagus spears on a serving platter taking care that all water has been removed. Spoon the mustard cream sauce over asparagus spears in a ribbon pattern. Sprinkle with salt and pepper. Top the sauce with parsley and place the asparagus in the refrigerator until the sauce is set. Serve very cold.

INGREDIENTS

1 pound asparagus, washed, broken off at stem end, with ends trimmed

1 cup cold heavy cream

2 heaping teaspoons dry mustard

½ teaspoon lemon juice

1 tablespoon minced parsley

Salt to taste

White pepper to taste

Serves 4

Creole Asparagus

ESPÁRRAGOS CRIOLLO

Unlike Julia Child and most other chefs I've read about or observed, I do not peel asparagus stalks. Perhaps it is wasteful, but I like fat asparagus stalks that have a definite breaking point where you can snap off the pithy end and trim the stalk on an angle. Instead of discarding the trimmings, I freeze them for later use in soups.

Directions

In a hot skillet, add the oil and sauté the garlic with the pieces of bread. Remove the garlic and bread mixture from the skillet, chop it and set it aside. Place the asparagus pieces in the hot oil. Add the onion, tomatoes, pimientos, salt, pepper and paprika. Stir-fry the mixture for 2 minutes. Sprinkle vinegar over the mixture and continue to stir-fry over a high heat for 1 minute. Remove the mixture to a serving dish and top it with the chopped garlic and bread. Garnish with egg slices.

*When cutting asparagus into smaller pieces for sautéing, I use a roll cut. This is a term I coined for cutting stalks of vegetables in the Oriental fashion: cut them on the diagonal and rotate the stalk 45 degrees after each cut so as to create larger surfaces for browning.

INGREDIENTS

- 3 tablespoons olive oil
- 3 garlic cloves, peeled
- ½ cup crouton-size bread bits
- 1 pound asparagus, washed, pithy end removed and roll-cut* into 2-inch lengths
- 1 large onion, chopped
- 3 medium tomatoes, chopped
- ⅓ cup chopped pimientos
- Salt and pepper to taste
- 2 teaspoons paprika
- 1 teaspoon white wine vinegar
- 2 hard-boiled eggs, sliced

Serves 4

Apple Soup

SOPA DE MANZANAS

Apples are uncommon in South America save
Argentina. Cold winter climates and appropriate soil are requisite to growing apples. Only
Argentina qualifies on both counts. To protect
against the salmonella bacteria, use a very fresh
egg with this recipe and wash the shell carefully
before cracking.

Directions
Place the apple chunks in a large saucepan and cover
them with cold water. Add lemon peel and sugar. Simmer
the mixture for about 25 minutes or until the apples break
up. Remove the mixture and strain through a sieve. Add
raisins to the strained apples and beat in the egg yolk.
Spoon the mixture into individual serving bowls. Top
apples with a dollop of yogurt and dust with cinnamon.
Serve warm.

INGREDIENTS

4   large tart green apples, cut
    into large chunks
    Peel of 1 lemon, cut in
    slivers
    Sugar to taste
8   raisins, soaked in hot
    water and drained
1   fresh egg yolk, beaten
    Plain yogurt
    Powdered cinnamon

    Serves 4

Thousand-leaf Pastry

PASTELITOS DE MIL HOJAS

These pastries, with their many petals, resemble flowers when they are constructed correctly. *Pastelitos* also may be filled with cooked meat or seafood and served as an appetizer course without the syrup, of course. Pick a day when you don t have much else to do to make *pastelitos* because they take a lot of time.

Pastry Directions

In a large bowl combine 4 cups flour, chilled butter and salt. Rub the flour and fat together with your fingertips until they form a coarse meal. Gradually mix in the lemon juice and add the egg yolks one at a time.

PASTRY

4½ cups flour

11 tablespoons unsalted chilled butter, cut into small pieces

¼ teaspoon salt

2 teaspoons fresh lemon juice

2 egg yolks

1 cup ice water

⅔ cup sweet dessert wine

1½ cups quince paste

Continue working the dough with your fingers while adding water, ¼ cup at a time. When all the water has been absorbed and the dough is smooth, place it on a lightly floured surface. Knead the dough by pressing it down, pushing it forward then turning it back on itself. Continue to knead in this manner for about 10 minutes, or until the dough is smooth and elastic. Cover the dough with a dry towel and let it rest for 30 minutes.

When the dough has rested, roll it into a rough square about 32 by 32 inches. Brush the dough evenly with some of the melted butter and sprinkle the butter with a small dusting of flour. Smooth the flour over the surface of the dough with the palms of your hands until the flour absorbs the butter and the surface looks dry. Fold the dough in half, creating a 16- by 32-inch rectangle. Butter and flour the top of the dough as before, spreading the flour carefully with your hands until it absorbs the butter. Bring the short ends of the dough together, creating a

16- by 16-inch square. Repeat the entire procedure 2 more times to produce a final 8- by 8-inch square. Now roll the dough into a 16-inch square, using the remaining flour to keep the dough from sticking to the surface. With a small knife or pastry wheel and a ruler, trim the dough to a 15-inch square. Measure to make sure the dimensions are correct. Cut the square into 36 squares that are 2½ inches square.

Assembly Directions

Mix the wine into the quince paste and place about 1 teaspoon of this filling in the center of each of 18 squares. Lightly moisten the dough around the filling with cold water. Top each filled square with an unfilled square, rotating it so that its 4 corners are offset from the 4 corners of the filled square, forming a total of 8 consecutive corners. Press the dough firmly around the filling to secure it. Then pinch the corners toward the filling to achieve a flower-like shape having 8 petals.

Syrup Directions

Combine the sugar and water in a small saucepan. Stir until the sugar is thoroughly dissolved, Bring it to a boil over high heat, stirring constantly. Boil steadily without stirring until the syrup reaches a temperature of 230°F on a candy thermometer, or until a bit of the syrup dripped into ice water immediately forms a coarse thread. Remove the pan from the heat and stir in vanilla extract. Cover the syrup and keep it warm while you deep-fry the *pastelitos*.

Deep Frying Directions

Divide the shortening equally between 2 deep fryers or 2 deep heavy saucepans. Make sure the melted shortening reaches a depth of 3 inches in each pan. Use more shortening if necessary. Simultaneously heat one pan of

SYRUP

1 cup sugar
¼ cup water
½ teaspoon vanilla extract
Vegetable shortening for deep-frying

Makes 18 pastries

shortening to 375°F and the other to 175°F. Drop into the 175°F fat as many *pastelitos* as the pan will comfortably hold. Fry for 3 to 4 minutes, basting constantly with the fat until the petals of the dough begin to separate and open a bit. Do not let the *pastelitos* brown. Immediately transfer the *pastelitos* to the pan of 375°F fat and fry on both sides for 2 minutes or until golden brown. Carefully remove the *pastelitos* from the fat and drain them on paper towels. Then dip them in the warm syrup and place them on a serving plate. Fry and glaze the remaining *pastelitos* as described. Serve at room temperature.

CHAPTER 4

Mar del Plata:

Argentina's Riviera

Mar del Plata

In summer—December through March—
Porteños head for the beach. The Atlantic
coast beaches have their Mecca in Mar del Plata, 250
miles southeast of Buenos Aires. Here, thousands of
Argentines are hoping for a vacation from their friends
and families. But, alas, they are fated to run into them on
the beaches.

Juan de Garay, the founder of Buenos Aires, sailed the
coast in 1581 and declared the area *muy galana* (very beautiful). A century or more later, Portuguese investors built
a pier and established a small town—El Puerto de Laguna
de los Padres (in honor of failed Jesuit missionaries)—that
was sold in the 1860s to Patricio Peralta Ramos. The settlement became Mar del Plata in 1874. By the early 1900s,
the city housed the exclusive Barrio Los Troncos where
upper class *Porteños* owned villas, many of which have
been handed down and continue to provide summer resi-
dences for the old families.

Like San Francisco, Mar del Plata is blessed with
numerous hills tiered along the coast, providing ocean
vistas from almost every street and residence. Strolling
past the stone and timbered mansions of the city conjures
up visions of the past in which wealthy Argentines
indulged themselves in an exclusive playground created
just for their pleasure. One envisions unblemished cream-
colored Bugattis racing around the hillsides and along the
coast, scarves whipping in the wind. In another scene,
formally garbed ladies and gentlemen are betting the
estancia at one of the 20 roulette tables in the elegant,
dimly lit casino. In yet another, sumptuous lunches and

dinners are served with centuries-old family silver to the glitterati in the massive dining halls of private villas.

Mardel, as it is known locally, is still a major port city as well as a resort town. Daytime activities center on the beaches of the area. All beaches are open to the public, however *balnerios* (bathing resorts) along the wide beaches are private. Most *balnerios* have shops, paddleball courts and *confiterías*. These *confiterías* are famous for their local pastries. Thus, they are jammed with sandy sun-worshippers throughout the season. Their favorites at teatime are *alfajores*—cookies filled with *dulce de leche* (sweetened cooked milk) and covered with chocolate or rolled in sweetened coconut.

As one of Argentina's most important fishing ports and seafood processing centers, Mar del Plata offers a glimpse of sea-faring life that is seldom, if ever, seen in large cities. Banquina de Pescadores, the port's picturesque wharf, is filled with busy stevedores and fishermen on their colorful wooden boats, going about their daily routine. Fleets of small fishing boats leave the harbor at dawn and return just before sundown, followed by a large colony of sea lions who make their home on the south side of the pier.

The cool waters here encourage abundant marine life. Naturally, seafood plays a large part in the area's gastronomical offerings. Typical are Spanish rice and seafood stews, octopus dishes, sautéed flatfish, squid cooked in its own ink and every kind of shellfish you can imagine.

Restaurants in the port complex offer a many-splendored dining experience. You can be sure of the best of the day's catch, expertly prepared and served in convivial surroundings by loquacious hosts who are understandably proud of their product. My favorite port restaurant is the Euzkadi family's Taberna Baska. As the name suggests, Taberna Baska is steeped in the Basque tradition of Spain, which is known for its exceptional cooking by men only. The restaurant offers myriad gifts of the sea: *lenguado* (flounder and sole), *besugo* (porgy), *lubina* (striped bass), *atún* (tuna), *merluza* (hake) and much more. And they come in various guises: *à la Roquefort, à la Baska, à la crema, à la manteca negra, albardados*—and even simply grilled. Taberna Baska's signature dish, risotto with baby squid in its own ink, is seasonal and, thus, not always available. It's an unusual taste that every "foodie" should try, and it's easy to make if your fish market has access to baby squid.

In town, restaurants are varied and plentiful: traditional *criolla* fare, *parrillas*, seafood, pizza or haute cuisine. Take your pick. But during the season, expect to wait in line because many restaurants in Mar del Plata don't take reservations. Vacationers dine earlier here than they would at home to beat the rush.

Big city that it is, Mar del Plata offers an exuberant nightlife including a large but elegant casino that caters to the tastes of rich *Porteños*. Translated, that means it's a far cry from the gaudy pleasure palaces of Las Vegas. Housed in the Gran Hotel Provincial, the casino, though a dim reflection of its past glory, remains a bastion of social privilege and a center for Argentina's summering beautiful people. Another casino—small, unlisted and very exclusive—can only be frequented by invitation.

The city also hosts an international film festival, the Festival Internacional del Cine, every other year in March. The opening night of this event brings out Argentina's finest in droves, competing for the title of most fabulous rich couple—he in his Dior summer tuxedo and she bejeweled and clad in her one-of-a-kind formal gown by Lagerfeld. Cinemas and theaters provide diversions for the more "fiscally challenged." The discos are another option bringing both locals and vacationers an all-night venue for dancing and socializing in egalitarian circumstances.

Away from the city of Mar del Plata are numerous beachside communities and resorts that range from the democratic to the severely and exclusively grand. A short drive south of Mar del Plata offers a rewarding view of steep bluffs along the beaches. Go north and you see massive sand dunes. Go a little farther

Pinemar north of Mar del Plata.

north and you can soak up the tony atmosphere of the Pinemar and Villa Gesell beach resorts. These resorts are the headquarters of *truly* wealthy Argentines who spend their summers in reclusive splendor. I'm not sure what they eat, but I'm willing to bet they don't suffer a shortage of caviar and champagne.

Shrimp and Vegetable-Stuffed Tomatoes

TOMATES RELLENOS

This recipe provides a guilt-free as well as delicious way to dispose of leftover vegetables.

INGREDIENTS

- 4 large ripe tomatoes
- 2 cups small cooked, shelled and deveined shrimp
- 2 cups cooked vegetables, any combination of peas, carrots, green beans, corn kernels and lima beans
- ½ cup garlic alioli (page 197) or homemade mayonnaise
- Dash of Tabasco or pepper sauce
- 2 garlic cloves, minced
- 6 green onions, chopped
- 2 teaspoons chopped fresh dill

Serves 4

Directions

Make the tomato shells by cutting the tops off tomatoes and carefully scooping out the pulp and seeds. Turn the tomato shells upside down to drain. Toss the shrimp and your choice of vegetables with the alioli or mayonnaise. Stir in Tabasco, garlic, onions and dill. Fill the tomato shells with the shrimp salad and chill until ready to serve.

Fish Soup

Most Argentine soups start out as a broth derived from a *puchero*. That is not the case with fish soups—they are constructed along the lines of hearty Mediterranean fish soups with a home-made fish broth as the base. And, of course, the garnish is a generous dollop of garlic alioli.

Directions

Boil live crabs in a large pot of salted water for 5 minutes. Remove and cool. In a 10-quart kettle, combine fish bones and heads with bay leaves, allspice, 1½ teaspoons salt and the water. Bring to a boil then reduce the heat to low and simmer for 20 minutes. Strain and reserve the stock; discard solid materials.

Rinse out the kettle and add olive oil. Heat the oil then add onions, celery, peppers and garlic. Sauté for 5 to 10 minutes or until the vegetables are tender. Add tomatoes, sugar, remaining 1½ teaspoons salt, pepper and reserved fish stock. Simmer for 10 minutes over medium heat. Add seabass and sherry and bring to a boil, stirring often. Add prawns, mussels and clams. Continue cooking until the prawns are pink and the mussels and clams are open, discarding any mussels or clams that do not open. Place ½ cup crab pieces in the shell in each soup bowl. Remove the soup from the heat and ladle it over the crab in the soup bowls. Garnish each bowl of soup with a dollop of alioli and a dill sprig. Serve hot with garlic toast. Offer cocktail forks and pincers.

INGREDIENTS

- 6 small live hard-shelled crabs, about ¼-pound each or 1 large Dungeness crab, cooked, cleaned, cracked and broken into claws and 4 body sections
- 1½ pounds fish bones and heads
- 4 bay leaves
- 1 teaspoon allspice
- 3 teaspoons salt
- 5 cups water
- ¾ cup olive oil
- 3 medium onions, chopped
- 2 cups chopped celery
- 1 large red bell pepper or pimiento, seeded and chopped
- 5 garlic cloves, minced
- 1 29-ounce can Italian roma tomatoes
- ¼ teaspoon sugar
- 1 teaspoon freshly ground pepper
- 1 pound seabass, cut in pieces
- 1¾ cup dry sherry
- 1 pound prawns in the shells, heads removed, cleaned and deveined
- 1 dozen mussels in the shell, rinsed and debearded
- 1 dozen clams in the shell
  Alioli (page 197)
- 8 sprigs fresh dill

Serves 6 to 8

Mar del Plata   125

Fish Soufflé

SOUFFLÉ DE PESCADO

Light and airy, *soufflé de pescado* is the perfect centerpiece for a light supper. Serve it with a salad of steamed and chilled vegetables sprinkled with olive oil.

Directions

Preheat the oven to 375°F. Butter the bottom and sides of a 6-cup soufflé dish, or individual soufflé dishes, and sprinkle with grated Parmesan cheese.

Simmer the fish in salted water until cooked through, approximately 5 minutes. Drain thoroughly and discard the water. Make a medium white sauce: stir flour into hot butter and continue stirring with a wire whisk while adding milk ¼ cup at a time. Blend well and add salt, pepper and nutmeg. Continue stirring until the mixture thickens, about 5 minutes. Flake the fish with a fork and combine it with the sauce. Add a little salt and the egg yolks one at a time, beating after each addition. Beat the egg whites until they are stiff but not dry. Fold the fish sauce into the egg whites and spoon the mixture into the soufflé dish. Bake in the center of the oven for about 30 minutes, or until the soufflé is puffed up and browned on top. Cut the soufflé into 4 portions—if using the large soufflé dish—and serve napped with the mustard sauce. Serve immediately.

INGREDIENTS

Butter for greasing soufflé dish

2 tablespoons grated Parmesan cheese

¾ pound firm white fish fillets

1½ tablespoons flour

1 tablespoon butter, melted

1 cup milk

Salt and white pepper to taste

1 teaspoon freshly ground nutmeg

4 eggs, separated

Mustard sauce, (page 102)

Serves 4

Baked Seabass Mar del Plata Style

A cousin to the famed *Pescado à la Veracruzana* of Mexico, *Corbina à la Mar del Plata* is at least as delectable.

Directions

Scrub the potatoes and boil them in salted water for about 20 minutes. Set aside and keep warm. Season the fish with salt and pepper and sprinkle with lemon or lime juice. Heat the oil in a skillet and sauté the onion and garlic until they are soft. Add the tomatoes to the skillet with capers, green peppers, olives, cinnamon and fish. Simmer over a low heat until the fish is tender and the sauce is slightly thickened, 10 to 15 minutes. Transfer the fish to a warmed platter, surround it with the potatoes and nap with some of the sauce. Cut the bread in 6 triangles, sauté them in butter until they are golden and arrange them in a border around the edge of the serving platter.

INGREDIENTS

12 small red potatoes
2 pounds seabass fillets
    Salt and pepper to taste
    Juice of 1 small lemon
    or lime
⅓ cup olive oil
2 medium onions, minced
2 garlic cloves, minced
6 medium tomatoes, peeled
    and puréed
2 tablespoons rinsed and
    drained capers
3 green peppers, seeded
    and cut into strips
2 dozen pimiento-stuffed
    green olives
1 teaspoon ground
    cinnamon
3 slices firm white bread
3 tablespoons butter

Serves 4

Stuffed Striped Bass

LUBINA RELLENA

In Mar del Plata, this dish is made with whole striped bass. A good substitution is red snapper. Serve with rice and a green vegetable or salad.

Directions

Preheat the oven to 400°F. Rinse the fish and pat it dry with paper towels. Season the fish cavity with salt and pepper. Combine the onion, garlic, parsley, breadcrumbs and additional salt and pepper to taste. Moisten the mixture with a small amount of milk and stuff the fish with the mixture. Fasten the cavity together with toothpicks. Butter a shallow, flameproof casserole that is just big enough to hold the fish. Place the fish in the casserole and dot it with butter. Pour the oil and then the wine over the fish. Bake for 40 minutes or until the fish feels firm when pressed with your finger.

When the fish is done the pan drippings and wine will have reduced to form a sauce. Cut the fish into quarters and serve with the stuffing. Ladle a small amount of the sauce over each piece of fish before serving.

INGREDIENTS

3 to 3½-pound striped bass, cleaned, scaled and boned with head and tail intact
1 tablespoon kosher salt
2 teaspoons freshly ground black pepper
1 medium onion, minced
3 garlic cloves, minced
½ cup minced parsley
1 cup fresh breadcrumbs
Milk
1 tablespoon butter
1 tablespoon olive oil
1 cup dry white wine

Serves 4

Baked Fish in Casserole

CAZUELA DE PESCADO AL HORNO

Originating near Cadiz in Spain, this dish is based on besugo fillets or porgy. I have substituted Chilean seabass and red snapper fillets with good results.

Directions

Preheat the oven to 350°F. To make the sauce, heat the olive oil in a skillet. Add the onions and sauté for 10 minutes, stirring frequently. Add tomatoes, water, saffron, salt, pepper and bay leaf. Cook over low heat for 15 minutes or until the mixture reduces slightly and thickens. Set aside.

Place the fillets in a buttered, flameproof casserole. Arrange potatoes, green peppers and peas around the fillets and pour the sauce over them. Place sliced pimientos on top of the fillets and bake in the oven for 20 minutes or until the fish flakes easily with a fork. Serve from the casserole.

INGREDIENTS

½ cup olive oil

2 onions, thinly sliced

3 tomatoes, peeled and chopped

½ cup water

½ teaspoon saffron

2 teaspoons salt

½ teaspoon freshly ground black pepper

1 bay leaf

6 firm-fleshed fish fillets

6 cups miniature red potatoes, scrubbed but not peeled

2 green peppers, seeded and thinly sliced

½ cup shelled green peas, fresh or frozen

3 fresh pimientos, thinly sliced (or canned pimientos)

Serves 6

Fish in Black Sauce

PESCADO EN SALSA NEGRA

Here is another Argentine interpretation of a Spanish baked fish dish. Dried porcini mushrooms and their soaking water are responsible for the intriguing color and hence the name of the dish.

Directions

Preheat the oven to 350°F. Soak the mushrooms in the warm water for at least 30 minutes. Drain the mushrooms, remove any woody stems, chop coarsely and strain, reserving the soaking liquid. In a flameproof casserole, heat the oil and sauté the onions and garlic until soft. Add salt, pepper, nutmeg and ground nuts. Cook over a medium heat for about 5 minutes. Add mushrooms, mushroom soaking liquid and bay leaf. Continue cooking and stirring for about 8 minutes. Add the fish fillets and spoon the sauce over them. Place the casserole in the oven and bake for about 20 minutes or until the fish flakes easily with a fork. Remove the casserole from the oven and sprinkle with parsley. Serve directly from the casserole.

INGREDIENTS

½ cup dried porcini
   mushrooms
1 cup warm water
2 tablespoons olive oil
2 onions, minced
3 garlic cloves, minced
   Salt and pepper to taste
½ teaspoon nutmeg
½ cup ground walnuts
1 bay leaf
2 pounds striped bass or
   red snapper fillets,
   dredged in flour
2 tablespoons minced
   parsley

Serves 6

Baked Dover Sole in Garlic Sauce

LENGUADO AL HORNO CON SALSA DE AJO

This is the basic recipe for baking any firm-fleshed fish. On the East Coast, Dover sole is usually available, but on the West Coast, Petrale sole is the best bet. Garlic sauce is a particularly tasty accompaniment, but other fish sauces will work as well. An important note: one should not expect a condimented sauce to mask the off flavor of less than pristine fish. Make sure yours is the freshest.

Directions

Preheat the oven to 350°F. Cut the fillets in half and sprinkle them with salt and pepper. Place the butter in small shallow baking dish and set it in the oven until it melts. Roll the fillets in the butter until they are well coated. Sprinkle with breadcrumbs on both sides and arrange the lemon slices on top. Bake, uncovered, for 15 to 20 minutes. Remove to serving dishes napped with garlic fish sauce.

INGREDIENTS

¾ pound Dover sole fillets

½ teaspoon salt

⅛ teaspoon pepper

¼ cup butter

¼ cup soft breadcrumbs

1 lemon, thinly sliced
   Garlic fish sauce (recipe
   follows)

Garlic Fish Sauce
SALSA DE PESCADORES CON AJO

Don't be alarmed by the amount of garlic in this sauce—an entire head. Somehow, the other ingredients tame the garlic flavor. In addition to baked fish, this sauce is great with sautéed or grilled fish.

Directions
Prepare a roux: melt the butter in a small skillet, add the flour and stir. Continue stirring until the roux is lightly browned. Add the broth, salt and pepper. Continue cooking over medium heat, stirring rapidly with a whisk until thickened. Stir in the garlic and simmer for 5 minutes. Stir in pine nuts and remove from the heat. Stir in parsley. Ladle a small amount of sauce on heated serving plates. Place the fish on top of the sauce and serve.

INGREDIENTS

1   tablespoon butter
1   tablespoon flour
½   cup fish broth or bottled
    clam juice
    Salt and freshly ground
    pepper to taste
1   head of garlic, skinned
    and chopped
½   cup lightly toasted
    chopped pine nuts
¼   cup minced parsley

Serves 2

Shrimp with Rice

ARROZ CON CAMARONES

Long-grain rice is grown in small quantities in Argentina. However, Spanish and Italian short-grain rice is always available. I prefer the short-grain rice in this dish, but either type will work. Use small to medium-sized fresh or fresh-frozen shrimp with the tail on and the head removed.

Directions

In a large saucepan sauté the garlic in butter for 2 to 3 minutes. Add shrimp, Tabasco, salt and just enough water to cover. Bring to a boil and simmer for 5 minutes or until the shrimp turn a light pink. Drain, reserving the liquid. Set shrimp aside and keep them warm. Discard the garlic. Measure the reserved liquid and add just enough water to make 2¾ cups. Return the liquid to the saucepan and bring it to a boil. Add the rice and level it gently with a fork. Cover and simmer it on low heat for 25 minutes or until the rice is completely cooked and all the liquid has been absorbed. Fluff the rice with a fork and place it in a serving dish. Top the rice with the shrimp and sprinkle it with lemon juice. Garnish with egg slices and cheese.

INGREDIENTS

3 garlic cloves

1 teaspoon butter

1 pound raw or defrosted fresh-frozen shrimp, shelled and deveined

Dash Tabasco or pepper sauce

¾ teaspoon salt

1 ½ cups raw rice

Few drops lemon or lime juice

2 eggs, hard-boiled and sliced

Grated Romano cheese

Serves 4

Creamed Mussels

MEJILLONES À LA CREMA

Creamed mussels the Argentine way equal or surpass any I have eaten in Belgium or France. The inclusion of fresh mushrooms is a master touch—so Argentine. One must take care not to boil the sauce after adding cream or it may curdle.

Directions

Place the mussels in a heavy pot with the salt, pepper and wine. Cover and cook on high heat until the shells open, about 7 minutes. Discard unopened mussels. Strain the liquid through a double layer of cheesecloth and reserve the liquid. Remove the mussels from the shells. Heat the butter, add the mushrooms and sauté for 5 minutes. Stir in the flour and add the strained cooking liquid. Continue cooking until thickened, stirring constantly with a whisk. Add the brandy, lemon juice and nutmeg. Mix thoroughly and gradually pour in the cream. Return the shelled mussels to the sauce and reheat, but do not boil or the sauce will curdle.

INGREDIENTS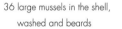

36 large mussels in the shell, washed and beards removed
½ teaspoon salt
Freshly ground black pepper
1 cup dry white wine
4 tablespoons butter
1 cup sliced mushrooms
4 tablespoons flour
2 tablespoons brandy (Spanish Fundador if available)
Juice of 1 lemon
¼ teaspoon freshly grated nutmeg
1 cup heavy cream

Serves 4

Rice with Squid in its own Ink

Down in the wharf area of Mar del Plata is a small Basque restaurant, Taberna Baska, that lives up to the reputation of Basque cooking. On a cool and foggy night, it's wonderful to be seated alongside fishermen and their families in the cocoonish atmosphere of the restaurant, inhaling the complex odors emanating from the kitchen. On one such night I was introduced to a specialty of the region—squid in its own ink. The idea of fish cooked in a black liquid may seem a bit strange to those not familiar with this delicacy. However, the ink imparts a subtle flavor that is sublime. Most who have tried this dish consider it one of the most delicious rice preparations ever concocted. The recipe, courtesy of Taberna Baska, is a dish that's easy enough to make if you can get your fishmonger to special order baby squid complete with ink sacs.

INGREDIENTS

- 2 pounds baby squid with ink sacs
- 4 tablespoons olive oil
- 1 large onion, chopped
- 1 fresh pimiento, seeded and chopped
- 2 garlic cloves, minced
- 1 medium tomato, chopped
- 1 tablespoon minced parsley
  Salt
  Freshly ground black pepper
- ½ dried red chili pepper, seeds removed and crushed
- 3¾ cups fish broth or bottled clam juice
- ¼ cup dry red wine
- 2 cups short-grain rice

Serves 4 to 6

Directions

Preheat the oven to 325°F. Clean the squid (see page 136 for instructions), reserving the ink sacs and tentacles. Cut the squid into ½-inch rings. Chop the tentacles. In a wide, shallow flameproof casserole, heat the oil and sauté the onion until it is soft. Add the squid rings and tentacles and sauté for 5 minutes. Add the chopped pimiento, garlic, tomato, parsley, salt, black pepper, chili pepper and fish broth. Cover and simmer 30 minutes.

Break the ink sacs into a cup and mix the ink with the wine. Pass this liquid through a sieve several times, pressing with a wooden spoon, until most of the ink is extracted. Set aside. Add the rice to the casserole. Stir in the ink mixture and season to taste with salt and pepper. Bring the mixture to a boil and cook over medium-high heat, stirring occasionally for about 10 minutes.

Place the casserole in the oven and bake, uncovered, for about 20 minutes or until most of the liquid is absorbed. Remove the casserole from the oven, cover lightly with foil and allow the dish to rest for 10 minutes. When ready to serve, garnish with pimiento slices. If desired, serve with garlic sauce (page 132). A green salad and a full-bodied Chardonnay should accompany this dish.

HOW TO CLEAN SQUID

Pull the tentacles from the body of the squid and peel off the silvery ink sac from beneath the tentacles. Cut off all waste material but leave the tentacles in one piece. Remove the skin from the body of the squid, pull off the fins and rinse well. Turn the squid body inside out, remove the cartilage and rinse the body under running water. Turn the squid body right side out, rinse and dry on paper towels.

Stuffed Squid in its Own Ink

CALAMARES EN SU TINTA

When calamare are in season, vacationing *Porteños* can't get enough of them. Stuffing them opens up all sorts of possibilities. The following version is served at the La Terraza Restaurant in the Five-star Costa Galana Hotel across from the beach in Mar del Plata.

Directions

Chop the tentacles and mix them with the ham. Stuff the bodies of the squid with this mixture. Place the ink sacs in a strainer over a small bowl. Press them with a wooden spoon to extract the ink. Pour ¼ cup of the wine through the strainer. Pass the liquid from the bowl through the strainer several times until most of the ink color is removed from the remaining material. Set aside.

In a large flameproof casserole, heat the oil and sauté the onion and garlic until they are soft, Add the tomato and parsley and cook 5 minutes. Stir in the flour and add the broth and the remaining ¼ cup wine. Pour in the ink mixture (the sauce should be black, but don't worry if it's not). Season with salt and pepper. Add the squid and simmer covered over a low heat for 2 hours. Serve with steamed rice and a salad. A full-bodied Chardonnay is a good choice for wine.

INGREDIENTS

2 pounds baby squid, cleaned with ink sacs reserved

4 tablespoons finely chopped cured ham

Ink sacs from 1 pound large squid, squid discarded or used for another purpose

½ cup dry red wine

2 tablespoons olive oil

1 medium onion, chopped

2 garlic cloves, minced

1 medium tomato, peeled, seeded and chopped

1 tablespoon chopped parsley

1 tablespoon flour

1 cup fish broth or bottled clam juice

Salt

Freshly ground pepper

Serves 4

Stuffed Squid

CALAMARES RELLENOS

If squid ink isn't your cup of tea, the following recipe for stuffed squid is an honorable alternative and quite impressive as a company dish on its own.

Directions

Preheat the oven to 350°F. Chop the tentacles and mix them with the ham, breadcrumbs, parsley, lemon juice and melted butter. Season with salt and pepper and stuff the mixture into the bodies of the squid. Roll the squid in flour and fry them in hot oil for about 5 minutes. Remove the squid to a flameproof casserole and place them close together. Add the broth and wine. Season with salt and pepper to taste, cover tightly and simmer in the oven for 40 minutes, basting occasionally with the pan juices.

Fry the onion in the oil remaining in the skillet. Add the green pepper. When the squid are done, remove them from the casserole and place them on a heated serving platter. Pour the cooking liquid from the casserole into the skillet containing the onions and green pepper. Turn the heat up to high and reduce the cooking liquid by half. Pour the reduced liquid over the squid and serve immediately.

INGREDIENTS

12 medium squid, cleaned with tentacles removed

6 thin slices cooked ham, chopped

4 cups fine breadcrumbs

Juice of 1½ lemons

4 tablespoons butter, melted

½ teaspoon salt

Freshly ground pepper

Flour

3 tablespoons olive oil

¼ cup fish broth or bottled clam juice

¼ cup dry white wine

1 onion, chopped

1 green pepper, chopped

Serves 6

Partridge with Cabbage

Lovely to look at, delightful to taste, this game dish makes a great impression at a dinner party for special guests. If partridge is not available, squab is the best alternative.

Directions

Brown the birds in oil in a heavy, flameproof casserole. When browned, remove the birds and set them aside. Place the onions in the casserole and sauté them until golden. Add the carrots, garlic, parsley and pancetta. Sauté for a few minutes more, and then add cabbage. Continue cooking while stirring until the cabbage is slightly brown and wilted. Add juniper berries, thyme, rosemary, cumin, paprika, caraway seed and salt and peppercorns. Stir in the apples and wine and bring the mixture to a boil.

Toast the flour in a hot skillet without oil until it is lightly browned. Sprinkle the toasted flour over the cabbage mixture and stir. Reduce the heat to low and return the birds to the casserole. Cover the casserole tightly and simmer for 20 minutes. When the birds are done, place the cabbage mixture on a serving platter and top with the partridge halves. Spoon a dollop of sour cream on each partridge half and garnish with a sprig of rosemary.

INGREDIENTS

6 partridges, cleaned and cut in half lengthwise

3 tablespoons olive oil

2 onions, thinly sliced

1 large carrot, chopped

4 garlic cloves, minced

3 tablespoons minced parsley

3 ounces finely chopped pancetta (or blanched bacon)

1 head of savoy cabbage, washed and cut in narrow strips

12 juniper berries, crushed

1 teaspoon ground thyme

2 tablespoons chopped fresh rosemary leaves

½ teaspoon ground cumin

1 tablespoon sweet paprika

½ teaspoon caraway seed

   Sprinkling of coarse kosher or sea salt, to taste

12 whole black peppercorns

2 green apples, sliced

1 cup red wine

1 tablespoon flour

¾ cup sour cream

6 rosemary sprigs

Serves 6

Veal with Noodles

CARBONADA CON REFALOSAS

Because veal is dependent upon condiments and seasonings for an interesting flavor, most veal dishes are highly seasoned. This carbonada is an exception. It calls for no spices—not even salt or pepper—but has the intensely fresh flavor of individual vegetables partnered with tender bits of veal and bow-tie pasta. Thus, children usually like it and it's good for them. For adults with jaded palates, you might want to serve a condiment on the side such as seeded and sliced serrano or jalapeño chilies marinated in soya sauce.

INGREDIENTS

2   large onions, minced
6 to 8 garlic cloves, minced
1   sprig parsley, minced
1   large or 2 medium red bell peppers, roasted, peeled, seeded and roughly chopped
2   tablespoons olive oil or lard
4   medium tomatoes, peeled and sliced
1 ½ pounds veal, cut into 1-inch squares
4   large white potatoes, peeled and cut lengthwise in eighths
1   turnip, coarsely chopped
2   carrots, minced
    Boiling water
3   tablespoons tomato paste
1   cup dry white wine
8   ounces bow-tie pasta
½   cup shelled peas, fresh or frozen
½   cup fresh corn kernels, cut from the cob
6   fresh serrano or jalapeño peppers, seeded and thinly sliced into rings (optional)
½   cup soya sauce (optional)

Serves 6 to 8

Directions

Sauté the onions, garlic, parsley and red pepper in oil until they are soft. Add tomatoes. When the mixture starts to bubble, stir in the veal, potatoes, turnip and carrots. Pour boiling water over the mixture to cover. Add the tomato paste and wine. Mix thoroughly. Cover and simmer over low heat for 25 minutes. In a large pot, bring the water to a boil. Add the noodles and cook them according to the package instructions. Drain the noodles, reserving a little of the pasta water. Five minutes before the stew has completed cooking, add the peas, corn, cooked pasta and a little of the pasta water. Continue cooking for 5 minutes.

Serve with crusty bread, a watercress salad and a buttery Chardonnay. If desired, mix the peppers into the soya sauce and serve as an optional condiment for the stew at the table.

Filet of Beef, Mar del Plata Style

Even by Argentine standards, this party dish is a showstopper. Of course, one must have access to only the very best beef. The dish is usually reserved for special occasions because it is not inexpensive—even in Argentina. However, the oohs and aahs from guests after tasting this incredible piece of beef make it worthwhile. Serve it with *Papas Fritas* (French-fried potatoes) or *Papas al Horno* (oven-roasted potatoes), steamed carrots and a green salad.

Directions

Preheat the oven to 350°F. Place the pancetta across the bottom of a heavy flameproof casserole. Melt the butter in a skillet. Brown the filet on all sides over medium heat and place it on top of the pancetta. Mix egg yolks, mushrooms, parsley and olive oil together and spread the mixture on top of the filet, pressing down on the mixture to compress it and keep it in place. Wrap the filet with the loose ends of the pancetta. Add wine, broth, onion, bay leaf, peppercorns and thyme. Roast the filet, uncovered, in the center of the oven for 30 minutes. Sprinkle the filet with breadcrumbs and cheese and continue roasting for another 20 minutes for medium rare.

Remove the roast from the casserole and keep it warm. Remove the pancetta and save it for another use or discard. Mix the flour and water to make a smooth paste and add it to the juices in the casserole. On medium heat, cook the sauce for 5 minutes or until thickened, stirring constantly. Taste for seasoning. Remove the bay leaf and spoon 3 tablespoons of the sauce in the center of a serving

INGREDIENTS

6   slices pancetta
3   tablespoons butter
4-pound filet of beef in one
    piece
2   hard-boiled egg yolks,
    chopped
½   cup chopped mushrooms
2   tablespoons chopped
    parsley
2   tablespoons olive oil
1   cup dry white wine
½   cup beef broth
1   onion, chopped
1   bay leaf
3   peppercorns
¼   teaspoon fresh thyme
¼   cup dry breadcrumbs
¼   cup grated Parmesan
    cheese
2   tablespoons flour
2   tablespoons water
    Salt and pepper to taste

Serves 8

platter. Cut the filet crosswise into ¼-inch slices and place them over the sauce on the platter. Pour the remaining sauce in a sauceboat and serve separately.

Sautéed Chard
ACELGAS SALTADA

The following recipe partners well with any seafood or roasted or braised meat preparation. It can be used to prepare many kinds of green vegetables: spinach, borage, kale, broccoli, brussels sprouts, green beans, peas, cabbages, etc.

INGREDIENTS

¼ cup raisins
1 onion, minced
2 tablespoons olive oil
2 garlic cloves, minced
4 cups chopped cooked chard
Salt to taste
1 teaspoon freshly ground nutmeg

Serves 4

Directions
Soak the raisins in hot water for 30 minutes and drain. Sauté the onion in oil over high heat. Add garlic and sauté for several minutes more, being careful not to brown the onions or garlic. Squeeze the chard in a towel until it's dry. Add the chard to the onion mixture and sauté it until it is heated through and coated with the oil. Season with salt and nutmeg. Mix in the raisins and serve while hot.

Meringue Stacks

POSTRE DE CHAJA

The cooking secrets of the convents came to the New World with the Jesuits and have stayed on, mainly in the hinterlands of Argentina. *Postre de Chaja* is typical of the old way with *postres* (desserts). Meringue-based pastries with fresh fruit, eggs and cream are still made by Argentine nuns.

Meringue Directions

Preheat the oven to 325°. Beat the egg whites, salt and cream of tartar until the mixture is stiff but not dry. Add the vinegar and gradually add the sugar a spoonful at a time, beating constantly until ⅔ cup of the sugar is used. Fold in the vanilla and the remaining ⅓ cup of sugar, mixing well. With a tablespoon or pastry bag, drop the mixture onto a Silpat-lined or oiled baking sheet. Form the meringues into 18 flat rounds, 3 inches in diameter. Bake for 30 minutes or until the meringues are dry and lightly browned. Remove the meringues from the baking sheet with a spatula and set them aside to cool.

MERINGUES

6 egg whites

⅛ teaspoon salt

⅛ teaspoon cream of tartar

½ teaspoon vinegar

1 cup sugar

1 teaspoon vanilla

Frosting Directions

Combine sugar, water, and cream of tartar in a saucepan. Boil until very syrupy. A candy thermometer should register 238°F, and a thread should form if a spoonful of the mixture is lifted out of the pan. Beat the egg yolks in a bowl and gradually add syrup, beating constantly until the mixture is cool and thick. To make the buttercream frosting, cream the butter until fluffy and soft then gradually add it to the syrup mixture. Stir in the brandy.

FROSTING

¾ cup sugar

¼ cup water

¼ teaspoon cream of tartar

5 egg yolks

½ pound unsalted butter

1 tablespoon brandy

Assembly Directions

Place a meringue on each of 8 serving plates and spread the meringue top with a thin layer of buttercream. Top with a slice of sponge cake or 2 ladyfingers. Divide the fruit equally and arrange it on top of the cake slice or ladyfingers. Cover the fruit with whipped cream. Spread the buttercream frosting on a second meringue and place it on top of the whipped cream, frosting side down. Spread each meringue stack with a covering layer of buttercream mixture. Crumble the 2 extra meringues with your fingers and sprinkle them over each meringue stack.

ASSEMBLY

8   slices sponge cake or 16
    ladyfingers
1   cup strawberries
2   cups heavy cream

Makes 8 meringue desserts

Caramel-filled Butter Cookies

ALFAJORES

Most Argentines adore *alfajores* and consume them at breakfast, lunch, tea, after dinner and between meals. They are a particular favorite at beach resorts like Mar del Plata where you can buy them at any one of numerous kiosks catering to the sandy set.

Directions

Combine flour, salt, sugar and baking soda in a bowl. Cut in the butter with a pastry blender or 2 knives. Work in the lemon zest then mix in the egg yolks and vanilla. Shape the dough into 2 balls and chill for 2 hours.

Preheat the oven to 325°F. On a floured surface, roll out each ball of dough to a thickness of ¼ inch. Cut into 2-inch rounds and transfer the rounds to a Silpat-lined cookie sheet with a spatula. Bake 15 minutes or until done. The cookies will be dry but not brown.

When the cookies are cool, spread a ¼-inch-thick layer of *dulce de leche* (caramel filling) on one cookie and top it with another. Press together gently and roll the seam of each sandwiched cookie in grated coconut.

INGREDIENTS

1¾ cups sifted flour
⅛ teaspoon salt
½ cup sugar
1 teaspoon baking soda
¼ pound butter, softened
1 teaspoon lemon zest
4 egg yolks, lightly beaten
1 teaspoon vanilla
1 recipe dulce de leche
   (recipe follows)
1 cup grated and sweetened
   coconut, fresh or dried

Makes 25 sandwiched
cookies

Caramel Filling

DULCE DE LECHE

Dulce de leche—or milk pudding—is an Argentine staple. In the old days, home cooks made it in quantity because it keeps indefinitely and they wanted to always have some on hand. Nowadays, it's available in tins in Argentina and in some Latin American markets in North America. Argentines spoon *dulce de leche* over ice cream or puddings. They even ice cakes with it. Sometimes flavorings are added. Cinnamon, lemon peel or ground almonds are frequent additions. The recipe that follows is the traditional one.

INGREDIENTS

2   cups milk
¾ cup sugar
    Dash baking soda
1   teaspoon vanilla

Makes about 1 cup of dulce de leche

Directions

Combine milk, sugar and baking soda in a saucepan. Bring the mixture to a boil. Lower the heat and keep the mixture barely at a simmer for about 2½ hours, stirring occasionally. When the mixture forms a soft ball in cold water, remove it from the heat and stir in the vanilla. Cool before using.

Variation: For a quick and easy dulce de leche, make it with canned, sweetened condensed milk. Merely cover an unopened can with water in a large saucepan, bring it to a boil and continue cooking over medium heat for 3 hours. Cool before opening the can. An even quicker method is to cook the canned milk in a pressure cooker filled three-quarters full with water for 45 minutes. CAUTION: DO NOT ALLOW THE SAUCEPAN OR PRESSURE COOKER TO RUN OUT OF WATER OR THE CAN MAY EXPLODE.

CHAPTER 5

Mesopotamia:

Flavors of the
Great Waters Rain Forest

Mesopotamia

There are three reasons to visit Mesopotamia and, particularly, the province of Misiones. The first is to experience mysterious mission ruins that lie crumbling and entwined in tangles of lush vines and epiphytic orchids. The second is to gaze awestruck at the spectacular cascades of Iguazú Falls plummeting down from a mountainous jungle to the river almost 250 feet below. And the third is to sample the tropical exotica of local foodstuffs.

In the aftermath of the Jesuits' expulsion from South America, the missions fell into decay amidst the heat and humidity of tropical Argentina. These ghostly reminders of lost colonies lend an aura of mystery to Mesopotamia as thick as the mists that hang heavy over the rivers and the jungles hiding pumas and jaguars from view. You tend to look over your shoulder to see if anyone or anything is approaching you from behind. Could it be aboriginal ghosts bidding you to follow them into the mists? But, no. It's merely furtive lizards scurrying out of your way. And thus, you return abruptly to an exotic but comfortable reality.

Iguazú Falls is Mesopotamia's jewel in the crown. Situated at the confluence of the Paraná and Iguazú rivers bordering Argentina, Brazil and Paraguay, the falls are viewed by most tourists from the Brazilian side. This is unfortunate because the Argentine side offers a far more spectacular view. Numerous river channels form dozens of cataracts that spill over rocky, jungle-draped outcroppings. More than a mile across, the falls pump at least 16,000 cubic feet of water per second into the sedimentary terrain below.

Jesuit ruins in Mesopotamia.

Iguazú Falls.

If the scenery looks familiar it's because Iguazú Falls was one of the stars of the movie *The Mission*, with Robert De Niro and Jeremy Irons. Like the missions, the falls are usually shrouded in mist. Then when the sun breaks through the mist in shafts of dazzling light, it's as if the heavens have opened and angels are raining down upon the waters.

While there are many hotels, hostels and *residencias* (bed and breakfast accommodations) on the Brazilian side of the falls, the place to stay close to the falls in Puerto Iguazú is the Hotel Internacional on the Argentine side. This modern, five-story hotel sits in contrast to the surrounding natural landscape. Like an ocean liner anchored on a sea of velvety lawns, clipped hedges and disciplined flowerbeds, the hotel stands in romantic isolation. Beyond the lawns, the site is enclosed on all sides by an untamed tropical rainforest. Hundreds of brilliantly colored toucans flit from tree to tree while calling raucously to their mates. And then, when you enter the hotel's open-air lobby—with its resident flock of airborne parakeets—you are astonished to see the west-facing cascades through a three-story wall of glass.

Exploring different levels and vantage points in and around the falls is the primary activity for visitors to Puerto Iguazú. Numerous, well-maintained paths make it possible to be in close contact with the falling waters as you walk over, under and around various cataracts. The distant sounds of the thundering falls make first-timers reach for their rain gear—slickers or raincoats are *de rigueur* but not really necessary. Climb up a nearby tower and the panoramic view of the falls is breathtaking. With only tropical birds as companions—rarely are there crowds of people on the Argentine side of the falls—visitors find a magic here they remember the rest of their lives.

Naturally, a day spent walking the up-and-down trails can work up a ravenous appetite. And Mesopotamia's original approach with local food products does not disappoint. Heading most local menus are suribi and dorado—weighing in at more than 150 pounds—pulled fresh from the rivers. These flavorful, white-fleshed fish are superb whether grilled, baked, or breaded and sautéed. Accompaniments usually consist of boiled rice along with green salads and local fruits: papayas, mangoes, bananas, avocados and some that seem to be nameless. *Churrasco Espadin* (Chop on a Sword)—usually roasted ox—is a favorite dish borrowed from Brazil across the river. Another Brazilian specialty—*cachaca* (brandy)—is the local preference for after-dinner toasts.

Paraguayan Indian specialties are also an unusual local treat with *locros* (a type of stew), fried cakes and Paraguayan soup, which, despite its name, is a bread of white maize, flour, cheese, onion and spices. Paraguayan rum is appreciated, too.

The food in either of the hotel's two dining rooms is almost as stunning as the falls. Extravagant buffets feature local provender arranged as art. In the evening, as you descend the grand floating staircase from the lounge to the dining rooms below, you get a parakeet's- eye-view of the candle-lit buffet tables. One night jewel-like fresh fruit compotes in large, cut-crystal bowls adorned one buffet table, whose centerpiece was a huge arrangement of whole fruits surrounded by a ring of orchids.

Another buffet table offered dozens of different composed salads creating a kaleidoscope of colors and shapes. A third buffet table displayed a variety of hot main courses and side dishes in heavy, domed, highly polished silver vessels reflecting the candlelight a thousand-fold. Arranged on outsized silver trays were whole poached suribi and dorado decorated with pipings of red and green alioli (a freshly made highly seasoned mayonnaise) and butter-colored cream cheese, along with thinly sliced rounds of radishes, zucchinis and limes representing fish scales. In the center of this table was a gigantic arrangement of purple caladiums, salmon-colored ginger flowers, coral and lime green-tipped heliconias, and sunset-pink cattlea orchids piled high and interspersed with giant-sized philodendron leaves fresh from the rain forest. Fortunately, the dessert table was beyond my view else I might have lapsed into sensory overload.

Mesopotamian Gazpacho

This version of gazpacho is more of a soupy salad. As it happens, it's a favorite of mine because I love the tartness of the limes, the zip of the seasonings, the crunch of the chunky vegetables and the silkiness of the chilled chicken broth. It's especially nice served in individual chilled crystal compote bowls.

For a slightly different version, substitute ripe melon for the cucumbers and sliced scallions for the red onions.

Directions

Mix tomatoes and their juices with green pepper, onion, cucumber and garlic in a bowl. Stir in the chicken broth and add lime juice. Taste for tartness, adding more lime juice if necessary. Add cayenne or chilies and stir in dill, oregano, thyme, cumin, salt, pepper and olive oil, mixing well. Cover and chill the mixture for at least 8 hours in the refrigerator. When ready to serve, stir in the avocado and garnish with radish slices and cilantro. Serve very cold in individual bowls.

INGREDIENTS

4   medium tomatoes, chopped
1   green bell pepper, seeded
    and finely chopped
1   red onion, chopped
1   cucumber, seeds removed
    and chopped
3   garlic cloves, minced
6   cups chilled chicken broth,
    fat discarded
    Juice of 1 fresh lime, or
    to taste
½   teaspoon cayenne (or
    crushed dried chili
    peppers)
¼   teaspoon powdered dill
¼   teaspoon crushed dried
    oregano
¼   teaspoon crushed dried
    thyme
¼   teaspoon powdered cumin
    Salt to taste
    Freshly ground black
    pepper to taste
2   tablespoons olive oil
1   ripe avocado, cut into
    ½-inch pieces (optional)
4   red radishes, sliced
2   tablespoons chopped
    cilantro

Serves 4 to 6

Fruit Salad

ENSALADA DE FRUTA

The heat and humidity of Misiones inspire light food, especially salads. Splendid tropical and subtropical fruits are featured in many of these salads. And local chefs are adept at arranging them as works of art.

INGREDIENTS

2   bananas, sliced
2   peaches, peeled and
    sliced
2   pears, peeled and sliced
1   cup cubed pineapple
5   dates, finely chopped
½   cup chopped walnuts
¼   cup mayonnaise
1   cup heavy cream,
    whipped until it holds
    a peak
4   large lettuce leaves
    Sweet paprika

Serves 4

Directions
Mix bananas, peaches, pears, pineapple, dates, walnuts and mayonnaise together. Fold in whipped cream. Place a lettuce leaf on each serving plate and spoon the salad on top of each leaf. Dust the top with paprika.

Piquant Fruit Salad

ENSALADA "DERNIER CRI"

White wine vinegar dressing adds sweet and sour zip to simple, readily available fruits.

INGREDIENTS

¼   cup olive oil
3   tablespoons white wine
    vinegar
1   teaspoon salt
¼   teaspoon freshly ground
    pepper.
1   head iceberg lettuce, cut
    into ⅜-inch strips
1   apple, peeled, cored and
    sliced
1   firm banana, sliced

Serves 4

Directions
Beat oil, vinegar, salt and pepper together with a whisk. Toss the lettuce with the fruit. Just before serving, pour the dressing over the salad and toss.

Stuffed Avocado Salad

Prawns and fresh heart of palm in half an avocado dressed with salsa golf is an impressive first course or luncheon dish. Of course, the prawns must be impeccably fresh or fresh-frozen, and the avocados must be perfectly ripe and unblemished.

I make this dish often in California because of the year-round availability of fresh prawns and avocados. Sources for fresh hearts of palm are listed in the section entitled, "How to Cook the Argentine Way," on page 11.

If you are unable to obtain fresh hearts of palm, use the canned product. To remove the briny taste, submerge the hearts of palm in cold water for several hours and then drain them thoroughly before slicing into rounds. If you can possibly find the fresh product, do so because the taste and texture of fresh heart of palm really has no adequate substitute.

Directions

When ready to serve, pile ½ cup of lettuce on 8 salad plates. Place an avocado half on the lettuce and fill the center of each avocado half with 2 tablespoons of *salsa golf*. Top the sauce in each avocado half with 2 or 3 slices of heart of palm, 2 prawns and a sprig of fresh dill.

INGREDIENTS

4 cups mixed lettuce leaves, torn into bite-sized pieces

4 ripe avocados, pitted, peeled and cut in half lengthwise

1 recipe *salsa golf* (recipe follows)

4 or 5 fresh hearts of palm, sliced into ½-inch rounds (or canned hearts of palm)

16 large prawns, boiled, peeled and deveined

8 fresh dill sprigs

Serves 8

Flavored Mayonnaise
SALSA GOLF

Salsa golf makes a great dressing for salads, fish or shellfish. Different versions are available throughout Argentina. But my favorite comes from the Hotel Internacional just steps from the falls in Iguazú. When I asked an Argentine about the etymology of the name *golf*, I was told it was like Kleenex—a made-up name that doesn't mean anything.

Although eggs contaminated with salmonella are very rare, it's important to note that this recipe incorporates raw eggs. To be on the safe side, use very fresh eggs and wash the shells thoroughly before cracking.

INGREDIENTS

2   egg yolks
1   teaspoon Dijon mustard
    Dash of cayenne, Tabasco
    or pepper sauce
    Salt to taste
2   teaspoons lemon juice
1   tablespoon white wine
    vinegar
1 ¼ cups olive oil
2   tablespoons tomato paste
1   tablespoon cognac

Makes about 1 ½ cups

Directions
Beat the egg yolks in a blender with mustard, cayenne or Tabasco, salt, lemon juice and vinegar until well mixed. Beat in the oil, drop by drop, until the mixture begins to thicken, then beat in the remaining oil in a thin, steady stream. Add the tomato paste and the cognac, mixing well.

Avocado Mousse with Shrimp

CREME DE PALTA

Avocados with shrimp or prawns come in many guises in the northeast provinces. This recipe for a cold molded avocado mousse is a warm-weather favorite among both locals and tourists.

Directions

Mix the mashed avocados with the salt. Mix the gelatin in cold water and heat it in a double boiler over boiling water. When the gelatin is completely dissolved, stir in the avocado and add lime juice and onion. Refrigerate until the mixture thickens. Fold in the whipped cream and ½ cup of the alioli. Correct the seasoning and spoon the mixture into a 5-cup ring mold. Cover tightly with foil and chill in the refrigerator. When ready to serve, unmold the mousse on a bed of watercress and garnish with the shrimp and dollops of the remaining ¼ cup alioli.

INGREDIENTS

4   cups mashed avocado

1   teaspoon salt

2   envelopes unflavored gelatin

½   cup cold water

1   tablespoon lime juice

2   tablespoons grated onion

½   cup heavy cream, stiffly whipped

¾   cup alioli (page 197) or flavored mayonnaise (page 156)

    Watercress

⅓   cup chilled cooked shrimp

Serves 4

Baked Dorado
DORADO AL HORNO CON PANCETA

Dorado and suribi are huge river fish—some over 150 pounds—from the tropical regions of Argentina. But unfortunately, you are unlikely to see these fish in your local supermarket. And while they are impressive when you see them whole, they don't taste that much different from any white, firm-fleshed fish. I suggest you make a substitution accordingly.

INGREDIENTS

6   potatoes, peeled and thinly sliced
2   pounds white fish fillets (halibut, seabass, etc.), bones removed
2   onions, sliced into thin rings
¼   pound chopped pancetta
3   eggs, slightly beaten
2   tablespoons olive oil
2   cups milk
2   tablespoons flour
1   teaspoon salt
½   teaspoon freshly grated nutmeg
½   teaspoon powdered oregano
1   teaspoon sugar
¼   teaspoon freshly ground pepper
    Few drops of lemon juice
¼   cup grated Parmesan cheese
    Dusting of sweet paprika

Serves 4

Directions

Preheat the oven to 325°F. Distribute potato slices evenly over the bottom of an oiled baking dish. Cover with the fish fillets and top with onion rings and pancetta. Mix beaten eggs with oil, milk and flour. Season the milk mixture with salt, nutmeg, oregano, sugar, pepper and lemon juice. Pour the mixture over the fish, top with Parmesan cheese, dust with paprika and bake for approximately 1 hour, or until the fish can be flaked with a fork, the potatoes are done and the sauce is lightly browned on top.

Suribi in Tropical Sauce

SURIBI TRUCHI EN SALSA DE TROPICALE

Suribi is not available in many—if any—North American fish markets. Don't let that stop you from experimenting with what is available. In California, I use imported Chilean seabass with excellent results.

Directions

Dust the fillets with flour, dip them in beaten eggs and roll them in breadcrumbs. In a skillet sauté the fillets quickly in olive oil until they are golden and crisp outside, but tender and flaky inside. Place the fish on a heated serving platter and top with lime slices. Keep the fish warm while making the sauce.

Using the same skillet in which the fish was sautéed, sauté the onions, adding more oil if necessary. Turn the heat up to high and add tomatoes with juices, garlic, jalapeño, cilantro, cinnamon, lime juice, salt and pepper. Cook the mixture for a minute or two while stirring. Remove the sauce from the heat and quickly beat in the butter. Pour the sauce over the fish and garnish with radish flowers and cilantro sprigs.

INGREDIENTS

2   pounds white fish fillets
    Flour for dredging
2   eggs, beaten
2   cups dry breadcrumbs
3   tablespoons olive oil
2   limes, thinly sliced
1   small red onion, chopped
8   green onions, sliced
4   ripe tomatoes, chopped
3   garlic cloves, minced
1   jalapeño pepper, seeded
    and chopped
½   cup chopped cilantro
½   teaspoon cinnamon
4   tablespoons lime juice
    Salt and freshly ground
    pepper to taste
2   tablespoons chilled butter,
    cut into small pieces
4   radishes, cut into flower
    shapes and chilled in
    ice water
    Cilantro sprigs

Serves 4

Stuffed Zucchini

ZUCCHINI RELLENOS

Vegetables stuffed with grains originated with the Moors, but their repertoire was limited until Spanish conquistadors returned to Spain with seeds obtained from New World produce. Potatoes, tomatoes, peppers and squashes are all part of the tradition today. Interestingly, this dish made a complete circle, coming to Argentina from Italy.

Directions

Preheat the oven to 350°F. Steam or boil the zucchini for about 3 minutes or until barely tender. Drain, dry with a paper towel and cut off the ends. Cut the zucchini in half lengthwise and hollow them out with a spoon, making sure the "boats" stay intact. Mix the zucchini pulp with the cooked couscous. Add olives, 1 cup of yogurt, the basil, salt and pepper. Fill the zucchini boats with this mixture and dot with butter. Bake for about 10 minutes. Serve hot with a dollop of yogurt dusted with paprika.

INGREDIENTS

4 zucchini
1 ½ cups cooked couscous
     (semolina)
½ cup pitted, chopped black
     olives
1 ½ cups plain yogurt
½ cup chopped fresh basil
     Salt and pepper to taste
1 tablespoon butter, melted
     Sweet paprika

Serves 4 to 8

Potato and Pancetta Cake

TORTILLA DE PAPA Y PANCETA

When properly prepared in a copper cooking vessel, this cheese-filled potato and pancetta side dish is a delight to the eye as well as to the taste buds. Only attempt this dish if you have a copper skillet or casserole. Otherwise the dish will suffer from a poor distribution of heat and won't deliver the buttery, golden brown results it should.

Directions

Preheat the oven to 350°F. Heat the butter in a deep copper skillet or casserole. Place the pancetta in a skillet in spokes, leaving 1 end hanging over the rim of the skillet. Place a layer of potatoes, salt, pepper, paprika and grated cheese in the bottom of the skillet. Follow with a second, third and fourth layer of potatoes, seasonings and cheese. Cover the potatoes with the overlapping pancetta tails. Cover the skillet or casserole and bake for 1½ to 2 hours. Press the pancetta from time to time to release fat. Continue cooking, covered, until the tortilla is a golden brown. Turn upside down on a platter and serve with steamed cabbage seasoned with salt, pepper and oregano.

INGREDIENTS

3 tablespoons butter

12 slices pancetta

1 pound potatoes, peeled and cut into ¼-inch slices

Coarse salt (kosher or sea salt) to taste

Freshly ground pepper to taste

2 teaspoons hot paprika

¼ pound Gruyère cheese, coarsely grated

1 medium napa or savoy cabbage, cut in wide bands and steamed

1 tablespoon chopped fresh oregano

Serves 4 to 6

Cassava Meal

Mandioca is both the name of this dish as well as a method of cooking cassava meal. Cassava originated with the Guaraní Indians native to the northeast of Argentina as well as in Paraguay, western Uruguay and Brazil. Poisonous before processing, cassava roots are boiled and dried, then ground into a fine meal that is used in breads, cakes and stews. It keeps well in any climate, has a pleasant nutty taste and is highly nutritious. In the United States, it is available as manioc meal in Latin American markets.

INGREDIENTS

¾ cup manioc meal
2 tablespoons butter
6 scallions, trimmed and thinly sliced including greens
1 cup or more beef broth
Salt and pepper to taste

Serves 6 to 8

Directions

Remove any rocks or dirt from the manioc meal. Melt the butter in a skillet. Add manioc meal and sauté it over medium heat, while stirring, until the meal becomes lightly browned. Add the scallions and continue to sauté for several more minutes, stirring continuously and being careful that the mixture doesn't burn. Add the broth a little at a time while stirring. The manioc meal will absorb the liquid and begin to coagulate. When you have added a cup or more of broth and the mixture is the consistency of a gluey soft pudding, taste for seasonings, adding salt and pepper if necessary. Remove to a serving dish and serve it as an accompaniment to roasted meats or stews.

Piquant Sweet Potatoes

Batatas calientes is a tasty treatment for sweet potatoes—especially if you don't care much for the
usual sticky-sweet renditions that are standard
fare on North American tables at Thanksgiving
and Christmas. The combination of the natural
sweetness of this root vegetable with the heat
of red and green peppers makes for a surprising
taste sensation that is generally appreciated by
all but the most pepper-shy. This dish is a perfect
accompaniment to roasted fowl, particularly
turkey.

Directions

Preheat the oven to 350°F. Peel the sweet potatoes and
boil them in salted water until they are fork-tender.
Transfer them to a mixing bowl and mash with an electric
mixer. Alternatively, you may cook unpeeled sweet
potatoes in a microwave on high, following the appli-
ance's instructions. When cool enough to handle, peel
and transfer the sweet potatoes to a mixing bowl and
mash. Cut butter into small chunks and add to the sweet
potato mixture. Beat in the butter until well mixed. If the
mixture is too stiff, stir in the chicken broth a little at a
time. Fold in the peppers. Add nutmeg, salt and pepper
and mix well. Place the mixture in a buttered shallow
baking pan and dot with small pieces of butter. Bake,
uncovered, for about 20 minutes.

INGREDIENTS

6 large sweet potatoes or
   yams
½ cup sweet butter, at room
   temperature
¼ to ½ cup chicken broth
2 to 3 fresh jalapeños, seeded
   and finely chopped
2 to 3 fresh serrano chili peppers, seeded and finely
   chopped
2 teaspoons freshly ground
   nutmeg
   Salt and pepper to taste

Serves 6 to 8

Sweet Potato Pudding

BUDÍN DE BATATAS

Quick and easy to prepare, this side dish is both salty and sweet. It is best partnered with a simple roast chicken or duck.

Directions

Preheat the oven to 450°F. Mix together the pumpkin, bananas, sweet potatoes and coconut. Add salt, syrup, drippings or lard and pepper. Pour the mixture into a well-greased baking dish and bake for 30 to 40 minutes.

INGREDIENTS

2   cups grated fresh pumpkin

2   ripe bananas, finely chopped

4   sweet potatoes, grated

½   fresh coconut, grated

1   teaspoon salt

½   cup light corn syrup

2   tablespoons pan drippings from roasted meat (or lard)

½   teaspoon freshly ground pepper

Serves 6

Beef Japanese Style

BIFE À LA JAPONESA

Given that Argentina is a cosmopolitan country embracing many ethnicities, the Japanese-style dish that follows is not an anomaly. And, as more and more Japanese are finding Argentina hospitable, Japanese cuisine is adding a whole new layer to the gastronomic mix.

Directions

Remove as much fat as possible from the tenderloin and rub it all over with salt and pepper. Tie the meat into a compact bundle and sauté it in 3 tablespoons of vegetable oil. When the meat is a golden brown on all sides, add wine and 1 tablespoon of soya sauce. Continue to cook for 6 to 8 minutes. Remove the meat from the skillet, wrap it in aluminum foil and allow it to cool. Then place it in the freezer until it is firm enough to slice paper-thin.

Make a sauce by mixing vinegar and the remaining 3 tablespoons oil and 4 tablespoons soya sauce with the ginger. Pour into a sauce dish and set aside. Steam the asparagus for 2 minutes and set aside. Remove the meat from the freezer. Using a mandoline or meat slicer, slice the meat paper-thin and arrange it on a large platter in a slightly overlapping spiral that covers the platter. Place the scallion in the center and distribute the asparagus and radish slices over the beef. Garnish with watercress and serve at room temperature. Serve sauce separately.

Variation: In place of the beef, use veal tenderloin. In place of the sauce, sprinkle the sliced veal with 8 tablespoons of olive oil and the juice of 1 lemon.

INGREDIENTS

1 ½-pound beef tenderloin
    Kosher or sea salt
    Freshly ground pepper
6 tablespoons vegetable oil
2 tablespoons red wine
5 tablespoons soya sauce
4 tablespoons rice vinegar
3 tablespoons peeled and grated ginger
3 stalks fresh asparagus, trimmed and roll-cut in ¼-inch lengths (see page 114)
1 scallion, julienned
1 radish, sliced very thin
    Watercress sprigs

Serves 8

Beef and Peach Pie

PASTEL DE POSADAS

Posadas is in Misiones Province in the north of Argentina near the Brazilian border. *Pastel de Posadas* is a traditional dish at local wedding feasts.

PASTRY

- 4 cups flour
- 1 cup sugar
- 1½ cups chilled butter, cut into small pieces
- 5 egg yolks
- 1 cup sweet dessert wine

Pastry Directions

In a large bowl, combine the flour, sugar and butter, mixing it together with your fingers until the dough looks like a coarse meal. Add 4 egg yolks one at a time. When each yolk is absorbed into the dough, mix in the wine ¼ cup at a time. Shape the dough into a compact ball, wrap it in waxed paper and refrigerate it for 1 hour or until thoroughly chilled.

FILLING

- ½ cup seedless raisins
- 1 cup hot water
- 2 tablespoons olive oil
- 2 pounds top sirloin, cut into ¼-inch cubes
- 1 cup coarsely chopped onions
- ½ cup dry white wine
- ⅓ cup sugar
- ½ teaspoon ground cinnamon
- ½ teaspoon ground cloves
- ½ teaspoon minced fresh oregano
- 1 bay leaf
- 1 teaspoon salt
- ¼ teaspoon freshly ground pepper
- 1 tablespoon breadcrumbs
- 6 fresh peaches, peeled, pitted and halved (or 12 canned peach halves)

Filling Directions

Place raisins in the hot water and soak for 30 minutes. In a heavy 10- to 12-inch skillet, heat the oil over high heat. Add the beef and brown it well on all sides, stirring constantly and regulating the heat so that the beef browns quickly without burning. Add the onions, lower the heat to medium, and cook, stirring constantly, until the onions are soft. Stir in the wine, sugar, cinnamon, cloves oregano, bay leaf, salt and pepper. Bring the mixture to a boil and cover the skillet. Reduce the heat to low and simmer for 25 minutes. Drain the raisins and stir them into the meat mixture. Remove the bay leaf, transfer the meat mixture to a bowl and allow it to cool.

Assembly Directions

Preheat the oven to 375°F. Remove the dough from the refrigerator and cut it in half. On a lightly floured board, roll the halves one at a time into 2 rectangles about 12 by 16 inches and ⅛ inch thick. Drape one rectangle of dough loosely over a shallow, lightly buttered baking dish— approximately 8 by 12 inches. Gently press the dough against the bottom and sides of the dish. Pour in the cooled meat mixture, spreading it evenly with a spatula. Sprinkle the meat with breadcrumbs and place the peach halves side by side atop the meat. Cover with the second rectangle of dough, letting it sink to about ½ inch below the dish's top rim.

Press the edges of the dough together all around the rim of the dish with the tines of a fork. Cut off all excess dough from the edges. Brush the top with the 1 remaining egg yolk mixed with 1 teaspoon water. Bake for 30 minutes or until the crust is golden brown. When the pie is done, remove it from the oven and set aside.

Meringue Topping Directions

In a large bowl (an unlined copper bowl is best), beat the egg whites with a balloon whisk or electric beater until they form soft peaks. Then beat in the sugar and continue beating until the meringue is firm and glossy. Spread the meringue thickly over the top of the pie, making decorative swirls with a spatula.

Final Baking Directions

Turn up the oven heat to 425°F. Return the pie to the oven and bake for 5 minutes or until the meringue is a light golden brown. When the pie is done, remove it from the oven and allow it to cool slightly. With a sharp knife, cut the pie into rectangles and serve immediately.

TOPPING

4   egg whites

¼   cup sugar

Serves 4 to 6

Beef with Fruit from Iguazú

CARBONADA CRIOLLA À LA IGUAZÚ

Here's another version of *carbonada criolla* but with a tropical touch.

Directions

Heat the oil and butter in a Dutch oven or heavy flame-proof casserole. Add the beef and brown it. Remove the beef and add the onions. Sauté the onions until golden. Stir in the wine, tomato paste, bay leaf, thyme, salt and pepper. Add the broth and return the beef to the casserole. Bring the mixture to a boil, cover and reduce the heat to low. Simmer slowly for 1 hour. Add sweet potatoes and simmer covered for 30 minutes more. Mix in the pears, peaches or apples, and currants or seedless raisins. Simmer uncovered for 10 minutes. Taste for seasoning, transfer to a serving bowl and sprinkle the bananas on top of the stew. Serve with *Mandioca* (page 162).

INGREDIENTS

2 tablespoons olive oil
4 tablespoons butter
3- pound chuck or rump
   roast, cut into 1-inch cubes
1½ cups chopped onions
1½ cups dry white wine
1 tablespoon tomato paste
1 bay leaf
½ teaspoon chopped fresh
   thyme leaves
2 teaspoons salt
½ teaspoon freshly ground
   pepper
1 cup beef broth
3 cups peeled and cubed
   sweet potatoes
3 pears, peeled and cubed
3 peaches or apples, peeled
   and sliced
3 tablespoons currants or
   seedless raisins
½ cup diced bananas

Serves 6 to 8

Avocado Mousse Dessert

In North America, avocados are usually considered a vegetable only appropriate for use in salads. But actually, avocados are a fruit, and they make a wonderful and unusual base for desserts. The following recipe is my interpretation of one such dessert I ate in Puerto Iguazú.

Directions

In a blender, mix the avocado, 1 tablespoon of confectioners' sugar, lime juice and salt until well blended and smooth. Beat the cream until it holds a soft peak. Add the remaining 2 tablespoons confectioners' sugar to the cream and beat for a few seconds more. Fold three-quarters of the whipped cream into the avocado mixture and spoon it into stemmed glasses. Chill the mousses in the refrigerator for several hours.

Cut the lime peel into julienne strips and simmer it in water for 10 minutes to remove bitterness. Rinse and drain it. Heat the water and granulated sugar in a small saucepan until it starts to boil. Reduce the heat and simmer while swirling the mixture for 1 minute or until the sugar is completely dissolved. Remove the syrup from the heat, stir in the lime peel and chill. To serve, garnish each glass of mousse with a dollop of the remaining whipped cream and top with candied lime peel.

INGREDIENTS

2 large ripe avocados, peeled, seeded and diced

3 tablespoons confectioners' sugar

¼ cup fresh lime juice

Dash of salt

1 pint heavy cream

Lime peel, washed

3 tablespoons water

½ cup granulated sugar

Serves 4

Banana Empanadas

EMPANADAS DE BANANA

Sweet empanadas are as much an Argentine tradition as savory ones. One of my favorite sweet empanadas from Mesopotamia is made with bananas and sour cream.

Directions

In a bowl, toss together the bananas, lemon juice, cinnamon, brown sugar, rum and sour cream or yogurt, making sure they are well mixed. Allow the ingredients to marinate for 15 to 20 minutes. Prepare the empanada pastry. Fill, seal and bake the empanadas as described. When cool, dust with confectioners' sugar.

INGREDIENTS

2   ripe bananas, sliced
2   tablespoons lemon juice
1   teaspoon cinnamon
2   tablespoons brown sugar
¼ cup rum
1½ cups sour cream or plain
    yogurt
6   empanada rounds (page
    33 or 64)
¼ cup confectioners' sugar

Makes 6 empanadas

Mango Pudding

There is something about a mango: it is both voluptuous and comforting. These characteristics are accentuated in this recipe for mango pudding. It is the creation of Chef Xavier Sanchez at the Hotel Internacional in Puerto Iguazú. The dining room manager, Pablo Lundhal, was most accommodating in obtaining the formula.

Directions

Preheat the oven to 375°F. Mix the mango pulp with the lime juice and salt. Sprinkle the mixture with the sugar and set aside for about 10 minutes.

Beat the egg whites until they hold a peak. Purée the mango mixture in a food processor or blender and add the egg yolks and lime zest. Mix well then blend in the cornstarch. Pour the mixture into a mixing bowl and fold in the beaten egg whites. Spoon the mixture into a well-buttered 1½-quart mold and bake for 10 minutes. Reduce heat to 350°F and bake for 30 minutes more. Remove the pudding from the oven and allow it to cool in the mold. Unmold the pudding in a serving dish and chill in the refrigerator until ready to serve.

INGREDIENTS

3   ripe mangos, peeled, sliced and cut into small pieces
2   tablespoons fresh lime juice
¼   teaspoon salt
⅓   cup sugar
3   eggs, separated
    Zest of 1 lime
2   tablespoons cornstarch

Serves 4

Mango Fool

MOUSSE DE MANGO

A fool is a dessert that that is enjoyed in many parts of the world. It merely requires equal parts puréed fruit and whipped cream mixed together and chilled. I suspect this particular recipe originated across the border in Brazil. Mango makes an exquisite fool—just the thing when it's too hot to cook.

Directions
Purée the mango pulp in a blender or food processor. Blend in the sugar, lime juice and orange juice. Cover the mixture and chill for 10 to 12 hours.

INGREDIENTS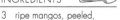

3 ripe mangos, peeled, sliced and cut into small pieces
⅔ cup confectioners' sugar
2 tablespoons lime juice
1 tablespoon orange juice
1¼ cups heavy cream, chilled
Fresh mint sprigs

Serves 4

Whip the cream until it holds soft peaks and fold it into the chilled mango purée. Pile into stemmed glasses and top with mint sprigs. Serve at once.

Apple Pudding

BUDIN DE MANZANA

Apples are a rarity in most of Latin America. But Argentina has the right combination of climate and soil around Mendoza, Santa Fe, Salta and Bariloche for apple growing. Surprisingly, I tasted this classic Moorish dessert in Puerto Iguazú where it is considered a specialty of *that* region.

This recipe calls for uncooked egg whites. To protect against salmonella, be careful to use very fresh eggs whose shells have been washed. As an alternative, eliminate the eggs and double the amount of whipped cream.

Directions

Peel the apples, remove the cores and chop them roughly. Cook the apples in a casserole with honey and water until the apples are soft. Cool the apples and add lemon juice, cinnamon and chopped almonds. Fold in the cream and beaten egg whites. Spoon the mixture into individual glass serving dishes and garnish with whole almonds. Chill the mousse in the refrigerator for about 3 hours. Serve with small biscotti.

INGREDIENTS

1½ pounds apples

7   tablespoons honey

5   tablespoons water
    Juice of 1 lemon, strained

½   teaspoon cinnamon

2   ounces almonds, chopped

2   cups heavy cream,
    whipped to soft peaks

3   egg whites, beaten to
    stiff peaks
    Whole almonds for garnish

Serves 6

Sweet Potato Candy

Where would Latin America be without sweet potatoes and yams? So versatile, they go into everything—from stews to desserts. From Misiones comes this sweet potato candy recipe.

INGREDIENTS

2 cups cooked, peeled and mashed sweet potatoes or yams

1 cup grated pineapple with juice

½ teaspoon salt

2 cups packed brown sugar

¼ teaspoon cream of tartar

⅔ cup hot water

1 cup coarsely chopped almonds or walnuts

Makes 40 pieces of candy

Directions

When the sweet potatoes are partially cooled, mix them with the pineapple. Add 4 to 5 teaspoons warm water. Simmer over a low heat, stirring continuously, until the mixture thickens. Dissolve the salt, sugar and cream of tartar in the hot water. Add this mixture to the sweet potato mixture and cook it until a spoonful forms a soft ball when dropped in cold water. Remove the mixture from the heat and beat it vigorously for about 5 minutes. Add the nutmeats and mix thoroughly. Drop the mixture by the spoonful on a buttered platter and allow it to rest until the candies harden.

CHAPTER 6

Patagonian Andes:

Alpine Ambiance with
a Latin Beat

Patagonian Andes

A magical wonderland, little known in North America, extends from the southern Andes to Tierra del Fuego in the far south of Argentina. There in the provinces of Nequén, Río Negro, Chubut and Santa Cruz are successions of frozen peaks, glistening lakes, imposing glaciers and fairy-tale forests—including one that's petrified.

The primary destination in Río Negro province is San Carlos de Bariloche. Situated at almost 3,000 feet above sea level on the southeastern shore of the cobalt-hued Lago Nahuel Huapi, Bariloche is confusing. It looks as if you have flown off course and have landed in the Swiss Alps instead of Patagonia. Mountain-hugging, chalet-styled buildings clearly indicate a climate and culture not Latin but Germanic. And because German is spoken along with Spanish, the illusion is complete.

This alpine ambiance is a result of the influx of a few hardy immigrants from Austria and Switzerland in the nineteenth century. Because Patagonia was empty and wide open at the time, the settlers had no need to assimilate and had carte blanche in establishing their societies however they liked. And what they liked was to bring the old country with them in so far as they could.

Today, Bariloche is a year-round resort that, among Argentines and the adventurous, is justly famous for its skiing in winter, its water sports in summer, and its gastronomy at any time of the year.

Lago Nahuel Huapi in Parque Nacional Nahuel Huapi is the center of activity here. Covering more than 300 square miles and over 62 miles in length, the lake is

Fitz Roy Range in Santa Cruz.

surrounded with snow-capped peaks. The scene is truly a nature photographer's dream.

In town, a large, fort-like square is surrounded by municipal buildings made of logs and extends from the lakeside to the town center. This square is the premier location for other photo opportunities as at least a dozen pairs of St. Bernard dogs—one full grown and the other always a puppy—pose daily with visitors.

In winter, the snow-clad landscape is a delft-like panorama of blue waters and titanium-white snow that frequently mounds like whipped cream above the rooftops. Long a favorite ski resort of the gentry, the area boasts fifteen miles of runs ranging from bunny slopes to killer courses challenging the best of world-class athletes. A five-star hotel, the fabled Llao Llao, is a little over nine miles to the west of town on a narrow peninsula surrounded by the waters of the Nahuel Huapi. The Llao Llao provides a rustic yet suitably grand hideaway for well-heeled skiers from Europe who appreciate shussing down the immaculately maintained trails in June, July or August.

Hotel Llao Llao in the distance at Parque Nacional Nahuel Huapi.

In the Argentine summer—December through March—the lakesides are carpeted with manicured lawns and awash with colorful banks of both wild and cultivated flowers. A visit to the area would not be complete without a boat trip to Isla Victoria, a large island in the middle of the lake. On the island, you can take a walk through the twisted trunks and branches of the Arrayanes Forest— reputed to be the inspiration for the forest in Disney's *Snow White and the Seven Dwarfs*. You might even glimpse a miniature Pudú deer here.

Summer activities are not limited to watersports and trekking. Hunting for wild game is a big draw, too. Among the quarry are boar and deer, including the red stag variety originally imported from Germany. And lake trout and rainbow trout from the rivers and streams practically jump into your creel. We're talking serious catches here—it's not unusual for the rainbows to weigh as much as 20 pounds.

Given the wealth of local fish and game in the region, it's fitting that these are the centerpieces of local menus. Pâtés and smoked foods play a large part as well. Other favorites include *curantos* (a mixture of shellfish, meat and vegetables cooked on hot stones), fish-farm salmon, cheeses, fondues, and no less than 130 different varieties of chocolate. And the profusion of wild and locally cultivated fruit has created a number of small artisan industries making cakes and jams for sale. The "stinky rose" is in a special category—garlic grown in the foothills of Río Negro province has exceptional flavor that gives foods an unusual depth and a heightened aroma. That's why it is in great demand by European chefs and is regularly exported to France and Italy.

In-town restaurant fare ranges from simply prepared fresh or smoked game and fish to elaborate seven-course presentations straight out of Tuscany. Two local restaurants stand out in my memory as excellent representations of both types of cuisine. Ahumadero Familia Weiss is known for its game and fish dishes—especially its *Trucha à la Crema* (Fresh Trout in Cream) and *Jabali y Ciervo* (Smoked Wild Boar and Venison)—as well as pâtés and smoked specialties you can take home.

La Rondine Ristorante in the Pan-Americana Hotel dishes up the best Italian food this side of Milan. The husband and wife chef team here—Noemi Barchetta and Guillermo Kempin Pugni—have created an oasis of classic Italian cuisine in an atmosphere of tasteful sophistication. Among their specialties are *Osobuco con Verduras Cocidas* (braised veal shanks with vegetables), *Cintas Cortadas con Hongos, Panceta y Crema* (pappardelle with mushrooms, pancetta and cream), and *Rellenos de Olivos* (olives stuffed with pâté then breaded and deep-fried).

While the Llao Llao dining room has spectacular lake views, the food is not always a match. With mostly international dishes on the menu, the personality and focus of a La Rondine or Ahumidero Familia Weiss are lacking. The best bet here is a substantial lunch of fresh pacific seafood flown in from Chile—always delectable—or the occasional game dish. But most diners who are not hotel guests come for the view. It is definitely worth a look.

This brings us to chocolate. With at least two chocolate shops in every block along Avenida San Martín, each more irresistible than the last, death by chocolate is a distinct possibility. As might be expected, the product leans to the Swiss-Austrian-German model—the richest chocolate flavor tempered by a light touch when adding sugar. There's no way you can get out of town without trying some. And it's the perfect gift for the folks at home.

Glaciar Perito Moreno in Santa Cruz.

Pâté Stuffed Olives
OLIVAS RELLENAS À LA RONDINE

Diners at La Rondine in Bariloche are crazy about *Olivas Rellenas*. This is a before-dinner tidbit served with aperitifs. My thanks to Chef Noemi Barchetta for this recipe.

Directions
Fill the cavity of each olive with pâté. Roll the olives in flour, dip them in the egg mixture and then roll them in breadcrumbs. When all the olives are coated, let them rest in the refrigerator until they are thoroughly chilled. Just before serving, heat the oil in a deep saucepan until it is almost smoking. Drop the olives into the hot oil and turn them gently until all sides are lightly browned. Drain them on paper towels and serve them immediately. Offer toothpicks to spear them with.

INGREDIENTS

10 jumbo green olives in brine, pitted, rinsed and drained
4 ounces goose or duck liver pâté
½ cup flour
1 egg, beaten
¾ cup fine dry breadcrumbs
Vegetable oil for deep frying

Serves 2 as an hors d'oeuvre

Lobster Empanadas

High in the Andes, near the border with Chile, is the all-season splendor of San Carlos de Bariloche. At Christmastime it's a fairyland of cobalt lakes, forested islands and manicured parklands surrounded by snow-capped alpine peaks. In the center of a small peninsula stands the rustic but elegant Llao Llao Hotel, a holiday mecca for the elite of Buenos Aires, Santiago and even Paris, Düssledorf, London, Madrid and Milan. When not attending the hotel's casino (closed as of this writing), guests spend their time dining in exquisite surroundings on international cuisine as well as impeccably fresh seafood from the Pacific coast of Chile. Hence, recipes such as *Empanadas de Bariloche* frequently straddle the border.

PASTRY

¼ pound unsalted butter, at
    room temperature
4 ounces cream cheese, at
    room temperature
2 cups unbleached flour
½ teaspoon baking powder
1 teaspoon ground cumin
¼ teaspoon cider vinegar
6 to 8 tablespoons very cold
    water
1 tablespoon vegetable oil

Pastry Directions
Using a fork, combine the butter and cream cheese. Sift the flour over the mixture. Add baking powder, cumin, vinegar and water and combine with a fork. Flour hands generously and work the dough until it becomes a smooth, elastic ball, 3 to 4 minutes. Flour both the work surface and rolling pin. Roll out the dough to about ⅛ inch thick and cut it into 6-inch circles for main course-sized empanadas. For appetizer-sized empanaditas, cut the dough into 3-inch circles. Cover the pastries with a lightly floured towel until you are ready to fill them.

FILLING

6 ounces fresh lobster or lan-
  gostino meat, cooked,
  shelled and roughly
  chopped (or saltwater or
  fresh water crayfish)
½ cup alioli or homemade
  mayonnaise
1 tablespoon tomato purée
1 tablespoon cognac
1 teaspoon Dijon mustard
⅓ cup finely chopped
  scallions, including
  green part
1 teaspoon coarse kosher or
  sea salt
¼ teaspoon white pepper
2 to 3 hard-boiled eggs, cut
  lengthwise into 8 pieces
16 to 20 pimiento-stuffed
  green olives
1 large egg, beaten
2 tablespoons water

Makes 8 to 10 main
course empanadas or 20
to 25 hors d'oeuvre-sized
empanaditas

Filling Directions

Combine the lobster, mayonnaise, tomato purée, cognac, mustard, scallions, salt and pepper and mix thoroughly. Set the filling aside and keep it cool until you are ready to fill the empanadas.

Assembly Directions

Preheat the oven to 400°F. Oil a large cookie sheet or line it with Silpat. Spoon the filling in the center of the pastry circles—about 2 tablespoons of filling for each main course empanada or 1 heaping teaspoon for empanaditas. Stuff an egg slice and 1 or 2 olives in the filling and fold the dough over the filling forming a half-moon. Beat the egg with the water to make a glaze. Moisten the open edges with the glaze and crimp the edges with a fork or your fingers to seal.

Place the empanadas on the cookie sheet and brush the top of each with the glaze. Bake them for 20 minutes, turn the heat down to 350°F and continue baking for about 5 minutes more or until the empanadas are golden. When the empanadas are done, remove them from the oven and cool them on racks for several minutes. Serve warm or at room temperature.

To freeze and reheat, place frozen cooked empanadas in a preheated 350°F oven for approximately 20 minutes.

Empanadas with Beef and Fruit

EMPANADAS CRIOLLA DE FRUTA

For a different kind of empanada, fresh fruits mixed with lean ground beef make a delightful summertime treat served along with tall, cool drinks on the veranda or patio.

Filling Directions

Heat the oil in a skillet and sauté the onion, garlic and bell pepper over moderate heat until they are soft. Add the meat, breaking it up with a fork or potato masher and sauté it several minutes longer. Add the tomato, pear, peaches, chili peppers, salt, pepper and wine. Simmer over low heat for 5 minutes. Cool.

Assembly Directions

Preheat the oven to 400°F. Spoon 2 tablespoons of the filling in the center of each pastry circle. Press an egg wedge and olive into the filling. Close, seal and glaze according to instructions on page 33 or 64. Prick the top of each empanada with a fork 2 or 3 times before glazing and baking.

Place the empanadas on a Silpat-lined or lightly oiled cookie sheet and bake for 10 minutes. Reduce the heat to 350°F and bake for 30 minutes longer, or until the empanadas are brown. Transfer them to a heated platter and serve at once.

Empanadas may be frozen and baked later if desired. Frozen empanadas must be thawed for 3 to 4 hours at room temperature before glazing and baking.

For a different look, you may curve the turnover slightly to form a crescent shape. Then instead of crimping the edges together with a fork, you can turn about ¼ inch of the pasty back over itself, pinching it between the thumb and forefinger to form a ropelike pattern along the edge.

FILLING

2   tablespoons olive oil
1   medium onion, finely chopped
3   garlic cloves, finely chopped
1   green bell pepper, seeded and chopped
1   pound lean ground beef
1   large ripe tomato, peeled and chopped
1   large pear, peeled, cored and chopped
2   large peaches, peeled, pitted and chopped
1   teaspoon crushed dried chili peppers
    Salt and pepper to taste
¼   cup dry white wine
1   recipe pastry (page 33 or 64) rolled and cut into 6-inch rounds
2   hard-boiled eggs, cut lengthwise into 16 wedges
16 pimiento-stuffed green olives
1   egg, beaten with ½ teaspoon water for glaze

Makes 8 to 10 empanadas

Ham Rolls Waldorf

ROLLOS DE JAMÓN WALDORF

The stuffing in this dish is reminiscent of a Waldorf salad. Rolled up in a thin slice of boiled ham or lightly smoked salmon, the yogurt-based fruit and nut filling illustrates the creativity one finds in the foods of the Patagonian Andes.

INGREDIENTS

- ½ cup julienned celery, white part only
- 1 green apple, peeled and julienned
- 3 tablespoons lemon juice
- 2 ounces walnuts, skins removed and finely chopped
- 4 tablespoons freshly made alioli (page 196 or 197) or mayonnaise
- ½ teaspoon prepared mustard
- 1 teaspoon plus pinch sugar
- ½ teaspoon salt
- 8 thin slices boiled ham, about 5 inches in diameter
- 1 teaspoon freshly ground pepper
- 1 cup plain yogurt
- 1 tablespoon chopped parsley
- Butter lettuce leaves
- Radicchio leaves
- Bunches of parsley
- 6 radishes, slivered

Serves 4

Directions

Sprinkle the celery and apples with 1 tablespoon of lemon juice. Mix the nuts with the mayonnaise and mustard. Add the celery, apple strips, 1 teaspoon sugar and salt, mixing well. Spread the filling on the ham slices and roll them up jellyroll style. Sprinkle them with pepper.

Make a dressing with yogurt, remaining 1 tablespoon lemon juice, salt, pepper, and a pinch of sugar and parsley. Make a bed of green and red lettuce leaves in a deep dish. Add bunches of parsley and top with the yogurt dressing. Place the rolls on top of the parsley and sprinkle with slivered radishes.

Smoked Salmon Crêpes

PANQUEQUES DE SALMÓN AHUMADO

A Bariloche institution since 1969, Ahumadero Familia Weiss is known for its game and fish, both fresh and smoked. The proprietors have been kind enough to share some of their most requested recipes. This one features their cold-smoked salmon in an appetizer dish.

Directions

Preheat the oven to 325°F. Mix the ricotta and salmon together. Add 2 tablespoons of cream and the lemon juice. Mix well. Fill the center of each crêpe with 1 tablespoon of the salmon and ricotta mixture, wrapping the crêpe around the filling. Place each filled crêpe in a flame-proof casserole. Cover and bake the crêpes for 13 minutes or just long enough to heat through.

Add salt and white pepper to the remaining 1 cup cream and whip it until it holds a soft peak. When the crêpes are hot, remove to individual serving plates and top them with the whipped cream and a light sprinkling of paprika.

INGREDIENTS

1   pound ricotta cheese

3½ ounces smoked salmon, minced

6   radishes, slivered

1   cup plus 2 tablespoons heavy cream

Juice of 1 lemon

12 small crêpes (recipe follows)

¼   teaspoon salt

⅛   teaspoon white pepper

1   teaspoon sweet paprika

Serves 6 as an appetizer course

Crêpes

PANQUEQUES

INGREDIENTS

¼ cup sifted flour

Pinch of salt

2 large eggs

½ cup milk

2 tablespoons butter, melted

Makes 10 to 15 crepes,
about 6 inches in diameter

Directions

Sift the flour into a mixing bowl and stir in the salt. Mix in the eggs and then the milk. Beat the batter until it's smooth. The consistency should be like light cream. Add more milk if necessary. Stir in the butter and set aside to rest for 30 minutes. Stir just before using.

Heat a crêpe pan or nonstick pan and brush the bottom with a little butter. Ladle in just enough batter to coat the bottom of the pan, pouring off any excess. Cook for 2 to 3 minutes or until browned, turn over and cook for 1 minute more or until browned. Continue cooking the crêpes and stacking them on a plate until the batter is used up.

Pappardelle

CINTAS CORTADAS

There is a significant difference between home-made egg pasta and store-bought semolina pasta in packages. Homemade egg pasta is porous and absorbent. It hungers for butter and cream sauces. Store-bought semolina is hard and impenetrable. It is perfect for olive oil-based sauces that slip and slide instead of absorb.

Pappardelle is at its best as homemade egg pasta. It has a large surface ideal for sauces that have substance. But there's no machine that cuts this noodle, so it must be done by hand using a pastry wheel. A fluted one, cutting the pasta strips into ribbons approximately six inches by one inch, produces the prettiest pappardelle.

Pasta Dough Directions

On a pastry board, make a well of flour. Break the eggs into the well and scramble lightly with a fork, drawing some of the flour over the eggs. Use the fork to mix the eggs with the flour until the eggs are no longer runny. With your hands, draw the sides of the mound together, reserving some flour in case you need it later. Work the eggs and flour together using your fingers and palms of your hands, until you have a smooth mixture. If the dough is still moist, work in more flour.

When the dough is no longer is sticky, wrap it in plastic wrap and prepare to knead it. Divide the dough into 2 or 3 parts and knead each part for 8 minutes. Keep both unkneaded and kneaded dough tightly covered in plastic wrap. Roll out the dough to about ¼ inch thick with a long pasta pin. Allow it to dry for 10 minutes or more before cutting it into strips. (If drying for future use, make sure the noodles are cut, then thoroughly dried so that mold doesn't form. Once dried, homemade noodles can be stored for weeks.)

Assembly Directions

While the sauce is cooking, drop the cut noodles in 4 quarts of boiling salted water and stir with a long-handled wooden fork to separate the pasta strands. Cover the pot until the water again comes to a boil. Uncover and continue cooking at a low boil while stirring and separating the pasta—about 8 minutes or until they are cooked but not soft. Drain the pasta in a colander, shake it well and transfer it immediately to a warm serving platter. Toss the pasta with butter and cheese. When the butter is well distributed, toss the pasta quickly with the sauce until it is evenly distributed.

PASTA DOUGH

1 cup flour

2 large eggs

1 tablespoon chilled butter, cut into small pieces

⅓ cup freshly grated Parmesan cheese

Mushroom, pancetta and cream sauce (recipe follows)

Serves 4 as a main course, 6 as an appetizer

Mushroom, Pancetta and Cream Sauce

SALSA DE HONGOS, PANCETA Y CREMA

The chef at La Rondine in Bariloche created this divine cream sauce for her pappardelle. It's sinfully rich.

Directions

Sauté the shallots in olive oil until they are transparent. Add garlic and continue cooking just until the shallots turn a pale gold. Add all the mushrooms and sauté over medium-high heat. Shake the pan or stir until the mushrooms are very lightly browned. Add pancetta and sauté for about 3 minutes more, adding salt if necessary. Turn the heat down to medium. Cook for about 10 minutes or until the liquid from the mushrooms is absorbed. Add the cream, butter and pepper, then raise the heat to high. Cook, stirring, until the cream is reduced by half. Remove from the heat and serve with pappardelle or other pasta.

INGREDIENTS

4 shallots, minced

3 tablespoons olive oil

2 tablespoons minced garlic

¾ pound fresh white mushrooms, wiped clean and sliced

½ pound fresh shiitake mushrooms, wiped clean, stems removed and sliced

¼ pound pancetta, cut into thin strips

Salt

½ cup heavy cream

2 tablespoons butter

Freshly ground black pepper

Makes about 1½ cups of sauce

Prosciutto and Fresh Pea Sauce

SALSA DE PROSCIUTTO Y ARVEJAS CON CREMA

When I make pappardelle, I have a hard time deciding which sauce to use. The previous sauce is exquisite, but so is this one. I usually decide on the basis of the quality of the peas available. The peas for this recipe must be very young. Many grocers have fresh sugar peas during the spring and summer, which are ideal. Otherwise, substitute small frozen peas or cook larger fresh peas in salted water for about 10 minutes.

Directions

Heat the peas in 2 tablespoons of the butter for about 3 minutes. Set them aside and keep them warm. Place the remaining 2 tablespoons of butter in a heavy skillet on medium heat. Sauté the onion until it is a light golden color. Add the prosciutto, thyme and chili peppers. Cook, while stirring, for 1 minute. Add the peas and cook for 3 minutes on medium heat while stirring and coating them with the butter. Add the cream, salt and pepper. Turn the heat to high and reduce the sauce by a third while stirring. Keep the sauce warm until you are ready to toss it with the pasta.

INGREDIENTS

2 pounds shelled sugar
   peas, or 1 cup frozen
   peas
4 tablespoons butter
½ cup chopped onions
¼ pound prosciutto, chopped
1 teaspoon fresh thyme
   leaves
   Dash crushed dried chili
   peppers
½ cup heavy cream
   Coarse salt to taste
   Freshly ground black
   pepper to taste

Makes about 1 ½ cups
of sauce

Smoked Trout with Spaghetti

SPAGHETTI CON TRUCHA AHUMADA À LA FAMILIA WEISS

Here is another marvelous smoked fish dish from Ahumadero Familia Weiss. Most children are wild about it, but for their sakes, I recommend omitting the crushed red pepper.

Directions

Boil the spaghetti according to the package instructions. Drain it and keep it hot. In a saucepan over medium heat mix the cream, garlic, pepper and chili pepper (do not add salt as the trout is already salted). Continue to cook the mixture for about 5 minutes while stirring. When the sauce thickens and is slightly reduced, add the trout and heat through. Pour the trout mixture on hot spaghetti and toss. Serve immediately.

INGREDIENTS

1   16-ounce package
    spaghetti
¾   cup heavy cream
1   garlic clove, minced
    Freshly ground black
    pepper
    Pinch crushed chili pepper
    (optional)
3½ ounces smoked trout,
    minced

Serves 4

Trout in Cream

TRUCHA FRESCA À LA CREMA

This is Family Weiss' signature dish—my favorite from the Ahumadero Familia Weiss in Bariloche. The Mushroom Cream Sauce is sometimes alternated with an Almond Cream Sauce or Roquefort Cream Sauce. To make the almond version, *Crema con Almendras*, substitute ¾ cup blanched slivered almonds for the mushrooms. For the Roquefort variation, *Crema con Roquefort*, replace the mushrooms with ⅓ cup Roquefort cheese.

Directions

Preheat the oven to 350°F. Season the trout with salt and pepper inside and out. Place the trout in a flameproof casserole or baking dish and sprinkle it with lemon juice. Top with the butter. Bake the trout uncovered for 10 to 15 minutes or until it flakes easily with a fork. Remove the trout to a serving platter and keep it warm. Nap the trout with mushroom cream sauce and serve with boiled potatoes.

INGREDIENTS

4   trout, scaled and cleaned
    Salt and freshly ground
    pepper to taste
    Juice of 1 lemon
2   tablespoons chilled butter,
    cut in small dice
    Mushroom cream sauce
    (recipe follows)

Serves 4

Mushroom Cream Sauce
SALSA DE CREMA CON HONGOS FRESCOS

INGREDIENTS

2 cups sliced fresh
mushrooms

¼ cup olive oil

1 garlic clove, minced

Salt and white pepper to
taste

1 teaspoon freshly ground
nutmeg

1 cup heavy cream

Makes about 2 cups
of sauce

Directions

In a skillet, sauté the mushrooms in hot oil until golden brown. Add the garlic and sauté for several more minutes. Season with salt, pepper and nutmeg. Add the cream and mix well. Bring the mixture to a boil, reduce heat to medium and continue cooking and stirring until the cream mixture is reduced by a third. Remove the sauce from the heat and keep it warm until you are ready to serve.

Salmon Pie
EMPANADA GALLEGA

Not really an empanada in the Argentine sense of empanadas, *Empanada Gallega* is one big filled pastry. This recipe calls for fresh salmon which, in Bariloche, is usually shipped across the border from Chile. While fresh salmon is available in Bariloche, many busy Argentine housewives use canned salmon to make this dish. Fresh or canned tuna also can be substituted. Argentine cooks frequently make a bread dough with yeast for *Empanada Gallega*. This recipe calls for a lighter pastry.

Pastry Directions

Sift the flour and salt together. Cut in the shortening with a pastry blender or 2 knives until the mixture looks like coarse sand. Mix in the egg yolk and water with a fork. Form the dough into a ball and chill for 2 hours.

Filling Directions

In a skillet, sauté the onions in 3 tablespoons of the olive oil until they are soft. Add the tomatoes, garlic, parsley, salt, pepper, dill and wine. Cook over high heat until the liquid is reduced by half. Correct seasonings and cool.

Assembly Directions

Preheat the oven to 400°F. Roll out a little over half the dough and line a lightly oiled 10-inch pie pan with it. Layer the filling starting with half the onion mixture. Top the onions with half the salmon strips followed by half the egg slices and half the olive slices. Repeat the layering with the remaining ingredients. Roll out the remaining dough and cover the layered mixture. Seal the pastry edges and cut a small hole in the center of the top crust the size of a finger. Brush the top with the remaining 1 tablespoon oil and bake the pie in the center of the oven for 25 minutes or until the pastry is brown. Cool and cut into wedges to serve.

PASTRY

2   cups sifted flour
¾   teaspoon salt
⅔   cup shortening
1   egg yolk, beaten
3   tablespoons ice water

FILLING

2   cups chopped onions
4   tablespoons olive oil
2   tomatoes, peeled, seeded
    and chopped
1   garlic clove, minced
2   tablespoons minced
    parsley
1¼ teaspoons salt
½   teaspoon freshly ground
    pepper
2   tablespoons chopped
    fresh dill
¼   cup dry white wine
1½ pounds salmon fillets,
    lightly poached and cut in
    1½ inch strips (or canned
    salmon)
¼   cup pimiento-stuffed green
    olives, sliced crosswise
2   hard-boiled eggs, sliced
    crosswise

Serves 4 to 6

Partridges in Garlic Alioli Sauce

PERDICES EN SALSA DE AJO

Partridge will be tenderer if allowed to rest in the refrigerator for 2 days before cooking. Squab, though smaller, is a good substitute for the harder-to-obtain partridge.

Directions

In a heavy flameproof casserole, brown the partridge halves on both sides in butter. Add the onion, garlic, pancetta, salt and pepper. When the onions are golden brown, add the wine. Cover and simmer on low heat for about 20 minutes. Add the spinach and lemon juice. Raise the heat to medium and continue cooking while stirring until the spinach is tender, 4 to 6 minutes. Ladle a small amount of the spinach sauce on heated serving plates and place 2 partridge halves on top of the sauce. Top partridges with 3 tablespoons of garlic mayonnaise. Serve immediately.

INGREDIENTS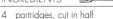

4 partridges, cut in half
   lengthwise
3 tablespoons butter
1 large onion, minced
3 garlic cloves, minced
¼ pound pancetta, chopped
   Salt to taste
   Freshly ground pepper
   to taste
1 cup white wine
2 bunches tender spinach,
   rinsed, dried and chopped
1 tablespoon lemon juice
   Garlic mayonnaise (recipe
   follows)

Serves 4

Garlic Mayonnaise

Serve garlic alioli with fish, game birds or rabbit. To guard against salmonella, be sure to use a very fresh egg in this recipe and wash the shell thoroughly before cracking it.

Directions

Mix the garlic and salt in a blender. Add the egg and lemon juice and beat until the mixture turns a pale yellow. While the blender motor is running, gradually add the oil in a thin stream. Stop the blender when the mixture holds a peak. Transfer the alioli to a serving bowl and serve it at room temperature.

INGREDIENTS

10 garlic cloves, crushed
1 teaspoon salt
1 egg
3 teaspoons lemon juice
1 cup olive oil

Makes about 2½ cups
of sauce

Braised Game Hens

POLLITO ESPECIAL

Pollito Especial makes a grand party dish or a special occasion family meal. The paper-thin slices of prosciutto inserted under the breast skin impart a lovely smoky flavor to the hens.

INGREDIENTS

4   small game hens, cleaned
    and plucked
¼   pound prosciutto, sliced
    paper thin
4   livers from hens
3   tablespoons butter
2   cups day-old breadcrumbs
    for stuffing
1   bunch parsley, minced
2   tablespoons olive oil
1   garlic head, separated
    and peeled
1   onion, chopped
4   carrots, chopped
3½ cups beef stock
    Giblets and necks from
    hens
1   cup red wine
¼   cup red wine vinegar
¼   cup dry vermouth
2   bay leaves
1   teaspoon crushed dried
    oregano
1   teaspoon crushed dried
    thyme
1   teaspoon ground cumin
    Salt and pepper to taste
¼   cup sherry
4   thick slices French bread,
    toasted
2   tablespoons clarified butter

    Serves 4

Directions

Preheat the oven to 325°F. Gently the lift the breast skin from the body of each bird and insert prosciutto, spreading it out to cover the breast meat. Sauté the livers in 1 tablespoon butter until they are lightly browned and chop them. Make a stuffing with the breadcrumbs, parsley and chopped livers. Fill the neck and body cavities with the stuffing. Truss the birds and sauté them in olive oil and 2 tablespoons butter over medium heat until they are browned on both sides. Place the birds in a flameproof casserole and set aside.

Sauté the garlic, onions and carrots for 3 or 4 minutes in the remaining oil and add the mixture to the casserole. In a large saucepan, add the beef stock, giblets, necks, wine, vinegar and vermouth. Bring the mixture to a boil and reduce the stock by half. Strain and discard the solids. Pour the stock over the birds and add the bay leaves, oregano, thyme, cumin, salt, pepper and sherry. Bring the mixture to a boil and place the casserole in the oven. Simmer, covered, for 50 minutes, checking to see that the casserole does not run dry. If it dries out, add a little more wine or water. Cover and return the casserole to the oven. Raise the heat to 450°F and continue cooking for 10 minutes more.

During the last 10 minutes of simmering the hens, sauté the bread in the clarified butter. When browned, place the croutons on a heated serving platter. Cut the trussing string from the birds and place 1 on each crouton. Strain the sauce into a saucepan. Over high heat, bring the sauce to a boil and continue cooking until it is reduced by half. Spoon a little sauce over each hen, garnish with a big sprig of watercress and serve.

Game Mélange
GASPADO DE CAZADOR

Here is a dish for those with large appetites. It makes a comforting cold-weather repast served right out of the stew pot, and it's perfect for the ski season. Restrict accompaniments to crusty bread, a simple green salad and a good bottle of Merlot from Mendoza. Substitute a Merlot from Chile or California if a good Argentine wine is not available.

Directions
Brown rabbit quarters, partridges and quail in oil in a heavy flameproof casserole. When the game is nicely browned on all sides, add garlic, onions, bay leaves, carrot, peppercorns, juniper berries, clove, tomatoes, salt and pepper. Cover and simmer the stew over a low heat until the game is tender, about 25 minutes. Serve with garlic alioli (page 197).

INGREDIENTS

1   rabbit, skinned, cleaned
    and quartered
2   partridges, cleaned and
    cut in half (or squab)
4   quail, cleaned and left
    whole
½   cup vegetable oil
4   garlic cloves, minced
2   onions, chopped
2   bay leaves
1   carrot, diced
10 whole peppercorns
12 juniper berries, crushed (or
    ¼ cup gin)
1   clove
4   pounds tomatoes, peeled,
    seeded and chopped
    Salt and pepper to taste

Serves 4 amply

Hunter-Style Venison

CIERVO À LA CAZADOR

Game dishes are the specialty of the Patagonian Andes. Because Bariloche attracts gourmets and a number of ambitious, talented chefs, simple game dishes have been elevated to epicurean heights. Here is one example.

Directions

Soak the mushrooms in wine for 30 minutes. Cut the venison into 1-inch cubes and sear them in a hot skillet without oil. Set aside.

In a flameproof casserole, sauté the onions, garlic and pimientos in oil. Add the venison cubes and sauté them until browned on all sides, 3 minutes per side. Remove the mixture from the casserole and set aside.

Deglaze the casserole with the mushrooms in wine. Add stock, juniper berries, red pepper, paprika, salt, black pepper and sage. Continue to cook over medium heat for about 10 minutes or until the liquid is reduced by half. Stir in the cream and continue cooking and stirring until the liquid is reduced by a third.

Return the venison mixture to the cream sauce and heat through. Remove the venison to a serving dish. Serve with a salad and steamed rice or boiled potatoes.

INGREDIENTS

1   cup fresh mushrooms
1   cup dry white wine,
    Chenin Blanc or similar
2   pounds fresh venison,
    preferably from the
    haunch, trimmed with
    tough connective tissue
    removed
3   medium onions, chopped
5   garlic cloves, skinned
2   fresh pimientos, minced
½   cup olive oil
½   cup venison stock made
    from trimmings (or beef
    stock)
12 juniper berries, crushed
½   teaspoon crushed chili
    pepper
1   tablespoon sweet paprika
    Salt and freshly ground
    pepper to taste
6   fresh sage leaves, minced
    (or 1 tablespoon dried
    sage)
¾   cup heavy cream

Serves 6

Veal Shanks à la Rondine

OSOBUCO CON VERDURAS COCIDAS

On my last visit to San Carlos de Bariloche, I arrived tired, hungry and cold—even though it was officially springtime in the Andes. I was tired because my flight from Buenos Aires was cancelled, and I waited three hours at the domestic airport for another. I was hungry because Aerolinas Argentinas, in its wisdom, did not provide a meal on this three-hour unscheduled flight (oh, for the days of the line's delicious *media luna* sandwiches with *jamón cruda* and *queso fresco*). And I was cold because when I arrived, snow was still on the ground, icy patches clouded the lake and a cruel wind blew down through the high mountain passes and through my light jacket.

Fortunately, I was booked into a hotel that featured an upscale new restaurant—La Rondine—promising classic Italian cuisine. Its Argentine chef, Noemi Barchetta, more than delivered on the promise. Her husband, Guillermo Kempin Pugni, is executive chef and manages the restaurant. Together, this talented young couple has created an elegant yet warm and friendly dining experience. *Osobuco con Verduras Cocidas* is the chef's signature recipe.

INGREDIENTS

2	tablespoons butter
1	tablespoon olive oil
8	1½-inch lengths veal shank with marrow
1	small onion, minced
1	small carrot, grated
1	cup peeled, seeded, chopped tomatoes
1	tablespoon chopped fresh sage
1	bay leaf
¼	cup flour
2	cups marsala wine
2	tablespoons minced garlic
1	tablespoon finely minced lemon zest
2	tablespoons minced tinned anchovies
4	pieces hot toast
2	tablespoons minced parsley

Serves 2

Directions

Heat the butter and oil in a shallow flameproof casserole. Sauté the veal shanks on both sides until they are golden brown. Add onion and carrot and continue sautéing until the vegetables begin to color. Add tomatoes, sage, bay leaf and flour, stirring constantly. Add marsala wine then cover and simmer for almost 3 hours. When the veal is tender, remove it to a heated serving dish. Skim the fat from the sauce and strain the sauce over the veal. At the last moment top the dish with a gremolata made of minced garlic, lemon zest and anchovies. Garnish with toasts and parsley. Offer marrow spoons for removing the marrow from the bones and spreading it on the toast. Serve with sautéed spinach seasoned with garlic and olive oil. A good Merlot goes well with this dish.

Steak with Roquefort Sauce

BIFE CON QUESO ROQUEFORT

This dish originated in the Asturias region of Spain where a strong blue cheese—*queso cabrales*—was and still is produced. The recipe came to Argentina with the Asturians and Galicians who immigrated in the late nineteenth century. The Argentine version of the sauce is based on Roquefort cheese, but any crumbly blue cheese may be substituted.

The steaks are pan-broiled in a well-seasoned cast-iron skillet over high heat and produce a lot of smoke. Be sure to have an adequate exhaust system if you do this. Otherwise, sauté the steaks over a medium heat for a longer period of time.

Directions

In a double boiler, mix together the cheese, wine, lemon juice, parsley, garlic, paprika and pepper. Cook, stirring occasionally, until the sauce is smooth. Remove the sauce from the heat and keep it warm over the hot water in the double boiler.

Marinate the steaks in olive oil for several minutes. Salt both sides lightly and shake off the excess. With the heat on high sear the steaks in a cast-iron skillet. When the steaks are seared on 1 side, turn down the heat to medium and continue to pan broil for 3 minutes for medium rare (more if you like your steaks well done). Turn up the heat to high, turn the steaks over and sear the other side. When the second side is seared, turn down the heat to medium and pan broil for another 3 minutes for medium rare. Remove the steaks to a serving platter and keep them warm.

Deglaze the skillet with water and add 2 tablespoons of this mixture to the cheese sauce. Taste for seasoning and add salt if necessary. Pour the sauce over the steaks and serve immediately.

A full-bodied Pinot Noir is the perfect wine accompaniment.

INGREDIENTS

¼ pound Roquefort or other blue cheese

4 teaspoons white wine

1 teaspoon lemon juice

1 tablespoon minced parsley

1 garlic clove, crushed

¼ teaspoon hot paprika

⅛ teaspoon freshly ground pepper

4 well-marbled steaks (such as filet mignon, New York or club), 1 inch thick

2 tablespoons olive oil

1 tablespoon coarse kosher or sea salt

Serves 4

Roquefort Potatoes and Brussels Sprouts

PAPAS Y REPOLLITOS EN SALSA ROQUEFORT

Potatoes turn up in combination with many other vegetables throughout Argentina, but especially in Mendoza where too much of a good thing is considered wonderful. Try to find tiny red potatoes that are about the same size as the brussels sprouts for this dish.

Directions

Boil the potatoes in their skins until soft. Drain, cool and remove the skins. Strip the outer leaves from the brussels sprouts and cut a cross in the stem end about ¼ inch deep with a sharp knife. Boil them until tender and drain. Melt the butter in a small casserole. Add the onion and flour and stir over low heat for about 50 seconds. Add milk and bring the mixture to a boil, stirring constantly until the mixture thickens. Add the cheese in small pieces and then the vinegar. Continue stirring until the cheese melts and is blended into the sauce. Add the potatoes, brussels sprouts, salt, pepper and nutmeg and continue cooking for about 5 minutes.

Remove the vegetables from the heat and stir in the parsley. Place the vegetables in a heated serving dish. Serve with sliced *jamón cruda* or prosciutto de Parma.

INGREDIENTS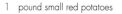

1   pound small red potatoes
¾   pound brussels sprouts
3   tablespoons butter
1   onion, chopped
3   tablespoons flour
2   cups milk
2   tablespoons Roquefort
     cheese
1   teaspoon balsamic vinegar
1   bunch parsley, minced
     Salt and pepper to taste
¼   teaspoon freshly grated
     nutmeg

Serves 4

Little Squash

In Argentina, pumpkin meat is the traditional
base for this dish. But any winter squash, such as
Hubbard or butternut, will do as well—in fact, I
prefer the squash to the pumpkin.

Directions
Sauté the onion and peppers in lard. Peel the pumpkin,
remove the seeds. Cut the pumpkin into 8 pieces. Place
the pumpkin pieces in a saucepan with the tomatoes. Add
the sautéed onions, peppers and salt and pepper. Cover
and simmer the mixture until it is tender. Add a little water
if the mixture becomes dry. Just before serving, add the
beaten egg and cheese, mixing well. Heat until the cheese
melts and serve.

INGREDIENTS

½ onion, chopped

3 sweet green bell peppers,
  seeded and chopped

2 tablespoons lard

2 pounds pumpkin meat (or
  winter squash meat)

1½ cups chopped tomatoes
  with juice
  Salt and freshly ground
  pepper to taste

1 egg, beaten

½ cup grated cheddar
  cheese

Serves 4

Candied Prunes
CARAMELOS DE CIRUELAS

Caramelos de Ciruelas make a delightful biteful with *mate* or after lunch or dinner.

Directions

In a heavy saucepan dilute the sugar in water. Bring to a boil while stirring. Continue to boil until the mixture reaches 220°F on a candy thermometer, or until a small amount of the mixture dripped from a spoon spins a thread. Remove the mixture from the heat and cool. Stir in the egg yolks and return to a low heat. Cook while stirring until the mixture pulls away from the sides of the pan. Cool the mixture and then shape it into small balls using a heaping teaspoonful of the mixture for each ball. Fill each ball with a prune. When all the candy balls are filled, roll them in confectioners' sugar.

INGREDIENTS

1½ cups sugar

½ cup water

5 egg yolks, beaten

1 12-ounce package prunes, pitted

½ cup confectioners' sugar

Makes about 40 candies

Patagonian Atlantic:

Appetite for Adventure

Patagonian Atlantic

Eastern Chubut Province is the Argentina of the great outdoors where the world's largest collection of marine mammals flourishes. It is a lonely, stormy place. Winds batter the buildings and people stay indoors for long periods. These rough coastal areas of southern Patagonia, however, are a paradise for the hardy naturalist. They provide an immense zoo without barriers where you can see vast seal colonies, southern whales, cormorants, Antarctic doves and Magellanic penguins. Upcountry, Patagonian hares, ñandus (rheas—South American ostriches) and guanacos run about the steppes.

A surprise to most visitors is the Welsh colony in lower Chubut Province. The first group of Welsh immigrants landed at Puerto Madryn after a hazardous voyage across the Atlantic Ocean in 1865. The impetus was to escape English domination in politics, language and religion. Misfortune met most of the early arrivals. Few of the newcomers had been farmers in Wales. Yet their destiny was an agricultural one. Nearly starving in the arid climate, the first colony eventually learned to build irrigation systems that would support crops as well as the next influx of immigrants from Wales.

The quaint village of Gaiman was founded by the next wave of Welsh immigrants in the late nineteenth century. Now as long ago, Gaiman and its outskirts boast a multitude of Welsh teahouses offering a welcome respite from the cold winds. The hot tea served with traditional Welsh cakes make these establishments popular stopovers on long motor trips.

A denizen of the Patogonian Atlantic.

The Welsh's gritty determination to maintain their identity persists up to the present day, although the Welsh language is losing its hold. But tradition dies hard and the people still celebrate their Welshness in song and verse at Eisteddfod folk festivals.

The Welsh influence is strongly reflected in local cuisine. Giant crabs, fish and a variety of smaller shellfish are readily available delicacies. But the mainstay of local menus is the lamb and mutton that is pastured here on salt marshes and fed nothing but marsh grasses so that it is butter-tender and has a delicate herb flavor. Among the local favorites are spit-roasted lamb, grilled baby milk-fed lamb, stuffed lamb shoulder, lamb stew, lamb neck soup, ground lamb, lamb chops, lamb's feet in vinaigrette sauce, marinated breast of lamb, lamb shoulder in mint sauce, lamb kidneys, and lamb intestines. The list is almost endless. And if you don't speak Welsh in this part of the country, selecting from restaurant menus should not present a problem. Whatever you point to will probably be lamb or mutton.

Puerto Madryn is the urban center closest to the Península Valdés. As such, it is the point of departure for visits to the renowned wildlife preserves in the area. You can choose among photo safaris, whale-watching or nature walks. There's even a tour by submarine.

Southwest of Puerto Madryn is the Reserva Faunística at Punta Loma, providing visitors with a good look at a sea lion rookery. A little to the north is Península Valdés with its sea lions, elephant seals, guanacos, rheas, Magellanic penguins and a variety of rare seabirds.

Further south lies the archipelago of Tierra del Fuego (Land of Fire). To most geography or nature buffs it evokes an isolated place at the end of the world, beaten into submission by gale winds and towering waves. Tierra del Fuego is *The Uttermost Part of the Earth*—according to the fascinating memoir of Lucas Bridges, long considered one of the world's great adventure stories.

Bridges was the son of one of the first settlers in Ushuaia on the Beagle Channel—now the capital of the Argentine province—when the Yahgan, Haush, Alacaluf and Ona Indians thrived. Primarily hunters and gatherers, these indigenous groups lived off the land and sea, eating guanaco, fish, shellfish and marine mammals. Despite the harsh climate, the native dwellers wore little or no clothing—a fact that amazed early settlers—and simply warmed themselves by the fires they built. Sadly, the opening of the area to European settlement led to the rapid demise of the indigenous groups thanks to imported diseases and violent persecution by sheep farmers. Charles Darwin, visiting the area in 1834, wrote that these Indians were "among the most abject and miserable creatures I ever saw."

Argentina didn't consider the area important until Chile established a presence and English missionaries were making inroads. A long-standing dispute over three small islands in the Beagle channel nearly brought Argentina and Chile to war in 1979. And, as late as 1984, Chile and Argentina still disputed sovereignty over the area.

Separated from the mainland by the Straits of Magellan, and bounded by the South Atlantic Ocean and the easternmost part of the Pacific Ocean, the archipelago has recorded temperatures along the Beagle Channel ranging from a high of 86°F in summer to a low of 7°F in winter. The climate has been called a perpetual but cool spring. Given the latitude, the presence of parrots, flamingos and hummingbirds here is astonishing. Notwithstanding the claims of a temperate climate, I would not come here without a serious parka.

Strictly speaking, Tierra del Fuego encompasses the land south of the Strait of Magellan and north of the Drake Passage, and is about the size of Ireland. But only one island—Isla Grande—is actually referred to as Tierra del Fuego. Surrounded by a maze of mountainous islands, islets, scenic glaciers, lakes, rivers, channels and fiords, Isla Grande is now politically divided between Argentina and Chile. Much of the surrounding territory is unexplored. But the growing interest among tourists to experience the end of the known world may change that.

Sheep farming, fishing and tourism are the mainstays of Argentine industry in Tierra del Fuego. Brown trout and rainbow trout fill the rivers, and Atlantic salmon is pulled from the sea daily. This is also the home of giant crabs. Unfortunately, they are getting fewer and more expensive. Thus, the cuisine is pretty much limited to lamb and fish in the restaurants of Ushuaia and Río Grande. Almost everything else is shipped in from more temperate climes.

Welsh Teacakes

Welsh teacakes are based on the age-old British tradition of baking cakes on a griddle. In the old days, every farmhouse in Wales and Scotland kept a peat fire going in a fireplace. Housewives suspended a flat, round iron plate over the embers for cooking cakes, pancakes and scones. Many old cottages in Wales and Scotland still house these traditional griddles. The Welsh of Argentina have continued this tradition. And on a harsh, bleak day in Patagonia, griddle-baked Welsh teacakes served with hot tea are a most welcome comfort food.

The following recipe was inspired by the teacakes from Ty Gwyn in Gaiman.

Directions

Oil a griddle or heavy skillet. In a bowl sift together the flour, baking powder, allspice, nutmeg, salt and sugar. Cut the butter and lard into the flour mixture with a pastry blender or 2 knives. Beat the egg into the milk with a fork and add the mixture to the flour mixture, blending well. Fold in the currants. Gather the dough together into a ball and roll it out on a floured board until it is about ¼ inch thick. Cut the dough into 2-inch rounds with a cookie cutter or glass. Heat the griddle or skillet until it is very hot. Cook the teacakes on 1 side until they are brown. Turn and cook on the other side until brown. Serve warm with clotted cream or butter with jam.

INGREDIENTS

2   cups flour
1   teaspoon baking powder
1   teaspoon powdered
    allspice
1   teaspoon freshly grated
    nutmeg
¼   teaspoon salt
½   cup sugar
¼   cup butter
¼   cup lard or shortening
1   egg
¼   cup milk
⅓   cup currants

Makes 18 to 20 teacakes

Salmon Mousse
BUDÍN DE SALMÓN

In Bariloche or Buenos Aires, this dish is made with fresh salmon. But in southeastern Patagonia, almost everyone uses the canned variety. The result is surprisingly good. Because this recipe calls for raw egg whites, salmonella contamination is a risk and care must be exercised in purchasing, storing and preparing the eggs. Use only the freshest eggs and make sure to wash the shells before cracking. As an alternative, use whipped heavy cream in the place of egg whites.

INGREDIENTS

2   1-pound cans red salmon
2   eggs, separated
¾   teaspoon salt
¼   teaspoon freshly ground
    pepper
½   teaspoon Worcestershire
    sauce
    Juice of 1 lemon
3   tablespoons olive oil
1   tablespoon butter
3   shallots, minced
2   tablespoons flour
½   teaspoon dry mustard
1   cup light cream
3   envelopes unflavored
    gelatin
3   tablespoons tomato catsup
1   bunch watercress, stems
    trimmed

Serves 10 to 12

Directions

Drain the salmon, reserving the liquid. Mash the salmon thoroughly with a fork and set it aside. Beat the egg yolks with the salt, pepper, Worcestershire, lemon juice and olive oil until well blended. Add the mixture to the mashed salmon and mix well.

Melt the butter in a saucepan. Add the shallots and sauté them until they are transparent. Stir in the flour and mustard, and cook for 1 minute while stirring. Gradually add the salmon liquid and cream. Continue cooking while stirring until the mixture thickens. Soften the gelatin in 1½ cups cold water. When softened, add the gelatin to the hot sauce mixture and stir until it's dissolved. Add the catsup and blend well. Allow the mixture to cool. Add the salmon mixture to the sauce and mix well with a wooden spoon.

Beat the egg whites until they hold a firm peak, then fold them into the salmon mixture. Pour the mousse into a

2-quart ring mold and chill until firm—preferably overnight. Unmold by dipping the mold into a bowl filled with hot water for about a minute. Cover the pan opening with the serving platter and hold them together firmly as you flip them over so the mousse slides out on the platter. Garnish with watercress.

Herring Salad
ENSALADA DE ARENQUES

Herring dishes came to Argentina with German immigrants. Fresh herring are very hard to come by in the United States unless you have a friend in the fishing industry. The best times to find fresh herring is in the spring and early summer. Trout, mackerel or salted herring fillets may be substituted. If using salted herring fillets, place them in a large bowl and cover them with cold water or milk. Refrigerate, covered, overnight. When ready to use, drain and rinse them and remove any spines. Dry on paper towels.

Directions

Boil the beets for 15 minutes in salted water. When cool enough to handle, peel the beets, slice them and set them aside. Sauté the herring in 2 tablespoons olive oil. Remove the herring to a plate and set it aside to cool. Cut the veal into 1-inch chunks and sauté for about 4 minutes in the herring cooking oil without browning, adding a little more oil if necessary. Add 2½ cups water, cover and simmer the veal over low heat for 30 minutes. Drain the

INGREDIENTS

4   fresh beets
4   fresh herrings, cleaned
2½ tablespoons olive oil
1   pound veal or tongue
3   shallots, chopped
2   carrots, julienned
4   small potatoes, boiled and
     roughly mashed
1   cup minced parsley
1   teaspoon red wine vinegar
     Salt and freshly ground
     black pepper to taste
4   large lettuce leaves
1   hard-boiled egg, sliced
12 pimiento-stuffed green
     olives

Serves 4

veal and mince. (If using tongue instead of veal, follow the directions for cooking on page 104. Drain the tongue, cut off about 16 ounces and mince, saving the remainder for another use.)

In a deep bowl, flake the herring fillets with a fork and mix them with the minced veal (or tongue). Add the shallots, carrots, potatoes and ½ cup of the parsley. Beat the remaining ½ tablespoon olive oil, vinegar, salt and pepper together with a whisk and combine with the fish mixture. Divide the mixture into 4 portions and place each portion on a large lettuce leaf. Garnish with slices of beet, hard-boiled egg and olives. Sprinkle the top with remaining ½ cup parsley.

Salt Cod with Chickpeas

BACALAO CON GARBANZOS

A staple in Spain, Italy and Portugal, bacalao is considered a delicacy in the cold regions of Argentina. Long soaking is required to remove the saltiness and to render the fish tender enough to eat.

Directions
Soak the cod for 12 hours in cold water, changing the water at least twice.

Preheat the oven to 350°F. Drain the cod and place it in a large, flameproof casserole. Insert cloves in the top and bottom of a whole onion. Cover the fish with fresh water and add the whole onion and bay leaf. Bring the mixture to a boil, then reduce the heat and simmer, covered, for 30 minutes.

Drain and flake the fish with a fork. Heat 2 tablespoons olive oil in a saucepan. Add the chopped onions and garlic. Sauté for 5 minutes or until golden. Add the flaked cod and chickpeas, mixing well. Spread the mixture in a buttered ovenproof baking dish.

Beat the eggs and add the remaining 3 tablespoons olive oil gradually while continuing to beat. Stir in the lemon juice, chili pepper, grated cheese and parsley. Pour the egg mixture over the fish, cover it with breadcrumbs and dot it with butter. Bake for 20 minutes. Garnish the finished dish with olives and serve from the baking dish.

INGREDIENTS

1 ½ pounds dried salt cod
3 cloves
1 whole onion, peeled with root and top ends removed
1 bay leaf
5 tablespoons olive oil
3 onions, chopped
3 garlic cloves, crushed
2 cups cooked and drained garbanzo beans (chickpeas) or canned garbanzos
3 eggs
3 tablespoons lemon juice
¼ teaspoon dried crushed chili pepper
4 tablespoons grated Parmesan cheese
4 tablespoons minced parsley
½ cup dry breadcrumbs
2 tablespoons butter
12 pimiento-stuffed green olives

Serves 6

Stuffed Squid Puerto Madryn

CALAMARES RELLENOS DE PUERTO MADRYN

Stuffed squid is a delicacy much appreciated by coastal dwellers in Patagonia, especially Puerto Madryn. A dish from Club Nautico in that city inspired this recipe.

Directions

Preheat the oven to 350°F. Chop the squid tentacles and mix them with breadcrumbs, salt, pepper, raisins, Parmesan cheese, hard-boiled egg, anchovies and melted butter. Stuff the mixture into the squid body cavities and place the squid close together in a baking dish. Bake, uncovered, for 30 minutes. Fry the onion in olive oil until golden. Add the tomatoes and simmer for 5 minutes. Pour the mixture over the squid and bake for 15 minutes more.

INGREDIENTS

12 squid, cleaned with
    tentacles removed and
    reserved
4 cups breadcrumbs
½ teaspoon salt
    Freshly ground pepper
½ cup raisins
¼ cup grated Parmesan
    cheese
1 hard-boiled egg, sieved
2 anchovies, minced
4 tablespoons butter, melted
1 onion, minced
2 tablespoons olive oil
6 tomatoes, peeled, seeded
    and chopped

Serves 6

Seabass in Egg Sauce
CORBINA ASADA CON SALSA DE HUEVO

Seabass is a delicious and versatile fish that lends itself to many different treatments. This recipe for baked seabass features a sauce made from the fish cooking liquid seasoned with lemon juice and thickened with egg yolks.

Directions

Preheat the oven to 350°F. Sprinkle the fillets on both sides with salt, pepper and lemon juice. Place them in a shallow baking dish. Arrange the onion slices on top of the fish and sprinkle them with the olive oil. Bake for about 15 minutes or until the fish flakes easily with a fork. Transfer the fish to a heated serving plate and strain the pan liquid into a small saucepan. Beat the egg yolks into the cream. Add a little pan liquid and beat it into the egg mixture. Remove the pan liquid from the heat and add the egg mixture, beating constantly with a whisk just until the mixture thickens enough to coat a spoon. Spoon the sauce over the fish and serve.

INGREDIENTS

1   pound seabass fillets
½   teaspoon salt
    Freshly ground black
    pepper
    Juice of 1 lemon
1   onion, sliced
½   cup olive oil
2   egg yolks
⅓   cup heavy cream

Serves 4

Seabass in Wine Sauce

CORBINA CON SALSA DE VINO

INGREDIENTS

1   pound seabass fillets
½   teaspoon salt
    Freshly ground black
    pepper
1   onion, sliced
½   cup olive oil
    Pan liquid from baked fish
1   garlic clove, minced
    Pinch of powdered
    bay leaf
1   cup dry white wine
2   tablespoons cider vinegar
4   tablespoons chilled butter,
    cut into ½-inch cubes

Makes 1 ½ cups of sauce

Directions

Cook the seabass as specified in the previous recipe, omitting the lemon juice, egg yolks and cream. Make a sauce from the pan liquid. Mix the fish liquid with garlic, bay leaf, wine and vinegar. In a small saucepan, heat the mixture while stirring until it comes to a boil. When the liquid is reduced to about half its volume, remove it from the heat and beat in the butter all at once. Pour the sauce over the fish and serve.

Chicken with Rice

ARRÓZ CON POLLO

What Spanish-speaking country does not include *Arróz con Pollo* in its culinary repertoire? The Argentine version is not that much different from the Spanish recipe except that it is usually made with long-grain rice instead of short-grain. Still, it's delicious, quick and easy to make on busy days.

Directions

Sprinkle the chicken pieces with salt and pepper. Sauté them in olive oil in a large flameproof casserole. When partially cooked, add the green pepper, onion, garlic and parsley. Continue sautéing for several more minutes. Add the tomatoes and cook for another 5 minutes. Stir in the boiling water. Cover and simmer over low heat for about 20 minutes, or until the chicken is almost tender.

Rinse the rice and add it to the chicken mixture, stirring gently with a fork to prevent the rice grains from sticking together. Season to taste and add the saffron. Cover and simmer the rice over low heat for about 30 minutes. Remove the cover and check the rice; it should be soft but not dry. If it's too dry, stir in a little boiling water before removing it from the heat.

INGREDIENTS

1   frying chicken, cut into
    serving pieces
    Salt and pepper to taste
3   tablespoons vegetable oil
1   green bell pepper, seeded
    and cut into 1-inch squares
1   small onion, minced
2   garlic cloves, minced
2   tablespoons minced
    parsley
2   tomatoes, roughly
    chopped
2¾ cups boiling water
1   cup plus 2 tablespoons
    long-grain rice
    Pinch of saffron

Serves 4

Welsh Chicken

A special occasion dish, Welsh Chicken is a favorite with the population in and around Gaiman. Many of the locals find it a welcome change from what they consider the monotony of lamb.

INGREDIENTS

1 stewing hen, about 4 pounds

1½ teaspoons salt

½ teaspoon freshly ground pepper

1 lemon, sliced

½ pound bacon

4 leeks, diced

4 carrots, diced

3 tablespoons flour

2 cups chicken broth

¼ cup minced fresh chervil

¼ cup minced fresh marjoram

¼ cup chopped fresh thyme leaves

2 tablespoons minced parsley

1 tablespoon butter, melted

1 small cabbage, shredded

Serves 6

Directions

Wash and dry the chicken thoroughly inside and out. Season the cavity with 1 teaspoon salt and the pepper, insert lemon slices and truss. In a heavy flameproof casserole, fry the bacon until it is crisp. Remove the bacon from the casserole, drain it on paper towels and allow it to cool. Discard all but 2 tablespoons of the bacon fat. Sauté the leeks and carrots in the casserole until they take on a little color but are still crisp. Remove them from the casserole and reserve.

Stir the flour into the fat remaining in the casserole and cook it for 1 minute. Crumble the bacon and add it to the flour mixture. Add the broth while stirring over low heat. Add the chervil, marjoram, thyme and parsley and bring the mixture to a simmer. Season with ½ teaspoon salt and pepper to taste. Place the chicken in the casserole and brush with melted butter. Cover the casserole with foil and a heavy lid to make a tight seal. Simmer slowly for an hour then add the reserved carrots and leeks. Again, cover the casserole with foil and the casserole lid. Continue simmering for 50 minutes.

Add the cabbage and simmer uncovered for 5 to 8 minutes, or until the cabbage bends but is not soft. Drain the cabbage and make a bed of the drained cabbage on a large platter. Place the chicken on top of the cabbage and arrange the carrots and leeks around the cabbage bed. Pour a small amount of the casserole juices over the top of the chicken and vegetables. Serve the remaining juices in a sauceboat at the table.

Rhea Steak

CHAYA DE AVESTRUZ

Rhea are the Argentine cousins of African ostriches. Ostrich meat is a new beef substitute you will find in many North American markets. It is interchangeable with rhea in cooking.

In Argentina, most rhea meat ends up as *charqui*—or jerky. This recipe calls for fresh rhea steaks cut from the thigh. Ostrich meat may be substituted and is available at many poultry retailers or wholesalers.

Directions

Prepare a marinade with vinegar, mashed garlic, peppers, Tabasco sauce, marjoram, nutmeg, cloves, ginger and bay leaf. Wash the steaks in salted water and then marinate them in the refrigerator for at least 2 hours, turning the steaks every 20 minutes.

Preheat the oven to 250°F. Dry the steaks and wrap them with a strip of pancetta or bacon fastened with a tooth-pick. Sprinkle the steaks with pepper. Heat a well-sea-soned cast-iron skillet and sprinkle coarse salt on the bottom. When the salt begins to smoke, add the steaks and sear for 1 minute on each side. Cover the steaks loosely with a piece of foil and place the skillet in the oven. Cook for 10 to 15 minutes. Serve with a simple wine sauce or a mushroom sauce (page 194). Crusty bread, a salad and a medium-bodied red wine round out the meal.

INGREDIENTS

1 cup red wine vinegar
4 garlic cloves, mashed
1 fresh jalapeño pepper, seeded and chopped
2 bell peppers, seeded and chopped
Dash of Tabasco or pepper sauce
1 teaspoon crushed dried marjoram
1 teaspoon freshly grated nutmeg
3 cloves
1 tablespoon grated fresh ginger
1 bay leaf
3 pounds rhea leg meat (or ostrich), cut into 6 steaks
6 strips pancetta or blanched bacon
Freshly ground pepper
Coarse kosher or sea salt

Serves 6

Lamb and Vegetable Casserole

CAZUELA DE CORDERO

Traditionally, this dish calls for goat's milk, but because so little is used, cow's milk is acceptable.

INGREDIENTS

2 tablespoons vegetable oil
2 teaspoons sweet paprika
3 lamb shanks, sawed in half lengthwise
1 large onion, chopped
2 large carrots, sliced
1 celery heart, minced
2 garlic cloves, minced
½ teaspoon ground cumin seeds
1 teaspoon crushed dried oregano
1 cup lamb or beef stock
2½ quarts boiling water
6 1½-inch cubes winter squash
6 small potatoes, peeled
3 tablespoons long-grain rice
1 tablespoon salt
½ teaspoon freshly ground pepper
1 cup shelled green peas, fresh or frozen
2 cups fresh green beans, trimmed and cut into 2-inch lengths
3 ears corn, cut in half
1 tablespoon butter
1 egg yolk
4 tablespoons milk
1 tablespoon minced parsley

Serves 6

Directions

In a heavy flameproof casserole, heat the oil on high and then turn the heat down to medium just before it starts to smoke. Stir in the paprika and add the lamb. Brown it well on all sides and remove it from the casserole. Sauté the onions, carrots, celery, garlic, cumin seeds and oregano in the casserole for about 5 minutes or until the onion is soft. Return the lamb to the casserole, add the beef stock and continue cooking for 4 minutes. Pour in the boiling water and bring the stew to a boil. Cover the casserole and turn the heat to low. Simmer for 1 hour then add squash, potatoes and rice. Season to taste. Continue simmering, covered, for 23 minutes. Add the peas, beans and corn, and continue simmering, covered, for another 8 minutes.

When the stew is done, remove it from the heat and beat in the butter. Beat the egg yolk with milk and stir the mixture into the stew. Sprinkle the stew with parsley and serve it directly from the casserole, making sure that each portion includes a piece of lamb, potato and squash.

Roasted Lamb Shoulder

CORDERO ASADO

Lamb shoulder has more fat than the leg. Extra juiciness and flavor is a payoff. That, plus a lower per pound cost, makes shoulder the favorite with locals and travelers on a budget.

Directions
Preheat the oven to 325°F. Place the lamb on a rack in a roasting pan. Top the lamb with the butter and bay leaf. Roast it in the oven and turn it when it's brown on 1 side. Add 1 cup wine and baste the lamb with the pan drippings. Continue to roast, uncovered, for about 2 hours. Remove the lamb to a serving platter and keep warm.

Just before serving, remove as much fat as possible from the meat juices and deglaze the roasting pan with a ½ cup wine. Sauté pimientos, garlic and parsley in the oil and add to the sauce. Heat the sauce until it starts to boil. Cook the sauce for 2 to 3 minutes while continuing to stir. Remove the sauce from the heat and season to taste. Slice the lamb crosswise about ¼ inch thick and keep it on a warm serving platter. Spoon the sauce over the lamb and serve.

INGREDIENTS

3½-pound shoulder or leg
   of lamb
1 tablespoon butter
1 bay leaf
1½ cups white wine
2 fresh pimientos, chopped
4 garlic cloves, minced
1 tablespoon minced parsley
2 tablespoons olive oil
   Salt and freshly ground
   pepper to taste

Serves 6

Marinated Roast Lamb

CORDERO AL HORNO

To approximate the roast lamb served in the Patagonian Atlantic, buy the youngest, smallest lamb available. If possible, cook it in an earthenware casserole. A reminder: Argentines like their lamb well done.

INGREDIENTS

2 tablespoons olive oil

1 teaspoon coarse kosher or sea salt

½ teaspoon freshly ground pepper

2 teaspoons chopped fresh rosemary or oregano leaves

1 side spring lamb

6 potatoes, peeled and quartered lengthwise

3 sweet peppers, halved lengthwise and seeded

3 large onions, halved

3 large sweet potatoes, peeled and halved lengthwise

6 2-inch chunks fresh or dried squash (recipe page 230)

½ cup beef stock

Salt and pepper to taste

2 tablespoons lard, melted

¾ cup red wine

½ cup chilled and diced butter

Serves 6

Directions

Make a marinade combining the olive oil, coarse salt, pepper and rosemary. Rub the lamb all over with the marinade. Let the lamb stand in the marinade for 6 hours in the refrigerator.

Preheat the oven to 350°F. Wipe the marinade from roast and place it on a rack in a roasting pan. In the bottom of the roasting pan, place the potatoes, peppers, onions, sweet potatoes, squash and stock. Season with salt and pepper. Baste the lamb and vegetables with melted lard. Continue to baste with the pan drippings every 20 minutes. Turn the vegetables regularly so they are uniformly browned. Roast, uncovered, until the lamb is well done or when the meat begins separating from the bone, about 2½ hours.

Remove the vegetables to a heated serving platter when they are done and keep them warm. When the lamb is done, remove it to a serving platter and let it rest for 15 minutes.

Remove as much fat as possible from the roasting pan and deglaze the pan with wine over a high heat. When the wine is reduced by half, remove the pan from the heat and beat the butter into the sauce all at once. Pour a little of the sauce over the lamb and serve the remaining sauce at the table in a sauceboat.

Lamb Stew

ESTOFADO DE CORDERO

This Spanish-style lamb stew has a tantalizing aroma as it simmers over low heat for the several hours it takes to cook. Redolent with garlic that complements older lamb beautifully, the stew is spiked with red wine vinegar adding an intriguing piquancy.

Directions

Heat the oil in a deep, flameproof casserole. Add the meat cubes and brown them well on all sides. Add the onion and sauté it until golden. Stir in the garlic cloves, bay leaf, paprika, vinegar, salt and pepper. Cover and simmer over a low flame for about 2 hours, or until the meat is tender. Add a little water or lamb stock during cooking if necessary. Serve with a green vegetable and a good Zinfandel.

INGREDIENTS

3 tablespoons olive oil

3 pounds boneless lamb, cut in 2-inch cubes

1 large onion, chopped

1 whole garlic head, separated but unpeeled

1 bay leaf

1 heaping tablespoon sweet paprika

½ cup red wine vinegar
Coarse kosher or sea salt to taste
Freshly ground pepper to taste

Serves 6

Lamb with Rice

CARBONADA CRIOLLA DE CORDERO

While classified as a *carbonada* in Argentina, this dish is more like an Italian risotto.

Directions

In a large casserole, sauté the lamb cubes and onion in oil over medium heat. Add parsley, celery, tomato sauce and 1 cup of the stock. Stir to blend. Add potatoes, rice, salt and pepper. Stir in more stock a little at a time and continue stirring while the rice absorbs the liquid. Continue adding stock while stirring constantly. When the rice has absorbed all the stock and is soft and creamy on the outside, remove it from the heat and serve it in individual rimmed soup bowls. Shave Parmesan cheese on top of the dishes before serving.

INGREDIENTS

1 cup cubed lamb
1 large onion, chopped
¼ cup olive oil
¼ cup minced parsley
½ cup chopped celery
1 cup fresh or canned
    tomato sauce
3 cups lamb or beef stock
1 cup peeled and cubed
    white potatoes
1 cup short-grain rice
    Salt and pepper
    Parmesan cheese, shaved

Serves 4

Ragout of Liver and Lights

CHANFAINA

This dish is included to demonstrate a bit of culinary history. In the early days of Argentina, hardy pioneers wasted nothing. They even came to develop a taste for some of the more unlikely morsels such as lights.

Lights are the lungs of an animal—in this case those of a lamb. The French and Argentines adore them. Most Americans, however, would be sure they were being fed a chopped rubber sponge. And large quantities of fresh, coagulated lamb's blood are not easy to come by—even in today's Argentina. At any rate, some bold soul may want to give it a try.

Directions

Heat the oil over low heat in a flameproof casserole. Add the onion, parsley, garlic and tomato. Cook slowly until soft and well blended. Season with marjoram, salt, pepper and chili pepper. Add the blood, liver, lights, broth, wine, vinegar and flour paste. Bring to a slow boil over medium heat while stirring continuously. Lower the heat, cover and simmer for 15 minutes. Serve if you dare!

INGREDIENTS

4   tablespoons olive oil
1   onion, minced
2   sprigs parsley
2   garlic cloves, minced
1   large tomato, chopped
½   teaspoon marjoram
    Salt and pepper to taste
2   teaspoons crushed dried
    chili pepper
4   cups diced coagulated
    lamb's blood, (or 4 blood
    sausages such as biroldo)
1   lamb's liver, cleaned and
    chopped
1   pair lamb's lights, cleaned
    and chopped
½   cup beef broth
½   cup white wine
2   tablespoons red wine
    vinegar
1   tablespoon flour, dissolved
    in a little cold water

Serves 4 bold souls

Dried Squash

CHICHOCA DE ZAPALLO

Dried squash extends meat stews, *carbonadas* and *locros*. It is especially important in the cold winters of southern Argentina when there is a scarcity of fresh vegetables. The people in this area prepare *chichoca* well ahead in large quantities and freeze it after drying. Some of the locals still dry squash in the sun, but it's easier and more sanitary to dry it in an oven or food dryer.

INGREDIENTS

1 Hubbard squash, halved, skinned, seeded and membranes removed

1 cup rock salt per squash

Yield depends on the number and size of squash

Directions
Preheat the oven to 200°F. Place the squash halves on a cookie sheet and dry in the oven for about 30 minutes. With a sharp knife, cut narrow spiral strips, about ¼ inch thick around each squash half. Sprinkle the squash generously with rock salt. Return it to the oven and continue drying for about an hour. When the squash is thoroughly dry, cool it and pack it in airtight containers. Freeze it until ready to use. Add to *locros* and simmer along with stews, *carbonadas* and *pucheros*.

Baked Chickpeas
GARBANZOS AL HORNO

Here is Argentina's answer to Boston Baked Beans.

Directions

Rinse the chickpeas and soak them overnight in cold water. Drain the chickpeas and place them in a large, flameproof casserole. Add 6 cups water, onion, bay leaf, parsley, thyme, cloves, garlic and peppercorns. Bring the mixture to a boil, cover it and simmer it slowly for 2 hours. Add salt and salt pork and continue simmering for 1 hour more, or until the beans are tender and the liquid is almost absorbed.

Preheat the oven to 350°F. Stir the mustard and corn syrup into the bean mixture. Pour the mixture into a buttered baking dish. Bake for 45 minutes, or until the top is browned.

INGREDIENTS

2 cups dried garbanzo beans (chickpeas)
6 cups water
1 medium onion, chopped
1 large bay leaf
¼ cup minced parsley
½ teaspoon dried thyme
2 whole cloves
4 garlic cloves, crushed
8 peppercorns, crushed
½ teaspoon salt
1 pound salt pork, cut into small pieces
1 tablespoon dry mustard
¼ cup dark corn syrup

Serves 6

Sherry Trifle

SOPA INGLESA

Many English settled in Argentina when they came to build the railroads. They yearned for English food, not the barbaric fare eaten by their Argentine hosts. Somehow, they managed to keep a stiff upper lip until the next ship came in with tinned pound cake and a dusty bottle of Jerez sherry.

This is an Argentine interpretation of an English Trifle. If you don't have sweet sherry on hand, use brandy or rum.

INGREDIENTS

1 shortcake or pound cake
½ cup Oloroso sherry (or any sweet sherry)
1 recipe dulce de leche (page 146)
1 teaspoon vanilla
2 teaspoons sugar
½ pint heavy cream

Serves 6

Directions

Cover the bottom of a deep transparent serving bowl with a layer of shortcake or pound cake, about ¾ inches thick. Pour ¼ cup sherry over the cake. Spread a layer of *dulce de leche* on top, about ¼ inch thick. Add another layer of cake and sprinkle it with the remaining ¼ cup sherry. Add vanilla and sugar to the cream and whip it until it holds a peak. Spread a thick layer of whipped cream over the cake. When served, sprinkle the top with additional sherry.

CHAPTER 8

Salta:

The Last Outpost
of the Great Northwest

Salta

Salta, Jujuy, Tucumán, and Catamarca comprise the provinces of Argentina's Northwest Territories. It is a multifaceted land with much to see and do. Inhabited for more than 10,000 years, the area is filled with traces of past cultures. It is the center of the country's colonial period and pre-Columbian cultures, and there are many archeological parks featuring pre-Hispanic relics here. Furthermore, it is home to most of the indigenous populations living in Argentina today. And only here can you see them practice the old ways in cooking, crafts and music.

Topographically, this territory can be divided into three regions, each quite different from the others. The high-and-dry mountains of the Andes foothills are the ultimate in "painted desert" landscapes. No visitor ever forgets the multicolored canyons of El Toro and Cafayate. Vermilion and pink strata sweep across steep cliffs while the purple shadows of deep canyons and the ochre of wide valley floors fulfill painterly allusions.

Contrast this with El Parque Nacional El Rey in Tucumán province. Here, within a humid strip of subtropical forest, you will come upon an almost impenetrable mountain jungle and mist-shrouded green hills where toucans nest in vine-covered trees. The intense greenery, abundant bird life and snow-capped peaks surrounding this remote destination startle visitors traveling from drier climes. It all seems so unlikely.

And then there are the mostly frigid and barren plateaus of the Puna de Atacama with its scenic lakes and volcanoes. A hop, skip and a jump and you'll cross the borders into Chile on the west and Bolivia on the north.

But most of all, there's Salta, the provincial capital and the most intact colonial city in Argentina.

Established in 1582, Salta sits in the lovely Lerma Valley enclosed by shadowy foothills that are, in turn, surrounded by massive, fir-covered peaks. The valley's perpetual spring makes it one of the most delightful places in all of South America.

Any Saturday or Sunday will find the few tourists at the Indian market in town and the locals at a large cultivated park at the edge of a mountain that marks the

Salta is Argentina's most intact colonial city.

town's eastern limit. The Parque San Martín, with its immense man-made lake, is a magnet for the town's children who compete each weekend in miniature boat races.

Broad avenues lined with the Spanish-styled villas of the affluent lead uphill to the park. The succession of white stucco walls surrounded with lush plantings and capped by undulating red tile roofs create a cohesive whole interspersed with individual flourishes here and there. A central parkway here, dividing the street into east-west lanes, is punctuated with palo borracho trees. Their outsized trunks resemble huge distended barrels that are just about ready to pop. Off the avenues, smaller streets with smaller villas curl around and up the hills and disappear into the horizon.

Near the park and on a corner opposite my favorite *criollo* restaurant/bar in Salta—Mama Gaucha—is a monkey-puzzle tree. Next to the palo borracho, the monkey-puzzle tree is perhaps the strangest tree I have encountered in my travels. It's a plant form gone mad, branches turning in upon themselves in crazy convoluted patterns. Still, it's part of the charm of this most charming town.

Salta is one of the few places in Argentina where you can experience native culture and cuisine. Local dishes provide a taste adventure quite apart from the Italo-Spanish fare usually encountered in other provinces. In Salta you find the spicy, exotic foods of indigenous peoples. Tender maize and wheat form the basis for this cuisine with its vast spectrum of different *locros, humitas* and *pucheros*. Mama Gaucha Restaurant is my favorite purveyor of the local cuisine. The owner, Señora Maria Ercilia Praguglia, serves all the *criollo* dishes outside under a blue awning in a quiet residential neighborhood. Her restaurant is where I first experienced tripe—*and liked it!* That day's version of her *Locros de Trigo*, prepared by Chef Carmen Evelia Lopez, was wheat based with chunks of flavorful beef, perfectly ripened tomatoes, nutty garbanzos and chewy but tasty tripe. The flavor of this concoction was incredibly rich and beautifully seasoned. And I must say the tripe was a pleasant experience.

Humitas are another wonderful taste treat that must be sampled. There are as many versions of them as there are of empanadas—maybe more. And soups, which are sometimes hard to distinguish from stews, *locros* and *pucheros*, range from a lovely, creamed winter squash base to hearty beef with red wine, onions and lots of garlic. Especially delicious is a stew made of chicken, vegetables and short ribs cooked until the meat falls from the bones.

Along with the excellent white wines produced in the province are other local alcoholic specialties such as *chicha*. In pre-Columbian times *chicha* was made by chewing maize and then spitting it into an earthenware container—much like *kava* is still made in the South Pacific. Today, *chicha* is made from a more sanitary fermented maize flour. *Aloja* (fermented carob pods) is another alcoholic potion that is enjoyed by some of the native population. But both *chicha* and *aloja* are probably best avoided if you don't want to have a killer hangover.

Egg and Spinach Pastry

TORTA PASCUALINA

This dish originated in the Middle East and came to Argentina with Spanish immigrants. You can substitute filo pastry sheets for the pastry recipe that follows. They are available in the frozen food sections of most supermarkets. If using filo, you must brush melted butter on each sheet.

PASTRY

2   cups sifted flour
3   egg yolks
⅓   cup olive oil
½   cup lukewarm water

Pastry Directions

Place the flour on a pastry board, making a well at its center. Place the egg yolks and 3 tablespoons of the olive oil in the well. Gradually work in the flour, adding enough lukewarm water to make a stiff dough. Knead the dough until it is smooth and elastic. Cover with a cloth and set aside for 10 minutes. Roll out the dough as thin as possible on a lightly floured board. Brush the dough with a little of the oil. Cut the dough into 4 pieces, each large enough to fit an 8- by 15-inch baking dish. Grease the dish and place 2 layers of dough on the bottom.

FILLING

2   cups cooked, drained
    spinach, squeezed dry
¾   teaspoon freshly ground
    pepper
½   teaspoon freshly ground
    nutmeg
½   cup grated Parmesan
    cheese
9   eggs
2   teaspoons salt
1   egg, beaten
2   tablespoons water

Serves 8 as an appetizer

Filling Directions

Preheat the oven to 375°F. Combine the spinach, pepper, nutmeg and Parmesan cheese. Mix well and place evenly over the dough in the baking dish. Make 8 evenly spaced depressions on the spinach mixture, using the back of a large soupspoon. Break an egg into each depression and sprinkle it with salt. Cover with the remaining 2 layers of dough, sealing the edges carefully. To seal the pastry compartments, run a pastry wheel over the dough dividing it into 8 equal portions, each containing an egg. Make an egg wash by combining 1 egg, beaten with water. Brush the wash on top of the pastry. Bake the *torta* for 30 minutes or until the top is lightly browned. Serve hot or cold.

Winter Squash Soup

Squash and pumpkin soups are now all the rage in trendy restaurants throughout the United States. But they have long been commonplace in Argentina where they have a reputation for curing many ills. Consider this native recipe merely a beginning.

Directions

Melt the butter in large saucepan. Add the onion, tomato, garlic and peppers. Cook until the onion is softened and the mixture is thick and well blended. Add the squash, stock and milk, season to taste with salt and pepper and stir in the sugar. Simmer, covered, for 20 minutes, or until the squash has broken down into a mush and thickens the soup. Stir Parmesan cheese into the beaten egg yolks and stir this mixture into the hot soup. Continue stirring on low heat for about 1 minute. Pour the soup into a tureen and top it with croutons.

INGREDIENTS

4 tablespoons butter
1 medium onion, chopped
1 medium tomato, peeled, seeded and chopped
2 garlic cloves, minced
1 green pepper, seeded and chopped
1 fresh hot chili pepper, seeded and chopped
1½ pounds winter squash (preferably calabaza or Hubbard), peeled and cut into ½-inch cubes
3 cups beef stock
3 cups milk
   Salt and pepper to taste
½ teaspoon sugar
1½ tablespoons Parmesan cheese
2 egg yolks, beaten
   Croutons

Serves 8

Cold Pumpkin Soup

SOPA FRÍA DE ZAPALLO

In hot weather, this lavish cold pumpkin soup fills the void without making you lose your cool. Acorn squash may be substituted for pumpkin meat.

Directions

Place the pumpkin pieces in a large saucepan. Add stock, onion, green onions and tomatoes. Simmer on a low setting until the pumpkin is tender. Remove the soup from the heat and cool. When cool, purée the soup in a blender or food mill. Add light cream and season to taste with salt and pepper. Pour into individual, pre-chilled soup dishes and refrigerate for at least 3 hours. Just before serving, spoon a dollop of whipped cream on top of each portion. Dust the cream with paprika and serve.

INGREDIENTS

2½-pounds pumpkin meat, cut in pieces

5   cups chicken stock

1   medium onion, chopped

6   green onions, chopped

4   tomatoes, peeled, seeded and chopped

1½ cups light cream
     Salt and freshly ground pepper to taste

⅔ cup whipped cream

1   tablespoon sweet paprika

Serves 6

Chicken Soup, Creole Style

SOPA CRIOLLA DE POLLO

Probably every culture has a version of chicken soup. And probably this soup is equated with comfort, mother love, and well-being wherever it is eaten. This recipe came originally from mountain dwellers outside Salta. I have adapted it to suit North American ingredients.

Directions

In a soup pot, bring the chicken broth to a boil. Add the hen, onions, carrots, garlic, green pepper and tomatoes. Reduce the heat to low and add wine. Simmer, partially covered, for 1 hour and 15 minutes. Mix in the rice, potato, salt and pepper. Simmer for another 24 minutes. Add the cabbage and simmer for 6 minutes. Add the peas and continue simmering for 5 more minutes. Stir in the lemon juice off the heat and ladle into a soup tureen or individual soup bowls. Top with the pimiento strips and parsley.

INGREDIENTS

4   cups homemade chicken
     broth
4-pound stewing hen, cut in
     serving pieces
½   cup chopped onions
½   cup diced carrots
4   garlic cloves, minced
2   tablespoons seeded and
     diced green bell pepper
½   cup peeled, seeded,
     chopped tomatoes
1   cup dry white wine
½   cup raw rice
½   cup diced potato
     Sea salt to taste
½   teaspoon white pepper
½   cup shredded cabbage
½   cup fresh or frozen peas
     Juice of 1 lemon
     Pimiento strips, fresh or bot-
     tled
2   tablespoons minced
     parsley

     Serves 6 to 8

Cheese Filled Humitas

HUMITAS EN CHALA CON QUESO

Humitas were originally an aboriginal concoction. The Argentine versions of today are far removed from the originals. *Humitas* are similar to tamales. They are usually filled with cheese, meat or meat mixtures. They are either baked or steamed in banana leaves or corn husks.

Cheese-filled *humitas* make a good vegetable course or may be served as an accompaniment to a roast or steak.

INGREDIENTS

12 ears fresh corn

Husks from corn, rinsed

Salt and sugar to taste

Small onion, minced

4 tablespoons olive oil

1 tomato, skinned, seeded and chopped

½ cup minced fresh basil leaves

½ pound teleme cheese, sliced about ⅛ inch thick

Serves 6

Directions

Remove the husks from the corn and save the tenderest. Scrape the corn from the cobs with a sharp knife and season it with salt and sugar. Sauté the onion in oil until it's golden. Add tomato and mix well. When the mixture is smooth, add the corn and basil. Simmer for 3 minutes, stirring constantly. Remove the mixture from the heat and cool.

Assembly Directions

Using 2 husks per *humita*, overlap husks and place 2 to 3 tablespoons of corn paste and 1 cheese slice in each packet. Fold the husks to make a 5- by 1½-inch package and tie the ends with a strip of cornhusk. Place a thick layer of scraped corncobs in the bottom of a deep flameproof casserole. Add salted boiling water to almost cover. Arrange the *humitas* in a layer on cobs and cover with a thick layer of husks. Turn the heat on high, cover the casserole and steam the *humitas* for 20 minutes. Remove the packages from the pot and place them on a heated platter. Serve as you would tamales.

Pumpkin Humitas

HUMITAS MENDOCINAS

This *humita* is served in a pumpkin or large
winter squash. The squash or pumpkin meat is
scooped out and served along with the *humita*
filling.

Directions

Sauté the garlic and onion in lard until tender. Add green
peppers and cook 2 minutes more. Add 1 teaspoon salt,
bay leaf, black pepper, cinnamon, paprika and 1 cup
parsley. Mix well and cook 1 minute. Add the tomatoes
and simmer 10 minutes, covered. Add the corn and ½ cup
milk. Stir frequently while cooking on low heat for 15
minutes, or until the corn is tender.

Preheat the oven to 300°F. Wash the pumpkin or squash
and cut off the top, removing the seeds and membranes.
Pour 2 cups milk, 2 tablespoons butter, the sugar and 1
teaspoon salt into the shell and bake for 1½ hours, or until
the pumpkin meat is tender. Remove the shell from the
oven and raise the heat to 475°F. Pour off the milk and
save it for the cat.

Fill the shell with the *humita* mixture. Sprinkle the top with
breadcrumbs, dot with 1 tablespoon butter and sprinkle
the remaining 1 teaspoon parsley on top. Return the filled
shell to the oven and bake it for 15 minutes or until the
breadcrumbs are golden brown. Serve the humita filling
from the shell at the table, making sure that a scooped out
portion of the pumpkin or squash meat is served with the
humita filling.

INGREDIENTS

3   garlic cloves, minced
1   large yellow onion,
    minced
3   tablespoons lard
2   green bell peppers,
    seeded and chopped
2   teaspoons salt
1   bay leaf
½   teaspoon freshly ground
    pepper
½   teaspoon ground
    cinnamon
2   teaspoons sweet paprika
1   cup plus 1 teaspoon
    minced parsley
2   ripe tomatoes, peeled and
    chopped
12 ears fresh sweet corn, cut
    from cob (or 4 cups frozen
    corn, thoroughly defrosted
    and drained)
2½ cups milk
1   basketball-sized pumpkin
    or winter squash
3   tablespoons butter
1   tablespoon sugar
1   cup fine breadcrumbs

Serves 8

Corn Mousse

BUDÍN DE MAÍZ

Corn is the grain of life in the northwest provinces. As a mousse, corn achieves an exalted place in the *criollo* repertoire.

Directions

Preheat the oven to 350°F. Grate the corn off the cob into a bowl. Add the *Salsa Inglesa*, butter, salt, pepper, sugar and nutmeg. Add the eggs and beat well. Bake in a greased mold inside a pan of warm water, or bain-marie, until set—25 to 30 minutes.

INGREDIENTS

6   ears corn
1   cup Salsa Inglesa
    (page 57)
1   tablespoon butter
    Salt and pepper to taste
1   teaspoon sugar
1   teaspoon freshly grated
    nutmeg
2   eggs, lightly beaten

Serves 4

Corn Bread Pudding

PAN DE MAIZ

Is this a pudding or a bread? In Argentina the difference is irrelevant. But almost everyone who has tasted the dish asks for the recipe.

Directions

Preheat the oven to 350°F. Heat the olive oil in a saucepan. Add the onions and sauté 5 minutes, stirring frequently. Add the tomatoes and sauté 10 minutes more while stirring. Add the broth, salt and chili pepper. Cook over medium heat for 10 minutes. Remove from the heat and set aside.

Sift the cornmeal and baking powder together. Add cottage cheese and butter and mix well. Add milk, beating thoroughly, and combine with the tomato mixture. Pour the mixture into a buttered 8-inch square pan. Bake for 1 hour, or until lightly set. Turn out the pudding onto a platter and cut into 1-inch slices or rectangles. Serve as a side dish.

INGREDIENTS

3   tablespoons olive oil

3   onions, chopped

3   tomatoes, chopped

¾   cup beef or chicken broth

1   teaspoon salt

½   teaspoon crushed dried
    chili pepper

2   cups sifted yellow
    cornmeal

1   teaspoon baking powder

½   pound cottage cheese

3   tablespoons butter

1½ cups milk

Serves 6 to 8

Roasted Chicken with Corn

POLLO DE CHOCLO

Roast a chicken according to the recipe for squab on page 41. Reserve the pan drippings, as they will be used to flavor the sauce for this dish.

Directions

In a flameproof casserole, sauté the onion in oil until it's soft. Add the tomatoes and continue to cook over medium heat for 5 minutes. Add the jalapeño pepper, bay leaf, marjoram, sage, garlic, olives and corn, mixing well. Continue cooking for 5 minutes more. Remove the mixture from the heat and set aside.

Deglaze the roasting pan from the chicken with beer. Cook over high heat for 3 minutes and then add this sauce to the casserole. Carve the chicken into serving pieces and place them in the casserole. Baste the chicken with the sauce, then cover and simmer over low heat for 7 minutes. Remove the chicken to a warm serving dish, ladle some of the sauce over it and sprinkle the top with parsley.

INGREDIENTS

1   roasted chicken
    (page 41)
1   onion, chopped
2   tablespoons olive oil
2   tomatoes, chopped
1   fresh jalapeño pepper,
    seeded and minced
1   bay leaf
1   sprig fresh marjoram,
    chopped
    Pinch powdered sage
2   garlic cloves, minced
1   cup pitted green olives
6   pimiento-stuffed green
    olives
1   cup fresh corn kernels,
    grated from the cob
1   cup dark beer
½   cup minced parsley

Serves 4

Beef and Corn Custard Salta Style

PASTEL DE CHOCLO DE SALTA

Pastels are a kind of pie. Instead of pastry, the filling is sometimes encased in potatoes, rice, corn or cornmeal. In this recipe, the *pastel* is treated as a pudding without any outer "crust."

Directions

Soak the raisins in hot water for 10 minutes and drain.

Preheat the oven to 350°F. Heat the oil in a skillet and sauté the onion slices and green peppers for 5 minutes. Add the meat and brown. Sprinkle the mixture with flour, 2 teaspoons salt and the chili peppers. Stir in the tomatoes and broth. Cook over a low heat for 5 minutes, stirring frequently. Remove the mixture from the heat and add olives, cumin and drained raisins. Mix well and spoon the mixture into a 10-inch buttered pie pan.

Melt the butter in a skillet and sauté the chopped onions for 5 minutes. Mix in the corn and remaining 1 teaspoon salt. Cook over moderate heat for 5 minutes. Beat the egg yolks and cream together and add to the corn mixture. Spread the corn mixture over the meat mixture and bake for 20 minutes, or until the custard is firm.

INGREDIENTS

½ cup seedless raisins

3 tablespoons olive oil

1 cup thinly sliced onions

1 cup thinly sliced green bell peppers

1 pound top sirloin of beef, cut into ½-inch dice

1 tablespoon flour

3 teaspoons salt

½ teaspoon crushed dried chili peppers

1 cup chopped tomatoes

½ cup beef broth

¾ cup pimiento-stuffed green olives

½ teaspoon ground cumin

2 tablespoons butter

½ cup chopped onions

2 cups fresh corn kernels, cut from cob

2 egg yolks

½ cup heavy cream

Serves 4 to 6

Short Rib Casserole

PUCHERO COSTILLADRO DE SALTA

Pucheros are tasty stews of whatever can be found in the kitchen—assorted meats, vegetables and seasonings. In Salta, corn is always available and always part of a *puchero*.

INGREDIENTS

1   cup dried or 2 cups
    canned garbanzo beans
    (chickpeas), drained
4   quarts water
4   pounds beef short ribs
½   pound lean salt pork,
    diced into ½-inch pieces
3½-pound chicken, cut in
    serving-sized pieces
2   dried whole chili pods
6   carrots, peeled
6   small whole onions
6   garlic cloves, minced
1   small winter squash,
    peeled and sliced
3   sweet potatoes or yams,
    peeled and halved
6   tomatoes
1   green bell pepper, seeded
    and chopped
6   potatoes, peeled
6   leeks, cleaned and cut into
    3-inch lengths
2   tablespoons chopped
    parsley
4   chorizo sausages or a
    variety of spicy smoked
    sausages
1   cabbage, cut lengthwise
    into 8 wedges

Serves 6 to 8

Directions

If dried garbanzos are used, soak them overnight in water to cover. Drain the garbanzos before using. To cook the *puchero*, pour the water in large pot and add soaked and drained garbanzos. (If using canned garbanzos, add them to the pot when the vegetable are added.) Bring the water to a boil. Add beef, salt pork, chicken and chili pods. Cover and simmer over low heat for 2 hours.

Add beef and carrots and simmer for 30 minutes. Add sausages, onions, garlic, squash, sweet potatoes, tomatoes, green pepper, potatoes, leeks and parsley. Simmer for 25 minutes or until the potatoes are almost tender. Add cabbage and simmer for 5 minutes more. Correct seasoning and remove the meat and vegetables to a heated platter. Serve cooking broth separately in bowls.

Wheat Locro

Locros are basic to the way of life in northwest Argentina. The closest cousin to *locro* is a North African couscous—a clue to its origin. Coming to Argentina by way of immigrants from Spain, a *locro* is one of those flexible dishes of the provinces that can be made with almost any meat, depending upon what's available in the kitchen. Sometimes it appears as a thick gruel, sometimes it's a soupy stew. Whatever the form, *locro* is based on meat and vegetables thickened with corn, beans, hominy or wheat and seasoned with a combination of herbs and spices. *Mondongo* or *tripa gorda*—tripe or a near relative—is a standard ingredient along with various cuts of beef, salt pork, marrowbones and a tangy sauce.

Mama Gaucha in Salta is known for its *criolla* dishes—especially its *locros* and *humitas.* I had my first taste of *locro* at this restaurant. All the different ingredients seemed to stand out in relief against the creamy backdrop of wheat berries and yet, paradoxically, they blend into a sublime melange of flavors.

The following is my interpretation of Mama Gaucha's recipe. It calls for *chichoca de zappalo* (dried squash) but any fresh winter squash may be substituted. Increase the quantity of fresh squash to 1 cup.

INGREDIENTS

2 pounds tripe, trimmed of
   fat
5 peppercorns
   Salt to taste
1 bay leaf
2 cups whole wheat berries,
   soaked overnight in water
2- pound veal knuckle bone,
   broken in pieces
2 medium onions, chopped
2 large tomatoes, cut in small
   wedges
2 red bell peppers, seeded
   and chopped
2 pounds salt pork, cut in
   ½-inch cubes
1 pound lean tender beef,
   cut into finger-sized pieces
1 sprig parsley
   Juice of 1 lemon
1 cup potatoes, cut in 1-inch
   cubes
½ cup cubed chichoca de
   zappalo (page 230)
½ cup diced sweet potatoes
3 ears corn, cut in 1-Inch
   rounds
1 scallion, cut in fine strips
¾ pound black-eye peas,
   cooked
   Freshly ground pepper to
   taste
   Locro sauce (recipe
   follows)

Directions

Rinse the tripe, place it in a deep pot and cover with water. Bring it to a boil then remove the tripe and drain immediately. When cool enough to handle, cut the tripe into 1½-inch squares. Return the tripe to the pot, add 4 cups of water or enough to cover the tripe. Add peppercorns, salt and bay leaf. Bring the mixture to a boil, cover and turn the heat to low. Simmer for about 4 hours adding water if necessary. Set aside until you are ready to add the tripe to the *locro*.

Rinse out the pot, add the wheat berries, cover with water and boil on high heat until the berries are swollen. Add the knucklebone, onions, tomatoes, bell peppers, salt pork, cooked drained tripe, beef, sprig of parsley and lemon juice. Simmer until the meat is tender and the liquid has become creamy from the breaking up of the wheat berries—about 2 hours. Add potatoes, squash, sweet potatoes and corn, and cook for 30 minutes more. Mix in the scallions and black-eye peas and heat through. Season with pepper. Serve hot in a soup tureen with *locro* sauce on the side.

Locro Sauce Directions

Sauté the onions and scallion in lard over medium heat. When the onions are soft, add garlic and continue sautéing until golden. Add chili pepper, tomato paste and water. Continuing cooking until the mixture thickens. Add parsley, salt, pepper, oregano, cumin, coriander and paprika. Mix well and continue cooking for 3 minutes. Pour the sauce into a sauceboat. Serve with the *locro* at the table.

LOCRO SAUCE

2   onions, chopped
1   scallion, chopped
½   cup lard
3   garlic cloves, minced
1   dried chili pepper, crushed
1   tablespoon tomato paste
2   tablespoons water
1   teaspoon minced parsley
1   teaspoon salt
    Freshly ground pepper
    to taste
1   teaspoon dry oregano
1   teaspoon crushed cumin
    seeds
1   teaspoon crushed
    coriander seeds
1   heaping tablespoon sweet
    paprika

Serves 4 to 6

Corn Locro

LOCRO DE CHOCLO

Here is a relatively quick *locro* made without tripe. Fresh corn kernels are used instead of wheat. Serve it with the *locro* sauce on page 251.

Directions

Sauté the garlic in olive oil until brown, discarding the garlic. Add the onion to the oil and sauté until it is soft. Add the pork tenderloin and continue to sauté until it is lightly browned. Cut the pepper into strips and add them along with the tomatoes, salt, pepper, paprika and corn. Add water to barely cover and bring the mixture to a boil. Add squash and simmer gently for 30 minutes or until the meat and squash are tender. Ladle into individual rimmed soup dishes and serve with toasted French bread.

INGREDIENTS

3   garlic cloves, peeled

½   cup olive oil

1   small onion, chopped

1   pork tenderloin, cut into
    finger-sized pieces

1   green bell pepper,
    charred, skinned, seeded
    and veins removed

2   tomatoes, peeled and
    chopped
    Salt and freshly ground
    pepper to taste

2   teaspoons sweet paprika

6   ears fresh corn, cut from
    cob

6   cubes winter squash, about
    1½ inches square

Serves 6

Stuffed Peppers

AJIES RELLENOS

Ancho chilies have just a touch of heat—perfect for the sausage-based stuffing in this dish. For those who prefer a milder pepper, green bell peppers may be substituted.

INGREDIENTS

4 large fresh ancho chilies
1 cup minced onion
1 tablespoon olive oil
1 tablespoon minced garlic
1 pound chorizo sausage, casing removed and contents crumbled
1 cup cooked rice
1 cup roughly chopped teleme cheese
1 egg, lightly beaten

Directions

Cut the tops off the chilies and remove the seeds and membranes. Sauté the onion in olive oil until soft. Add the garlic and remove from the heat. Add the crumbled sausage to the onions along with the rice and cheese. Add the egg and combine the mixture thoroughly. Stuff the mixture into the pepper shells and replace the tops, attaching them with toothpicks.

Sauce Directions

Preheat the oven to 350°F. Place the tomatoes and their juices in a saucepan. Add garlic, chili pepper, salt and ground pepper and bring the mixture to a boil. Using a large spoon, break up the tomatoes into large pieces. Reduce the heat and simmer for 10 minutes. Pour the sauce into a baking dish and arrange the stuffed peppers on top. Cover the dish with foil and bake for 45 minutes. Remove the foil and bake uncovered for an additional 15 minutes. Spoon the sauce over the peppers and serve garnished with cilantro.

SAUCE

1 28-ounce can roma tomatoes
2 tablespoons minced garlic
2 teaspoons crushed chili pepper
½ teaspoon salt
½ teaspoon freshly ground pepper
1 bunch cilantro, coarsely chopped for garnish

Serves 4

Jerked Beef Stew

CHARQUICÁN DE SALTA

Charquican refers to a stew made with dry meat; *charqui* is the dried meat. Stews with dried or jerked meats are widely enjoyed having evolved from the gaucho culture when fresh meats were not always practical. In the northwest, *charqui* meat is made of beef, lamb or pork—whatever is at hand. Back on the pampas where the dish originated, it would include the rhea or guanaco, too.

After removing all the fat, the locals cut the meat into steaks and dry the meat in the sun. To prepare for the stew pot, the dried meats are chipped or pounded into flakes. When prepared with salt, *charqui* becomes *tasajo*.

As the following recipe demonstrates, you can build a satisfying and easy to prepare dish around *charqui*. Some specialty markets import beef *charqui* from Argentina. However, North American jerked beef (not dried beef) works just as well.

INGREDIENTS

- 1   red bell pepper, seeded and chopped
- 1   large onion, chopped
- 2   tablespoons lard
- 3   sliced tomatoes
- ½   pound jerked beef, chopped (or fresh beef, recipe follows)
- 1 ½ cups water
-     Salt and pepper to taste
- 2   teaspoons crushed dried marjoram
- 3   medium potatoes, cut in chunks
- 1   cup shelled lima beans, fresh or frozen
- 2   tablespoons raw rice

Serves 2 to 4

Directions

Sauté the red pepper and onion in the lard Add tomatoes. When this sauce is smooth and bubbling, add the jerked beef, water, salt, pepper, and marjoram. Stir until well mixed then add the potatoes, lima beans and rice. Cover and simmer over a low heat for about 30 minutes.

Jerked Fresh Rhea

CHARQUI

Almost any fresh meat lends itself to drying as a preservative and then rehydrating in a stew or casserole. One such meat that is available now in the United States is the rhea, Argentina's ostrich, that runs wild in the grassy areas of the country.

The taste and texture of the rhea is quite similar to beef and, thus, rheas and ostriches are being raised in North America as an alternative to the more expensive beef. Argentines, having little need for beef substitutes, eat rhea just because it tastes good. *Charqui* is frequently the method used to prepare rhea for snacking or adding to stews. Beef or pork can be substituted. The recipe that follows is the traditional way of making *charqui*—using salt and sunshine. I, however, recommend using an oven or food dryer according to the product directions.

Directions

Cut out as large a piece of meat as possible. Slice it into thin steaks and press with weights to extract excess juices. Rub salt into the steaks on both sides and stack them on top of one another without additional pressing. Let the steaks stand outside for 24 hours then drain and expose them to dry, fresh air. Protect the steaks with a covered wire screen to prevent dew from falling onto the steaks. After 4 or 5 days, place the steaks on a chopping block and pound them with a wooden mallet. Repeat pounding 2 or 3 times to obtain an even and tender *charqui*.

Pan broil the steaks in butter combined with oil and serve. Or freeze them in freezer wrap until you are ready to use.

INGREDIENTS

Tender parts of rhea, cut from the thigh

Coarse salt

Yield depends on size of meat

Sweet Potato Fritters

BUÑUELOS DE BATATA

As with many of the Argentine recipes calling for sweet potatoes, yams or pumpkins, these ingredients are pretty much interchangeable. Any one of them can make an exquisite side dish.

Directions

Purée cooked sweet potatoes in a food mill. Add eggs, baking powder and flour and mix well. Form tablespoon-sized fritters and fry them one at a time in hot oil until brown. Drain the fritters on several layers of paper towels and sprinkle them with sugar before serving.

INGREDIENTS

2½ cups peeled and cooked
   sweet potatoes
2 eggs, beaten
1 teaspoon baking powder
1 cup flour
   Vegetable shortening
2½ tablespoons confectioners'
   sugar (optional)

Makes 10 to 12 fritters

Squash Cakes

CROQUETAS DE ZAPALLO

Croquetas de zapallo are similar to *buñuelos de batata* except they are cooked on a griddle instead of deep-fried and use winter squash or pumpkin instead of sweet potatoes or yams. Both are frequently served with afternoon tea.

Directions

Purée cooked squash in a food mill. Add milk and eggs, beating well. Mix together cornmeal, flour, baking powder and salt and sift them into the squash mixture. Stir until the batter is smooth. Form small, flat cakes and bake on a hot, lightly oiled griddle, turning to cook both sides. When the cakes are done, place them on a warmed serving platter and sprinkle with confectioners' sugar. Serve warm.

INGREDIENTS

1   cup milk
2   eggs, beaten
1   cup cooked squash
1   cup cornmeal
1   cup flour
2   teaspoons baking powder
½   teaspoon salt
1   tablespoon peanut oil
2½ tablespoons confectioners'
    sugar (optional)

Makes 6 to 8 croquetas

Custard Cake

TORTA DE FLAN

This northwestern dessert is somewhere between a flan and a trifle. It's simple to make and the ingredients are usually on hand in most households.

Directions

Place the sponge cake pieces in a serving bowl and sprinkle them with wine. In a saucepan, heat 3 cups of milk, adding sugar and a cinnamon stick. Bring the mixture to a boil and remove it from the heat immediately. Beat the egg whites with the boiling water. When they are stiff fold them into the hot milk gently to coat them. Carefully lift the coated egg whites from the milk and place them on top of the cake pieces. Beat the egg yolks until lemon colored and stir in the cornstarch, salt and 1 cup cold milk. Pour the egg mixture slowly into the heated milk and cook the mixture over medium heat for 3 minutes while stirring. Remove the cinnamon stick, stir in the vanilla and ground cinnamon and set aside to cool.

When the mixture has thickened to a custard-like consistency, pour it over the cake and sprinkle the top with raisins. Chill thoroughly before serving.

INGREDIENTS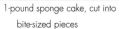

1-pound sponge cake, cut into
   bite-sized pieces
½ cup dessert wine such as
   Madeira
4 cups milk
½ cup sugar
1 cinnamon stick
3 eggs, separated
1 teaspoon boiling water
6 tablespoons cornstarch
½ teaspoon salt
1 teaspoon vanilla extract
½ teaspoon ground
   cinnamon
½ cup raisins

Serves 6

CHAPTER 9

Mendoza:

Celebrating the Good Life

Mendoza

Argentina is the third, fourth or fifth largest wine producer in the world, depending upon the source, and Mendoza Province is Argentina's wine country. Here, the melting snows of the Andes nurture the vines. Known by the locals as *La Tierra del Sol y Buen Vino* (Land of Sun and Good Wine), Mendoza, with its plentiful water, sandy soil, dry climate and year-round sunshine, has long been producing wines of character and substance. In spite of enormous yields, few Argentine wines are exported. That's why they are little known outside the country.

Mendoza Province also offers outstanding year-round recreational opportunities. Backpacking and horseback riding in the outback reward fit campers with fabulous views that can be seen nowhere else. Aconcagua—the highest peak in the Americas at 23,200 feet—is a climbing challenge for the hardiest mountaineer. Whitewater rafting through rushing, rock-strewn rivers is another way to get the adrenaline flowing. And in winter, you can ski elbow to elbow with champion skiers from around the world on expert slopes. Hot spring spas offer relaxation after a day of climbing or shussing. On occasion, you can even experience the thrills and chills of an earthquake—the only downside I can think of.

The city of Mendoza is the province's capital and its commercial and administrative center. It lies in the Río Mendoza Valley in the shadow of the Andes and Aconcagua—purported to be the tallest mountain in the world outside Asia. With vineyards stretching as far as the eye can see, it's not hard to intuit what's important here.

Wine first figured in the local economy as early as the colonial period, thanks to the existence of irrigation systems devised by aboriginal peoples to grow crops. This was followed by a period of decline after Argentine independence in 1816, and the loss of outlets on the Chilean side of the Andes. But by 1884, the railroad opened up the territory and wine production began again in earnest. Now, Mendoza boasts a much mod-

Vineyards in Mendoza.

ernized irrigation system that forms a perimeter around the city and lines the vineyards.

Until recently, most of the vineyards were relatively small, owner-operated enterprises. The seventies saw some importation of promising wines from Mendoza into the United States. By the eighties, Argentine wines had all but disappeared in North America. Seeing the success of Chilean wines in the United States, Argentine vintners are now expanding, modernizing and gearing up for a major onslaught on the U.S. market. Many of the wines are comparable to top California vintages and deserve a wider audience. Mendoza vintners have produced Cabernets that challenge the best of California vineyards. Rich, dark, subtly layered with nuances of oak, a Piedrahi from Casadé has all you can ask for in a Cabernet.

Some of the vintners in Mendoza and nearby San Juan are succeeding in producing outstanding Chardonnays that have both "nose" and "mouth." One in particular impressed me. The Catena Chardonnay from Agrelo Vineyards is a big, buttery Chardonnay—similar to California coastal Chardonnays—that has an exemplary fruitiness and a wonderful freshness. Another from Agricola in Mendoza—a 1998 Uvas del Sol—is another outstanding example of the Argentine winemaker's art.

Far from a dusty, rural outback town, the city of Mendoza is the site of a major university as well as a bustling city of trendy shops, restaurants and nightclubs. In spring and summer, the parks and rural roads are flooded with snappily clad joggers sporting the latest in running shoes. In winter, it's the ski crowd that dominates with their jazzy Spyder jumpsuits and their Rossignal boots and skis. At night—any time of the year—café life is buzzing.

Mendoza's weather in springtime couldn't be better—sunny and warm with gentle southeast breezes that flutter amiably through acres of leafy trees. The tree-lined streets and squeaky-clean sidewalks (it is claimed that residents and shopkeepers swab the sidewalks every day with kerosene to keep them shining) make Mendoza a most enjoyable city in which to stroll. Tranquil plazas hopscotch the central district providing delightful places to rest or have an impromptu picnic. Or you can meander down lovely country lanes where poplar trees stand at attention and colorful wildflowers carpet the fields.

Many attractive sidewalk cafés vie for the attention of the city's half-million population. Here you can relax with a glass of the exceptional wine from any of the local bodegas such as Agrícola, Martins, Esmeralda, Suter, or La Rural. Or you might take in a tasting tour of the wineries.

At Martins we were privileged to have a private wine tasting conducted by the bodega's charming general manager—Señora Susana Balbo. She has retrofitted the winery with oak barrels and the premium wines here were most impressive.

La Rural has a fascinating wine museum. And there's no telling whom you will meet on these excursions. As a visitor at La Rural, I was introduced to the Russian ambassador and his family who were also wine touring.

Many of Mendoza's restaurants are the epitome of chic in both ambiance and cuisine. One piqued my appetite for both. Estación Miró featured a dining room decked out in accouterments suggesting the surreal art of the Spanish master, Miró. And the imaginative, unexpected ways in which the kitchen partnered ingredients was a match for the décor. Consider *Suprême de Pollo* (boneless, skinless, tendonless chicken breasts in Roquefort sauce garnished with asparagus and walnut bits); or *Verdura à la Miró* (locally grown, lightly steamed miniature vegetables carved into flower shapes, napped with a lemon herb sauce and served in a pastry basket). More traditional fare is found at the Sarmiento where the specialty is *Chivito de Mendoza*—the best tasting grilled baby goat dish I can remember.

Mendoza is definitely a trendy, happening place. At the same time, it honors the long traditions of wine making and the lifestyle that is known as the "good life." I think I could live here happily.

Wine Punch

SANGRÍA

There is little to compare with the delight of sipping sangría in one of Mendoza's outdoor cafés in the freshness of a spring or summer evening. Some of the lighter red wines from Mendoza make the perfect base for this popular drink.

Directions

Place the peaches and apples in a large glass pitcher and mash them lightly with a large spoon. Pour in the wine. Add the brandy and gin. Add plenty of ice cubes and stir until the sangría is thoroughly chilled. Serve in chilled wineglasses garnished with mint.

INGREDIENTS

3 fresh peaches, skinned, pitted and sliced
2 apples, cored and thinly sliced
2 bottles red wine
¼ cup brandy, Spanish Fundador if available
¼ cup gin
Mint sprigs (optional)

Serves 8 to 12

Almond Horchata
HORCHATA DE ALMENDRA

Horchata originated with the Moors and they brought it to Spain when they occupied most of the Iberian peninsula. In Argentina, it is a concentrate that makes an interesting addition—along with a few dashes of orange flower water—to wine cups or fresh grape juice. While it's easy enough to make, it is sold in many Hispanic markets in North American under the name, *Orgeat*.

Directions

Soak the skins off the almonds by scalding them with hot water. Cover the blanched nuts with cold water and steep for 2 hours. Drain the nuts and mash them to a creamy paste with the sugar. Stir in the cold water and mix well. Pour the mixture into ice cube trays and freeze. When frozen hard, remove from the ice cube trays and place the cubes in a large, airtight container and store in the freezer. When ready to use, place a cube in each wineglass and fill with red or white wine. Add a thin slice of orange or a dash of orange flower water if desired.

INGREDIENTS

1   pound sweet almonds
20 bitter almonds
2   cups confectioner' sugar
2   quarts water

Makes about 72 horchata
ice cutes

Tossed Green Salad with Creamy Dressing

ENSALADA VERDE

Simple greens dressed with a cream dressing spiked with mustard are the perfect note with an otherwise heavy Argentine meal.

INGREDIENTS

½ cup heavy cream
1 tablespoon minced onion
1 tablespoon minced garlic
½ teaspoon ground dill seed
1 tablespoon Dijon mustard
¼ cup red wine vinegar
¼ cup olive oil
¼ cup grapeseed oil
3 or 4 drops beef flavoring such as Maggi
Salt and freshly ground pepper to taste
2 heads butter lettuce, washed, dried and broken into large pieces

Serves 4 to 6

Directions

Place chilled cream in a deep bowl and add onion, garlic, dill seed, mustard, vinegar, oils, beef flavoring, salt and pepper. Beat the mixture with a wire whisk until thickened. Cover and refrigerate the dressing for 2 to 3 hours. When ready to serve, place the lettuce in a salad bowl and toss with the dressing. Use only enough to lightly coat the greens.

Chicken Suprêmes in Roquefort Sauce

POLLO À LA ESTACIÓN MIRÓ

In France boneless, skinless chicken breast halves are known as *suprêmes*. A white tendon runs about two thirds of the way down the underside of the meat. This tendon is removed and the meat is flattened slightly with the side of a heavy knife or cleaver before cooking. Estación Miró follows the French method for preparing *suprêmes* of chicken breasts. It is a dish of rare finesse, but it is very important that the chicken is not overcooked or it will be dry and tough.

For wine, if you don't have access to good Chardonnay from Argentina, an Estancia or Meridian Chardonnay from the coastal region of California is a good match for this dish.

Directions

Preheat the oven to 400°F. Rub the *suprêmes* with drops of lemon juice and sprinkle them lightly with salt and pepper. Melt the butter in a heavy flameproof casserole. When it foams, turn the heat to medium, place the *suprêmes* in the casserole and quickly turn them in the butter. Lay buttered parchment paper over the *suprêmes*. Cover the casserole and place it in the oven. After 6 minutes, test to see if the *suprêmes* are done—press with your finger. If they are still soft, return them to the oven for a minute or two. If they are springy to the touch, they are done.

Remove them to a warm platter and cover them while making the sauce. Reserve the cooking butter in the casserole for the sauce.

Sauce Directions

Pour the chicken broth and wine into the casserole in which the *suprêmes* were cooked. Add the cheese and boil the mixture down quickly over high heat until the liquid is syrupy and the cheese has melted. Stir in the cream and boil down again over high heat until the cream thickens. Take the mixture off the heat, taste for seasoning and stir in a few drops of lemon juice. Pour the sauce over the *suprêmes*, sprinkle with parsley and walnut bits. Garnish with asparagus and serve immediately.

INGREDIENTS

4   *suprêmes* (half chicken breasts, skinned, boned and tendons removed)
½   teaspoon lemon juice
¼   teaspoon salt
    Generous pinch white pepper
4   tablespoons butter
    Roquefort cream sauce (recipe follows)
4   tablespoons walnut bits
8   asparagus spears, lightly steamed

SAUCE

¼   cup chicken broth
¼   cup dry white wine
½   cup cubed Roquefort cheese
1   cup heavy cream
    Salt and white pepper, to taste
    Lemon juice to taste
2   tablespoons minced parsley

Serves 4

Duckling in Wine Sauce

PATO EN SALSA DE VINO

Perfumed with cinnamon, cloves and allspice, this duckling in wine sauce has an irresistible aura straight out of *Arabian Nights*. It is always a big hit with guests.

Directions

Simmer the giblets, liver and neck in 2 cups water for 1 hour. Strain and reserve stock.

Preheat the oven to 350°F. Prick the duckling all over with a fork to help release excess fat. Season it inside and out with salt and pepper. Heat the butter and oil in a heavy flame-proof casserole and sauté the duckling until it is golden brown all over. Remove the duckling from the casserole and set aside. Spoon off all but 4 tablespoons of fat from the casserole. Add the onions and sauté them until they are soft.

Return the duckling to the casserole. Tie the bay leaf, cloves, cinnamon, allspice berries and jalapeño in a square of washed cheesecloth and place it in the casserole. Add the wine and 1 cup of reserved duck stock. Check the seasoning and add salt and pepper if necessary. Bring the mixture to a boil over high heat. Cover with aluminum foil, then with the casserole lid, making a tight seal. Place the casserole in the oven and simmer for 1½ hours, or until the duck is tender.

When done, lift the duckling out onto a heated serving platter and keep it warm. Remove the cheesecloth from the casserole and discard. Remove as much fat as possible from the liquid in the casserole, taking care not to remove any of the juices. Reduce the remaining liquid by half over high heat. Remove the casserole from the heat and correct the seasoning. Ladle a little of the sauce over the duckling and serve the rest separately in a sauceboat at the table. Serve with rice and a green or fruit salad.

INGREDIENTS

Duck livers, giblets and neck

5-pound duckling, cleaned and loose fat removed

Salt and pepper to taste

2 tablespoons butter

2 tablespoons olive oil

2 large onions, minced

1 bay leaf

2 whole cloves

1-inch cinnamon stick

4 allspice berries

1 fresh jalapeño pepper, whole

1 cup dry red wine

Serves 4

Drunken Chicken

POLLO BORRACHO

Chicken and boiled ham braised in white wine needs only plain boiled rice and a salad to make a complete and satisfying meal.

Directions

Rub the chicken with a mixture of salt, pepper, cumin and coriander. Melt the butter in a flameproof casserole. Layer a third of the ham on the bottom of the casserole. Add the chicken legs to the casserole and cover with another third of the ham. Arrange the chicken breasts over the ham layer and top with the remaining ham strips. Pour in the vinegar, wine and enough chicken stock to cover. Add the garlic and simmer, covered, over a low heat for 45 minutes, or until the chicken is tender.

Soak the olives in cold water for 15 minutes and drain. Remove the chicken and ham from the casserole and place them in a serving dish. Reduce the liquid in the casserole to about 2 cups over high heat. Moisten the chicken with a little of the liquid and serve the rest in a sauceboat. Garnish the dish with olives and capers.

Variation: You may thicken the sauce if desired by mixing 1 tablespoon of flour with 1 tablespoon of butter and stirring it into the liquid over low heat.

INGREDIENTS

3 ½-pound chicken, quartered
  Salt and pepper to taste
¼ teaspoon ground cumin
¼ teaspoon ground coriander
1 tablespoon butter
½ pound boiled ham, cut into
  2- by ¼-inch strips
¼ cup white wine vinegar
2 cups dry white wine
1 cup chicken stock
3 garlic cloves, minced
12 pimiento-stuffed green
  olives
3 tablespoons rinsed capers

Serves 4

Chicken in Grape Juice

POLLO AL JUGO DE UVA

The grapes in Mendoza are huge, and many cooks there use grape juice for cooking instead of wine. When freshly squeezed, grape juice imparts an elusive but agreeable flavor to chicken. If you can find grapes large enough to make the task of juicing them not overly burdensome, I think it's worth the extra effort. Pressing the grapes through a food mill and then straining the juices through a sieve is the method I use. I do not recommend bottled grape juice.

INGREDIENTS

1   frying chicken, cut into
    serving pieces
    Salt and freshly ground
    pepper to taste
1½ tablespoons butter, melted
1½ tablespoons olive oil
1   tablespoon minced parsley
¼   cup chopped fresh
    tarragon
2   pounds seedless white
    grapes, squeezed and
    strained
2   tablespoons chilled butter,
    cut into small pieces

Serves 4

Directions

Season the chicken pieces with salt and pepper. Add melted butter and olive oil to a heavy flameproof casserole and sauté the chicken until lightly browned on all sides. Add the parsley and tarragon and cook for 1 minute. Pour the grape juice over the chicken and bring the mixture to the boiling point. Cook, uncovered, for several minutes until the juice is reduced slightly. Reduce the heat and cover the casserole tightly. Simmer over low heat for about 45 minutes, or until the chicken is tender.

When done, place the chicken on a serving platter and keep it warm. On high heat, boil the liquid in the casserole until it is reduced by half. Remove the casserole from the heat and beat in the chilled butter pieces. Serve the sauce separately in a sauceboat at the table.

Chicken in Orange Sauce

POLLO EN JUGO DE NARANJA

Braised chicken in a creamy orange sauce was
the highlight of a dinner at the Restaurant Pampi
in Mendoza.

Directions

Season the chicken quarters with salt and pepper. Heat
the butter in a heavy flameproof casserole and sauté the
chicken quarters, 1 or 2 at a time, until golden brown on
all sides. Set the chicken aside.

Pour the fat from the casserole into a small bowl and
reserve. Return the chicken pieces to the casserole,
putting the legs and thighs in first and the breasts and
wings on top. Add the stock, orange juice and grated
orange rind. Cover and simmer for 45 minutes, or until
the chicken is tender.

Remove the chicken quarters to a serving dish and keep
them warm. Mix the flour with a tablespoon of the
reserved fat and stir it into the liquid in the casserole.
Bring it to a boil and cook, stirring, for 2 minutes. Reduce
the heat to low.

Beat the eggs with the cream. Stir a cup of the thickened
cooking liquid into the egg mixture, 1 tablespoon at a time.
Pour the egg mixture into the casserole. Continue cooking
and stirring with a wire whisk over medium heat for 1 or
2 minutes. Don't let the sauce boil or it will curdle. When
thickened, pour some of the sauce over the chicken and
serve the remainder in a sauceboat at the table.

INGREDIENTS

3 to 3½-pound chicken,
   cleaned and quartered
   Salt and pepper
3 tablespoons butter
1 cup chicken stock
1 cup orange juice
   Rind of 1 orange, grated
1 tablespoon flour
2 eggs
1 tablespoon heavy cream

Serves 4

Chicken Pie

PASTEL DE POLLO

INGREDIENTS

- 2 stewing hens, approximately 6 pounds each, cut into quarters
- 3 quarts cold water
- 2 medium onions, quartered
- 1 stalk celery, quartered
- 2 large carrots, quartered
- 2 bay leaves
- 6 sprigs parsley
- 1 tablespoon chopped fresh thyme leaves
- 8 black peppercorns

FILLING

- ½ cup butter
- 2 medium onions, chopped
- 4 garlic cloves, minced
- 2 green peppers, seeded and chopped
- 1½ cups diced cooked ham
- 1½ teaspoons crushed dry oregano
- 2 teaspoons salt
- 1 tablespoon vinegar
- 1 cup raisins
- 20 pimiento-stuffed green olives, sliced
- 5 tomatoes, peeled, seeded and chopped
- 3½ cups fresh corn kernels cut from cob
- 10 cups stewed chicken meat
- 1 tablespoon chopped fresh thyme leaves
- ¼ cup flour
- 2 cups reserved chicken broth
- 1 tablespoon tomato paste
- Salt and pepper to taste

Pastel de Pollo is a lovely dish for an informal party. It can be made ahead and refrigerated until it's time to bake it.

Directions

Place hens separately in 2 large pots. Divide the remaining ingredients in half and add to each pot. Cover the pots and bring to a boil. Lower the heat and simmer for approximately 2 hours, or until the chicken is tender. Let the chicken stand in the broth until it's cool. Skim the fat from the broth. Remove the meat from the bones and cut it into bite-sized pieces, discarding the bones and skin. Strain and reserve the broth, discarding the vegetables and seasonings.

Filling Directions

Melt ¼ cup butter in a large skillet. Sauté the onions, garlic, green peppers and ham until the vegetables are almost tender. Stir in the oregano, salt, vinegar, raisins, olives, tomatoes, corn, chicken and thyme. Melt the remaining ¼ cup butter in a saucepan and stir in the flour, cooking 1 minute. Blend in the chicken broth and tomato paste. Continue cooking and stirring until the mixture thickens. Season with salt and pepper. Combine the broth mixture with the chicken and corn mixture. Spoon the mixture into a lightly buttered 3-quart flameproof casserole or a 9- by 12-inch baking pan.

Pastry Directions

Preheat the oven to 425°F. Prepare the pastry. Roll it out so that it is 2 inches larger than the baking dish. Place the pastry over the chicken mixture. Crimp the edges and cut 1-inch vents in the pastry with a sharp knife. The pie may be refrigerated at this point and finished later or the next day. When ready to bake, brush the pie with egg white and bake for about 45 minutes—1 hour if the pie has been refrigerated—or until lightly browned.

Roll out any extra pastry dough slightly thicker than the crust. Cut out small shapes such as chickens or leaves. Lay these on a greased baking sheet and brush with egg white. Bake with the pie until they are lightly browned, about 5 minutes. When cool enough to handle, arrange them on top of the pie as decorations.

PASTRY

Pastry (page 33 or 64)
1   egg white, slightly beaten

Serves 8 to 10

Grilled Beef Tenderloin
BIFE À LA REBAUDO

As men do the outdoor grilling in Argentina, my spouse, Peter, brought the custom with him to California. Hence, I was reduced to groveling to obtain his secret recipe for barbecuing beef tenderloin Mendoza style. He developed this recipe after much experimentation with different marinades. And while it suggests an Asian sensibility, the recipe is a true reflection of the independent Argentine spirit. I should also mention that the Rebaudo way with grilled beef is famous within our circle.

Directions

Prepare a marinade mixing together the garlic, ginger, chili, cilantro, shrimp paste or fish sauce, onion, kaffir lime leaves, sugar, salt, lime juice and lime zest. Rinse the filet and wipe it dry with paper towels. Marinate it overnight in the refrigerator, turning frequently.

Prepare a fire in an outdoor grill with mesquite wood or hardwood lump charcoal (available in hardware and specialty stores). When only the glowing embers remain in the grill, place the filet on a spit or oil the grating and place the filet on top. Baste the filet with the marinade, turning several times if cooked on a flat grill. Close the lid on the grill, leaving a small opening and continue to baste with the marinade. When browned all over and cooked to your liking, remove the filet from the grill and let it rest for 15 minutes. Grilling should take about an hour. Serve well-done pieces from the ends and rare slices from the center of the filet.

Serve with *chimichurri* sauce (page 82), roasted potatoes, a variety of salads, roasted marinated peppers (page 55) and plenty of Cabernet wine.

INGREDIENTS

- 1 garlic head, minced
- 1 tablespoon minced fresh ginger
- 1 teaspoon minced fresh chili pepper
- 1 tablespoon chopped cilantro
- 1 tablespoon Thai shrimp paste or fish sauce
- 1 red onion, minced
- 6 Thai kaffir lime leaves, crushed (optional)
- 1 teaspoon sugar
  Salt to taste
  Juice of 2 limes
- 1 tablespoon finely minced lime zest
  5- to 6-pound beef filet

Serves 6 to 8

Roasted Kid with Rosemary

CHIVITO ASADO CON ROMERO

Most Argentines wouldn't think of using any herb but rosemary with *chivito*—whether grilled, roasted or stewed. And the herb does seem a perfect choice. Having experimented with fresh oregano and thyme, I'm partial to rosemary, too.

Directions

Preheat the oven to 350°F. Make a marinade with olive oil mixed with rosemary, salt and pepper. Rub the kid well on both sides with the marinade. Roast the kid uncovered in a roasting pan until it's well done or when the meat starts to separate from the bones. Baste frequently with rosemary sprigs dipped in chicken broth and pan drippings. When the roast is done, remove it to a heated serving platter. Top it with butter and allow the roast to rest for 20 minutes. Remove as much fat as possible from the roasting pan and deglaze it with white wine. Boil down the sauce until it is reduced by half. Serve the sauce separately in a sauceboat at the table. Serve the roast garnished with watercress, lemon wedges and broiled tomato halves.

INGREDIENTS

¾   cup olive oil
½   cup chopped fresh
     rosemary
1   teaspoon coarse kosher or
     sea salt
½   teaspoon freshly ground
     black pepper
1 2-pound whole kid (or lamb),
     butterflied
1   cup chicken broth
     Rosemary sprigs
3   tablespoons butter
1   cup white wine
     Watercress
     Lemon wedges
     Broiled tomato halves

Serves 6 to 8

Grilled Kid

CHIVITO À LA PARRILLA SARMIENTO

This recipe is based on the *chivito* served at Parilla Sarmiento in Mendoza. Young kid or *chivito*, as well as lamb, are usually grilled whole or in halves. Choose young animals insofar as possible to ensure tenderness and flavor—the smaller, the better. In North America, these are specialty items and must be ordered in advance from gourmet meat sources. But the wait will be well worth it. The natural tenderness of grilled *chivito* is in a class of its own.

INGREDIENTS

1 cup olive oil
½ cup minced fresh
   rosemary, pounded in a
   mortar
1 2-pound kid, butterflied
   Mild saline solution

Serves 6 to 8

Directions

Prepare a mesquite wood or hardwood lump charcoal (available in hardware and specialty stores) fire in the grill. When the fire progresses from blazing to hot gray ash, you are ready to cook the meat. Make a dry marinade by mixing olive oil and rosemary. A few minutes before cooking, rub both sides of the carcass with the marinade. Arrange the embers so as to have a milder fire under the breast and a hotter fire under the forequarters and hindquarters. Make sure the fire is never strong enough to scorch the meat.

Oil the grate before adding the meat. Place the carcass rib-side down over the coals. When it is brown, turn it over and brown the skin side. At this point, you will need to sprinkle the roast with the saline solution, brushing it on or dripping it on with a garden herb such as rosemary or parsley. Continue this sprinkling of salt solution on the cooked parts of the roast. Cooking should be very slow to minimize the number of times you must turn the roast until it is done. When done, the meat will come off the bones and the juices will be transparent. This will take at least 2½ hours, depending upon the age of the animal and the heat of the grill.

When done, allow the roast to rest for 20 minutes. Because this is a special party dish, presentation is important. A silver tray bearing the roasted animal, surrounded by bunches of fresh rosemary, makes an elegant statement. However, I suggest removing the roast to the kitchen for cutting into serving pieces.

Tongue in Almond Sauce

LENGUA CON ALMENDRAS

Bred to be tender, the grass-fed steers of Argentina have velvety, juicy tongues that need little gilding. Fortunately, tongue is available in most North American markets and the quality is very good. So, if you like tongue, I think you'll like the Argentine way with it.

Directions

Place the tongue in a large soup kettle, cover with cold water and bring it to a boil. Turn down the heat and simmer for 3 hours, or until tender. Drain the tongue, reserving 2½ cups of the cooking liquid. When cool enough to handle, skin the tongue and remove the roots, gristle and any small bones at the base.

Heat the oil in a skillet and sauté the onions and garlic for about 5 minutes, or until soft. Mix in the tomatoes and cook over a low heat for another 5 minutes. Stir in the almonds, thyme, parsley, reserved liquid, stock and wine. Cook over medium heat for 10 minutes. Mix in the olives and breadcrumbs and cook for 5 minutes more. Slice the tongue in long thin strips that follow the natural curves. Add the tongue slices to the sauce and simmer 5 minutes. Arrange the tongue slices on a heated platter, surrounded by sauce. Sprinkle with capers and serve.

INGREDIENTS

5- to 6-pound pickled beef
    tongue
2   tablespoons olive oil
¾   cup chopped onions
3   garlic cloves, minced
¾   cup peeled, seeded,
    chopped tomatoes
1   cup blanched ground
    almonds
1   tablespoon chopped fresh
    thyme leaves
½   teaspoon minced parsley
½   cup beef stock
½   cup dry white wine
½   cup pitted, chopped black
    olives
½   cup dry breadcrumbs
¼   cup rinsed capers

Serves 8 to 10

Potato and Cheese Cake

TORTA DE PAPAS Y QUESO

This recipe is from the kitchen of a lady I almost met. She heard I was writing an Argentine cookbook from the manager of a hotel where we were staying in Mendoza. She left this recipe for me in my mailbox as she was checking out but she didn't leave her name. I tried it, liked it, made a couple of small changes and now it's been recorded for posterity in these pages. I wish I could give proper credit to the contributor. Wherever you are, thank you.

Directions

Preheat the oven to 350°F. Cook the bacon until crisp, reserving the fat. Drain the bacon on a paper towel and crumble it. Mash the potatoes with salt, pepper and egg yolk. Sauté the onions in the reserved bacon fat until they are golden then add them to the potato mixture. In a separate bowl, mix the Tabasco and the cottage cheese. In a shallow, buttered 1½-quart rectangular or square baking dish, spoon in half the potato mixture and spread it with a spatula to cover the bottom of the dish. Spread the cottage cheese over the potato layer and top with a layer of the remaining potato mixture. Draw the tines of a fork over the top of the potatoes. Sprinkle the top with bacon bits and bake for 30 minutes. Cut into squares and serve directly from the baking dish. For a satisfying Lenten or vegetarian meal, omit the bacon and bacon fat.

INGREDIENTS

3   slices bacon

6   hot boiled potatoes

½   teaspoon salt

⅛   teaspoon freshly ground pepper

1   egg yolk, beaten

2   onions, chopped

1   tablespoon melted bacon fat (or vegetable oil)

½   teaspoon Tabasco or pepper sauce

1   cup creamed cottage cheese

Serves 4

Puréed Chickpeas

PURÉ DE GARBANZOS

Puréed, creamed chickpeas make a rich side dish that is best paired with a light main dish such as a simple chicken or fish entrée served without sauce. This recipe can be adapted to create a lighter dish by omitting the cream and substituting a seasoned vegetable or meat broth for the cooking water. The broth from a *puchero* would be ideal.

If using canned garbanzos, eliminate the soaking and cooking steps.

INGREDIENTS

1 cup raw garbanzo beans (or canned garbanzo beans)
1 bay leaf
1 teaspoon salt
½ teaspoon freshly ground pepper
2 tablespoons flour
2 tablespoons butter, at room temperature
½ cup heavy cream
2 tablespoons chilled butter, cut into small pieces

Serves 4

Directions

Soak the raw garbanzo beans overnight in water to cover. After soaking, boil the garbanzo beans in the soaking water for 10 minutes to remove the skins. Drain the soaking water and discard the water and skins.

In a heavy pot, bring 3 pints of cold water to a boil. Place the soaked, skinned garbanzo beans and a bay leaf in the pot and reduce the heat to the lowest setting. Cover and barely simmer the garbanzo beans until they are tender. This could take 30 minutes to an hour, depending upon the garbanzos. When the garbanzo beans are cooked and cooled, drain and purée them in a food mill or blender. Place the puréed garbanzos in a saucepan and reheat. Add salt and pepper. Make a paste of flour and the room temperature butter. Stir the paste into the purée and continue stirring until the mixture is smooth. Cook over a low heat for 15 minutes. Stir in the cream and continue stirring while cooking over a low heat for an additional 4 to 5 minutes, or until the cream is absorbed. Remove the mixture from the heat and beat in the cold butter pieces. Serve in a heated, covered vegetable dish.

Green Beans with Potatoes

Cooked vegetables combined with potatoes are commonly served in Mendoza. Broccoli or zucchini are good substitutions for the string beans.

Directions

Steam the beans for 8 minutes or until they are barely tender. Drain them and toss with the oil and lemon juice. Spread the beans on a heated platter and keep them warm. Purée the potatoes and mix in the butter, garlic, salt, pepper and cayenne. Mound the potato purée over the beans and garnish with red pepper slices.

INGREDIENTS

1 ½ cups cut string beans
2 tablespoons olive oil
2 tablespoons lemon juice
2 ½ cups cooked potatoes
1 tablespoon butter
3 garlic cloves, minced
  Salt and freshly ground
  pepper to taste
  Dash of cayenne
1 red bell pepper, seeded
  and thinly sliced

Serves 4 to 6

Deep-fried Squash

In Argentina, they grow a tender summer squash that looks like a miniature acorn squash. It can sometimes be found in specialty produce shops in North America. If you can't find it, substitute any small, round squash.

Directions

Mix the garlic with the breadcrumbs. Roll the squash slices in flour, beaten egg and breadcrumbs in that order. Season with salt and pepper and deep-fry in oil until lightly browned.

INGREDIENTS

3 garlic cloves, minced
  Breadcrumbs
4 zapallitos (squash),
  washed and cut into
  ½-inch slices
½ cup flour
1 egg, beaten
  Salt and pepper to taste
  Vegetable oil

Serves 4 as vegetable
course

Stuffed Chayote Squash

CHAYOTE RELLENO DE MENDOZA

Mendoza chefs work wonders with chayote squashes. This is but one of the many ways in which chayotes can add an unusual note to a family or company dinner.

Directions

Wash the chayotes, cut them in half lengthwise, and remove the seed. Steam them until they are tender, then set them aside.

Preheat the oven to 450°F. Remove the chayote pulp and mash it, taking care to preserve the shells. Mix the rice, crumbs, egg, salt, marjoram and lemon juice with the mashed pulp. Refill the shells with the mixture and cover with the bacon halves. Place the chayotes in a baking pan. Add water to cover the bottom of the pan. Bake for 15 to 20 minutes, or until the bacon strips are browned.

INGREDIENTS

3   chayote squashes

¼   cup cooked rice

¾   cup breadcrumbs

1   egg, beaten

½   teaspoon salt

1   teaspoon crushed dried
     marjoram

2   teaspoons lemon juice

3   slices bacon, cut in half
     crosswise

Serves 6

Cabbage Pudding

BUDÍN DE REPOLLO

I'm always surprised when people claim to hate cabbage. Maybe it's because they've experienced overcooked cabbage with its gruesome odor. But when it's cooked only to the point where its color is a lovely jade green and it is still slightly resistant to a fork, it's a marvelous vegetable. Some cooks microwave cabbage for 3 to 4 minutes in a plastic bag instead of boiling it. Cabbage is especially good in this first course dish.

Directions

Soak the breadcrumbs in the milk.

Preheat the oven to 400°F. Cook the cabbage in a small amount of boiling salted water until barely tender, about 5 minutes. Drain it, cut it into thin shreds and place it in a mixing bowl. Sauté the onion in butter until it's golden. To the cabbage, add onion, salt, pepper, eggs, soaked breadcrumbs, Parmesan cheese and nutmeg. Mix well and spoon the mixture into a shallow 3-quart baking dish. Place it in the oven and bake it for 20 minutes or until the custard is set.

Tomato Sauce Directions

Heat the oil in a saucepan until it is almost smoking. Seed and chop the tomatoes and add them to the saucepan. Cover the pan immediately to avoid splattering grease particles. Continue cooking until the oil is no longer sputtering. Remove the cover and reduce the heat to medium. Add cinnamon, parsley, vinegar, Tabasco, salt and pepper. Simmer over low heat for 8 minutes. Serve over the cabbage pudding.

INGREDIENTS

1   cup fine soft breadcrumbs

1½ cups milk

1½ pounds green cabbage, cored and quartered

1   cup chopped onion

2   tablespoons butter
    Salt and freshly ground pepper to taste

3   eggs, beaten

½   cup grated Parmesan cheese

¼   teaspoon freshly grated nutmeg

TOMATO SAUCE

3   tablespoons olive oil

2   cups canned roma tomatoes

1   tablespoon ground cinnamon

½   cup chopped parsley

2   tablespoons red wine vinegar
    Dash of Tabasco or pepper sauce
    Salt and freshly ground pepper to taste

Serves 6 to 8

Orange Custard

FLAN DE NARANJAS

Too many write off flan as an ordinary and boring dessert. But, in my book, orange flan is a dessert deserving of poetry. The rich, smooth, creamy consistency of a properly cooked flan is heavenly. Juxtaposed with the sweetly tart addition of freshly squeezed orange juice, it's divine. Topped with lightly sweetened whipped cream and fresh orange segments, it is simply God-given.

INGREDIENTS

2 cups orange juice
1 cup granulated sugar
5 whole eggs
⅛ teaspoon salt
Pinch of freshly ground
nutmeg
2 cups heavy cream
1 teaspoon vanilla extract
2 teaspoons confectioners'
sugar
8 fresh orange segments

Serves 6

Directions

To make the syrup, mix the orange juice and granulated sugar in a saucepan and bring the mixture to a boil. Cook without stirring over medium heat until the mixture reaches a temperature of 220°F on a candy thermometer, or until a small amount dropped from a spoon spins a thread. Remove the mixture from the heat and set it aside to cool. You should have about 1⅓ cups of syrup.

Preheat the oven to 350°F. Beat the eggs until they are frothy. Stir in the salt and nutmeg, mixing well, then stir in the syrup. Pour this mixture into a lightly buttered 8-inch cake pan. Set the pan in larger pan containing 1¾ inches of hot water. Bake in the oven for an hour or until the custard is set; test this by checking to see if a toothpick inserted into the center of the custard comes out clean. Cool thoroughly on a cake rack then turn upside down on a serving platter. Beat the cream with vanilla and confectioners' sugar until it holds a peak. Top the flan with dollops of whipped cream and decorate the top with orange segments.

Variation: A traditional way with many flans is to coat the inside of a flan baking pan with caramelized sugar and allowing it to cool and harden before adding the flan mixture.

The Great Pleasures of Argentine Wines

"Wine gives great pleasure, and every pleasure is of itself a good."
Samuel Johnson: in Boswell's Life.

Big! Big, I tell you! Like Texas, most everything in Argentina is king-sized. Steaks, Hailstones, Ranches. Egos. And it's especially true when it comes to the more than 516,000 acres devoted to the vine. It's the greatest undiscovered wine country in the world. It is also the last.

Argentina once made wines fit mainly for domestic consumption. Now its wines are of tremendous importance to the world of wine, as they stand on the brink of fulfilling fantastic promise. Depending upon who is doing the counting, Argentina ranks fourth or fifth in wine production just behind the United States, Italy, France and Spain. Moreover, Argentina's production potential is staggering and the country could, if it made the effort, beat the competition by significant numbers. Unlike the United States, Italy, France and Spain—and up-and-coming contenders from Chile, Australia and New Zealand—Argentina devotes huge plots of land to vineyards. Its production capacity is virtually unlimited. In addition, the diversity of the *terroir* and the varietals that flourish there make it possible to design fine wines in myriad styles.

ARGENTINE
WINE HISTORY

That Argentina produces wine at all is somewhat of a fluke. Legend has it that wine came to Argentina via a Spanish priest, Juan Cedrón, who brought Pais vine stalks from Chile in the mid-fifteen hundreds and planted them in Argentine soil as an experiment. These early grapes flourished and were well established in Mendoza by the late sixteenth century. Intended for local consumption, the wines were considered rustic by aristocratic European standards. Soon, however, word spread that they were far better than the imports from Spain—the only legal alternative at the time because Spain forbade its colonies to produce wine.

Edicts from the mother country were, of course, ignored and in time the local demand for Mendoza's wines grew exponentially. But expansion outside the growing areas was slow, given the distance and harsh terrain between wineries and the major market in Buenos Aires.

The British came to the rescue in 1885 by opening the first railroad in Argentina. Linking Mendoza and *mendocino* winemakers with Buenos Aires, the rails assured short transit time and safe delivery to a parched capital. Vineyards and bodegas proliferated at this point and the domestic market exploded.

Unfortunately, wine quality in the late 1800s was sacrificed to mass production, as the demand far exceeded the supply. Exceptions were the first French varieties introduced in Mendoza in 1880 by French botanist Aimé Pouget. One variety in particular—Malbec—did extraordinarily well in the western and northwestern territories of Mendoza. This lusty red wine was intensely colored, bright in flavor and traveled well. Today, it is at the top of the heap, far superior to the French version, and rules as the signature wine of Argentina.

While a few vintners set about to improve the general quality of Argentine wine, most bet on quantity over quality. Thus, Argentine wines virtually disappeared from North American wine shops by the late 1980s. Hyperinflation, poor fiscal control and international trade constriction caused by the war with the British over the Falkland/Malvina Islands delivered another decisive blow. Turnaround took almost ten years. But by the 1990s, the domestic market had learned that better quality could be delivered if demanded. And offshore markets were waking up to Argentina's status as a world-class wine producer.

Mendoza Province produces 75 percent of Argentina's wines and was the first region to make massive efforts to improve quality. Among exports, Mendoza accounts for 95 percent. Given the advantages of the *terroir*, the province is truly vineyard heaven. On the eastern slopes of the Andes foothill—some at high altitudes—Mendoza vineyards are irrigated with pollution-free waters from the Andes. Bright sunshine and year-round dry weather make it possible to grow superb fruit. And for devotees of organic produce, chemical use is almost non-existent.

Mendoza produces a full range of European style wines such as Merlot, Cabernet Sauvignon and Malbec as well as Syrah and some local varietals. Its Malbecs—emphasizing black currants and spice—are considered the standard by which other countries' Malbecs are judged.

Other important wine regions are located in San Juan, La Ríoja, Salta and Río Negro provinces. Huge investments have been made in San Juan, to the immediate north of Mendoza, where vintners are planting international varietals in new, irrigated vineyards. The province's potential is especially good in the warm El Pedernal Valley with plantings as high as 4,429 feet. Its Chardonnays are rich and buttery with spectacular "nose" and "palate."

La Ríoja, north of Mendoza, is hot and dry with mainly poor sandy soil. Its vineyards sit at almost 4,000 feet—a particularly good climate for growing red varieties but old habits die hard. In the past vintners here produced low cost white wines for mass domestic consumption. Now they are moving up to higher quality white wines that provide good value at a reasonable price. The district is best known for its Torrontés riojano grape. To avoid a conflict with Spain over the designation of Spanish "Ríoja," wines from this province are designated as "a product from the Famatina Valley in the foothills of the Andes north of San Juan, Argentina." There also are vineyards of note north of Rioja in the Catamarca region sitting at even higher elevations—over 6,000 feet.

Further north, Salta Province is a land of undulating mountains, foothills and valleys with gentle breezes cooling them in late afternoon. It is home to one of the loveliest wine producing valleys on the planet—Valles Calchaquies. Like Catamarca, vineyards rise to altitudes of over 6,000 feet here. Malbecs, Cabernet Sauvignons and Torrontés are among the district's outstanding products.

Río Negro in the south of Patagonia would be a desert it if weren't for irrigation. As it is, Río Negro sports patches of verdant green near the rivers that provide a cool climate particularly well suited to white wines. But it's still too early to tell if quality can consistently live up to the standards set by its northern neighbors.

Until recently, little wine was exported from Argentina to North America so few wine aficionados here have Argentine wines on their radar screens. But rapid change is afoot. And given the high quality of the wine today, the future appears limitless. Some distributors, however, feel that at the high end, Argentine vintners are pricing themselves out of the market. Discussions with Susana Balbo of Susana Balbo Wines revealed that pricing at the high end is a strategic move to change the image of Argentine wines from ho-hum to superior.

Price aside, more and more foreign wine interests are buying into the dream. New capital is coming from French, Italian, Dutch and United States investors. France's Domain and California's Kendall-Jackson are recent additions to the Argentine wine scene. Meanwhile, native vintners such as Catena, Trapiche and many others have retrenched and are producing fine red and white wines for both export and domestic markets. Establishing Argentine wines among the top wines of the world is the vision and the mission.

The following lists a host of Argentine vintners and asso-
ciated wines that are worthy of note. Most are available in
North America in various price categories.

The asterisk (*) indicates outstanding.

<u>Alta Vista</u>, Chacras de Coria, Mendoza.
Malbec
Chardonnay
Torrontés—Moderately priced.

<u>Altos de Medrano</u>, Mendoza.
de Hormigas Malbec*—Inexpensive. Serve with
  Tagliarini with Beef, Pork and Mushroom Sauce,
  page 44.

<u>Arnaldo B. Etchart</u>, Cafayette, Salta and Mendoza.
Cabernet Sauvignon, (Cafayette).* Serve with Beef Rolls
  à la Mutti Becker, page 47.
Malbec, (Cafayette).* Serve with Pan-Grilled Steak,
  page 75.
Chardonnay, (Cafayette)—Moderately priced. Serve
  with Pappardelle, page 188.
Merlot (Mendoza).
Torrontés, (Cafayette)—Inexpensive. Serve with Beef
  Japanese Style, page 165.

<u>Bianchi</u>, Mendoza.
Cabernet Sauvignon Particular
Chenin Blanc
Malbec—Moderately priced.

<u>Catena</u>, Mendoza.
Merlot Reserva

Alta Malbec.* Serve with Pork Loin in Milk, page 74.
Río Negro—Expensive.

Catena Zapata, Mendoza.
2001 Alamos Pinot Noir
2001 Alamos Chardonnay—Moderately priced. Serve
    with Duckling in Wine Sauce, page 268.
Catena Chardonnay, Agrelo Vineyards*—Moderately
    priced. Serve with Veal with Noodles, page 140, and
    Partridge with Cabbage, page 139.
Catena Malbec, Lunlunta Vineyards.* Serve with Rhea
    Steak, page 223, and Roasted Lamb Shoulder, page 225.

Chandon, Terrazas de los Andes, Mendoza.
Varietals

Chateau Mendoza, Mendoza.
Cabernet Sauvignon
Merlot

Crotta Wine, Mendoza.
Malbec
Chenin Blanc
Bonarda

Fabre Montmajou (French Ownership).
Gran Vin*

Familia Cassone Winery, Luján de Cuyo, Mendoza.
Malbec
Cabernet Sauvignon
Rosé
Chardonnay

Fapes Winery and Vineyards, Mendoza.
Malbec Premium Oak Reserve* (in 1999 rated best
    Malbec in the world at Vinales 2000, Paris). Serve
    with Grilled Beef Tenderloin, page 273.
Malbec
Malbec/Bonarda
Pedro Giménez

Finca Flichman, Mendoza.
Cabernet Sauvignon
Malbec
Syrah
Merlot
Chardonnay Origin Barrancas, (Maipú, Mendoza)
1999 Cabernet Sauvignon
Reserva Cabernet Sauvignon Barrancas—Moderately
    priced.
Reserva Chardonnay (Trapungato and Barrancas)
1998 Reserva Malbec (Trapungato). Serve with Beef,
    Currant and Almond Empanadas, page 33.
1997 Reserva Syrah—Moderately priced.

Jean Rivie, Mendoza.
Malbec
Cabernet Sauvignon
Bonarda
Chenin Blanc
Tocai Fríulano
Torrontés—Moderately priced. Serve with Beef with
    Fruit from Iguazú, page 168.
Tempanilla

Humberto Canale, Mendoza and Río Negro, Patagonia.
Cabernet Sauvignon
Pinot Noir

Malbec

Merlot

Torrontés

Chardonnay—Moderately priced. Serve with Drunken
   Chicken, page 269.

Sauvignon Blanc—Moderately priced. Serve with
   Creamed Mussels, page 134.

Semillon

Cabernet Sauvignon Reserva

Lagarde Wineries Group, Lujan de Cuyo, Mendoza.

Lagarde

Henry

Medrano

Letra de Tango

Atlas Cumbres

La Rural, Mendoza. San Juan, La Ríoja, Río Negro.

Chardonnay—Moderately priced. Serve with Chicken
   in Grape Juice, page 270.

Sauvignon Blanc—Moderately priced. Serve with Rice
   with Squid in its own Ink, page 135.

Chenin Blanc

Ugni Blanc

Tempranillo

Sangiovese

Cerea

Criolla

Cabernet Sauvignon

Merlot

Malbec

2000 Rutini Cabernet Sauvignon.* Especially good with
   Steak with Roquefort Sauce, page 202.

1997 Felipe Rutini Malbec

1997 Felipe Rutini Merlot

1997 Felipe Rutini Chardonnay—Moderately priced.
   Good with Partridges in Garlic Alioli Sauce,
   page 196.
Rutini Brut Nature (sparkling wine)

Leon Unzue, Mendoza.
Malbec

Lopez, Maipú, Mendoza.
Monchenont
Casona Lopez
Chateau Vieux
Rincon Formoso
Lopez
Traful
Vasco Viejo

Mapema, Mendoza.
Mapema, (blend of Cabernet Sauvignon, Malbec,
   Merlot)*—Moderately priced. Serve with Marinated
   Roast Lamb, page 226.

Mendoza Peaks, Mendoza.
Cabernet Sauvignon

Michel Torino, Mendoza and Cafayette.
Cabernet Sauvignon (Bodega La Rosa, Cafayate)

Navarro Correa, Mendoza.
Coleccion Privada Cabernet Sauvignon.* Serve with
   Roasted Kid with Rosemary, page 275.
Malbec.* Serve with Roasted Quail, page 68.

Nicolas Fazio, Mendoza.
Malbec.* Good with Braised Beef, Genoa Style,
   page 108.
Cabernet Sauvignon

Nieto y Sentiner Cadus, Mendoza.
Malbec.* Serve with Pampas Stew with Beef and
    Chicken, page 85.

Norton, Perdriel, Luján de Cuyo, Mendoza.
Merlot
Malbec
Cabernet Sauvignon
Petit Verdot
Chardonnay
Sauvignon Blanc—Moderately priced. Serve with
    Smoked Trout with Spaghetti, page 192.
Semillon—Moderately priced. Serve with Suribi in
    Tropical Sauce, page 159.
Riesling—Moderately priced. Serve with Lobster
    Empanadas, page 183.
Privada*—Moderately priced. Serve with Roast Suckling
    Pig, page 70.
1999 Malbec
1999 Cabernet Sauvignon.* Serve with Creole Roast
    Turkey, page 42.
1999 Merlot

Pascual Toso, Mendoza.
Cabernet Sauvignon.* Serve with Veal Shanks à la
    Rondine, page 201.

Salentein, Mendoza.
Malbec
Cabernet Sauvignon
Merlot
Chardonnay
Sauvignon Blanc—Moderately priced. Serve with Salt
    Cod with Chickpeas, page 217.
Tempranillo

San Telmo, Mendoza.
Malbec.* Serve with Beef and Peach Pie, page 166.
Cabernet Sauvignon
Chardonnay

Susana Balbo, Mendoza and Cafayette.
2001 Crios Syrah and Bonarda blend* (Mendoza). Serve
    with Empanadas with Beef and Fruit, page 185.
2002 Crios (Cafayete)

Tapiz, (Owned by Kendall-Jackson Wine Estates.)
Cabernet Sauvignon.* Serve with Filet Mignon in Egg
    Batter, page 49.
Merlot.* Good with Roulade of Flank Steak and
    Vegetables, page 50.
Malbec.* Excellent paired with Breaded Beef Buenos
    Aires Style, page 51.

Trapiche, Mendoza.
Malbec
Cabernet Sauvignon*—Moderately priced. Serve with
    Hunter-Style Venison, page 200.
Chardonnay—Moderately priced. Serve with Baked
    Dover Sole in Garlic Sauce, page 131.
1997 Iscay (Merlot and Malbec varietal from Finca Las
    Palmas)*—Expensive. Good choice for Lamb and
    Vegetable Casserole, page 224.
Medalla Merlot
Medalla Chardonnay
Caballero de la Cepa
Fond de Cave

Valentin Bianchi, San Rafael, Mendoza.
2001 Sauvignon Blanc*—Moderately priced. Excellent
    with Striped Bass Buenos Aires Style, page 39.

Vína Cobos, Marchiori Vineyard, Perdriel, Mendoza.
1999 Cobos Malbec*—Expensive. For a festive dinner,
serve with Filet of Beef, Mar del Plata Style,
page 141.

Viniterra, San Juan and Mendoza.
Malbec
Cabernet Sauvignon
Alto Agrelo Chardonnay—Inexpensive. Serve with
Baked Seabass Mar del Plata Style, page 127.
Semillion and Espumantes (Sparkling)
Blend of Chardonnay and Pinot Noir (Trapungo,
Mendoza)

Weinert, Mendoza.
Cavas de Weinert*—Moderately priced. Serve with
Short Rib Casserole, page 248.
Malbec*—Moderately priced. Serve with Lamb with
Rice, page 228.
Carrascal*—Moderately priced. Serve with Mixed Fry
from La Yaya, page 106.
Merlot*— Moderately priced. Serve with Game
Mélange, page 199.

Y Víñedos Santiago Graffigña, Tulum Valley, San Juan.
2000 Malbec Seleccíon Especial*—Moderately priced.
Don Santiago.

Index

W

X Y Z